28.00
24.40

OFFICIALLY
WITHDRAWN

Tradition and Change

in

Swedish Education

INTERNATIONAL STUDIES IN EDUCATION AND SOCIAL CHANGE
General Editor: Professor E J King

NOTICE TO READERS

Dear Reader

An Invitation to Publish in and Recommend the Placing of a Standing Order to Volumes Published in this Valuable Series.

If your library is not already a standing/continuation order customer to this series, may we recommend that you place a standing/continuation order to receive immediately upon publication all new volumes. Should you find that these volumes no longer serve your needs, your order can be cancelled at any time without notice.

The Editors and the Publisher will be glad to receive suggestions or outlines of suitable titles, reviews or symposia for editorial consideration: if found acceptable, rapid publication is guaranteed.

ROBERT MAXWELL
Publisher at Pergamon Press

Acknowledgments

This book seeks to give to those interested in education in
Sweden sufficient description and analysis to help them
understand current trends and developments.

I first visited Sweden as a student in the summer of 1948, to
teach at a Summer School in Stockholm for *Folkuniversitet*.
My wife teaches 10-13 year olds in *Mellanstadiet*; my daughters
have been educated there, both at school and university; and
as a family we commute, every month or so, between our homes
in England and Sweden.

Over the years, I have inevitably followed the press, radio
and television in Sweden, and have talked with people from all
walks of life; politicians, academics, administrators; those
in public service, business, industry, agriculture, the
professions; hundreds of teachers and pupils in schools.
They are far too numerous to name. I am sincerely grateful
to them for the insights they have given me. Errors of fact
and interpretation are, of course, my own responsibility.

In particular, however, I do want to thank Mrs Frankie Clark
for her care in preparing the text for the press. And most
of all, I am indebted to my wife, Ingegerd, and my daughters,
Karin and Louise, for their encouragement and their patience.

Chester, 1981   LEON BOUCHER

Contents

viii   Contents

List of Figures

xi

List of Tables

CHAPTER 1

National Sentiment and Educational Tradition

Education in Sweden is a massive enterprise which engages
directly some 40% of the total population of 8.3 million.
There are about half a million 2-7 year olds in various forms
of pre-school; over a million 7-16 year olds in the compulsory
basic school, *Grundskola*; a quarter of a million 16-19 year
olds in the integrated upper secondary school, *Gymnasieskola*;
150,000 in an integrated system of higher education, with an
annual entry of about 35,000; 270,000 adults are taking school-
level courses run by the local authorities;[1] 100,000 are taking
job retraining courses; 15,000 students aged from 18 attend
every year residential courses of at least 15 weeks at the folk
high schools; and nearly two million adults enrol in study
circles run by various adult education associations, in addition
to the courses run by trade unions and employers. To staff all
these courses, there are about 150,000 teachers – understandably,
some of the teachers in the formal school and higher education
systems also staff the adult courses; and about 100,000
administrators, clerks, school nurses, school meals staffs,
caretakers. The total enterprise costs over 7% of the GNP, a
little over half of the money coming from central government
and the rest from the local authorities. For the pupil, tuition
is free within the formal school and higher education systems,
and at minimal cost for all other courses.

This scale of educational provision is a relatively modern
phenomenon, and clearly relates to the affluence of the country.
With a wealth per head of population which places it among a
very select group at the top of the international league table
in terms of GNP, Sweden certainly presents a picture of well-
being, of a people who have "never had it so good". It is a
picture in sharp contrast to the poverty and harshness of life
which encouraged large-scale emigration to the USA between
1850 and 1920, or the social unrest of the world-wide economic
depression of the 1930s. It is in sharp contrast, too, to

the caricature of Sweden as a land ridden with discontent, of
social licence where illegitimacy and divorce are the norm,
where there is ready access to pornography and narcotics, and
where people have pronounced tendencies to suicide all brought
about by too ready access to liberal social welfare services in
a secular half-socialist paradise or hell.

Such an image is no more true than that of Paris as the sin
capital of the "naughty nineties", or that of an 18 year old
English boy who, on being introduced for the first time to a
Swedish lady, was heard to remark "I thought all Swedes were
blonde and sexy". There are indeed many human tragedies in
Sweden behind the social security statistics of drunkenness,
drug addiction, broken families, and social inadequacy in a
modern complex society. Many Swedes deplore the sight of youngsters, *raggare*, in their leather jackets riding round the town
square in large cars or on noisy motor cycles. Many dislike
the high level of taxation which finances the extensive network
of social services. Many no doubt feel they are over-governed
by a bureaucratic, computer-controlled, machine. Many find it
hard to understand, let alone to sympathise with, that 10-15-20%
of an age-group who are tired of school, who play truant or
vandalise the facilities, who treat so casually and wastefully
opportunities of which their parents and grandparents could only
have dreamed.

The visitor to Sweden, however, can hardly fail to see a quiet,
calm, clean, modern, well-ordered country. There is, inevitably,
noise and bustle in the centre of large conurbations such as
Stockholm, Göteborg and Malmö; about a third of the population
now lives in the major towns. But Sweden is still essentially
a country of small towns and scattered communities. Half the
population still live in local authority areas of less than
30,000, and a "populated area", *tätort*, is defined as one where
there are more than a mere 200 people. In the built-up areas,
even in the largest cities, the apartment blocks and houses are
likely to stand in green lawns with well kept shrubs and
borders; an extensive, and expensive, system of housing grants
and very long loans make for a social mix which is quite
different from the usual western European or American scene
where the social class composition of an area is clearly visible
in the type of housing available: by and large, Sweden has no
slums. In the relatively sparsely populated countryside the
red wooden farmhouses and barns with their white framed windows
make idyllic pictures against the background of yellow corn-
fields, green conifer forests, copses of silver birch, and

thousands of lakes twinkling in the summer sun;[2] or in winter
look like traditional Christmas cards, the pines and firs heavy
with snow.

If.increased wealth has made possible increased educational
opportunities, it has been the purpose of increased education
to provide a highly skilled as well as a socially responsible
source of labour. The interaction between school and the society
of which it is a part is an essential characteristic of the
period since 1945, and the argument that school reform would
promote economic change by its contribution to productivity and
bring about social change by its contribution to the formation
of more harmonious, thoughtful, critical, independent-minded
people, is balanced by the argument that a more affluent, more
leisured, more technocratic society required reform of an out-
dated school system. Whether the motive for change was social
egalitarianism, the need for skilled labour, or merely the
aspirations of people emerging from the social and economic
strains of the 1930s - and there are strands of all of these
movements - all the major political parties became united in
their desire to see a rapid expansion of educational opportunity.
This consensus remains undisturbed. The election debate in 1979,
for example, showed agreement between the parties that all was
not well within the schools; that many pupils were bored;
teachers felt themselves under stress; the function of schools
to transmit knowledge, especially in the basic skills, needed
to be re-emphasised; the more high-flown goals of a generation
of reform had not been realised. But there was not the slight-
est suggestion that there should be a return to the system of
parallel elementary and selective grammar schools: only that
the traditional values of these schools, especially in their
norms of social behaviour and their stress on scholastic achievement, should be maintained or, in the eyes of some, restored.[3]
The source of these traditional values is to be found in history:
and while the major purpose of this book is to describe and
analyse aspects of the contemporary education scene, to ignore
not only the Sweden in which the older generations of today grew
up but also the Sweden of historic tradition would be to mislead,
to distort understanding of the present context.

The Historic Past

Sweden, or more accurately that part of Scandinavia which now
forms the soverign state of Sweden, is an integral part of the
Greco-Roman European tradition, and has long been a centre of
human settlement. There are extensive stone-age remains; there

was extensive trading contact with the Roman Empire; over two
thousand rune-stones have been found, with their alphabet
adapted from Greek and Roman characters; the nordic Vikings
travelled to the Americas, and across Russia and the Ukraine
to the Black Sea as well as to northern France and the British
Isles. Following conversion to Christianity by missionaries
from England and Germany around the ninth century, a degree
of national unity was achieved about the year 1000 between the
kings of Götaland and Svealand with a "capital" at Stigtuna,
a few miles north of present day Stockholm, and, in 1164, an
archbishopric centered at Uppsala. For several centuries there
was rivalry between branches of the noble families who also
held power in parts of what is now Norway and Denmark: there
was a personal union with Norway in 1319 at a time when Gotland,
Skåne and Blekinge were lost to Denmark, and in 1389 at Kalmar,
a union was proclaimed between Denmark, Norway and Sweden which
lasted until 1521. It was during these centuries that Sweden
saw its first parliament, *Riksdag*, 1434 in Arboga; and that
formal education began under the auspices of the church. Lund,
then part of Denmark, had a cathedral school in the twelfth
century, and other cathedral and monastic schools were founded
in the thirteenth century. In 1477, a university was founded
at Uppsala. But as the Swedish educational historian,
Landqvist, commented: "Medieval schooling in Sweden used the
same texts and methods as the rest of Europe. There is no
trace of any national contribution: the church and education
were international ... The foreign universities in this sense
were part of the educational system of medieval Sweden".[4] The
pupils learnt the stories of the saints and the rules of the
monastic order; but they also had access to manuscripts which
introduced them to a world of geography, ancient history,
astronomy, medicine and music. The monk who read these scripts
aloud and added his own comments to the text was called
"reader", *lektor* - a title which has an honoured place in
academic schooling.

The sixteenth and seventeenth centuries are particularly important in that they established a national monarchy under the Vasa
family, with the coat of arms still used today and formed by the
"Three Crowns" of the people of Svea, Göta and Vende. This
centrally administered and powerful Lutheran empire controlled
Finland and the coastal areas of the eastern and southern Baltic,
and even had for a brief period (1635-55) a colony in America
in what is now Delaware. But in education, perhaps the most
important development was the fusion of church and state, in
line with the formula of the Peace of Augsburg, "to each prince

his own religion". As Landqvist said, "From the Reformation in
general, and especially in Sweden, developed the educational
ideas of nationalism and democracy ... that these ideas developed
this character in Sweden more than in other protestant countries
is a consequence of the fact that religious development and the
struggle for national unity came together with the same goals".[5]
The church, which in 1541 had a Bible in Swedish, became in
effect a department of state, and thus spared Sweden the worst
excesses of the religious factor which loomed so large elsewhere
in Europe. The cathedral schools became the state grammar
schools.

In 1525 Gustav Vasa appealed to the bishops to halt the contemporary decline in schools which followed the initial opposition to the ideas of Luther, and gave monies to re-establish
teaching posts in twenty-two towns. In 1571 the first statutes
were proclaimed, establishing a grammar school with the
curriculum based on that of Melanchthon, with Latin as the main
subject, the Latin of Caesar, Cicero and Virgil, along with
music, biblical studies and moral teaching. There were four
classes covering eight years of schooling, and the school-master
was called *Rektor* and the *Lektor* taught theology. This was
followed in 1611 by a further statute for the provision of two
more classes, to cover four more years, in the schools of the
cathedral cities. An idea of making these cathedral schools
into *gymnasia* on the German model developed around 1620 and
Gustavas Adolphus (or as the Swedes say, Gustav the Second,
Adolf) established three royal schools in Västerås (1623),
Strängnäs (1626) and Linköping (1627). Partly to prevent these
schools competing with the universities, the statutes of 1649
set up lower and higher *trivial* schools, so called because they
taught the *trivium*, the first three of the seven liberal arts:
grammar, rhetoric and logic. Each of these schools lasted four
years and were followed by a further four years in the *gymnasium*.
In all of the schools, the teachers were called *Lektor*, and had
the help of *Adjunkter*. After the *gymnasium* there were academies
at the universities of Uppsala, Åbo (now in Finland, founded
in 1640) and Greifswald (now in Northern Germany, founded in
1456) and then Lund (1668). In 1693 a statute extended the
trivial school to five years, added Hebrew to the curriculum of
the *gymnasium* and set up a leaving examination for those who
were to continue their studies in the university.

But in the long run the most important development at this time
was the beginning of popular education. The Protestant church
rested on the idea of "the priesthood of all believers", an idea

which pre-supposes the ability to read the Bible. In 1548
Archbishop Petri urged priests to provide schooling for the
children of their parishes to teach reading and the Lutheran
faith. It was not until 1656, however, that church law made
the parish priest responsible for teaching the catechism and
for the curate to teach reading. By 1700 about 10% of the population were receiving schooling: by 1800 it had reached around
50%.

The eighteenth century saw the end of Sweden as a major international power. Charles XII was defeated by the Russians at
Poltava in 1709 and by the 1720s all possessions, other than
Finland, were lost. A period of weak monarchy was paralleled
by a period of rivalry between political factions, increasing
resentment of aristocratic and ecclesiastical privileges, and
an intellectual ferment as lively as elsewhere in the "age of
enlightenment" in Europe.

Swedish law was codified in 1734; a popular census started in
1949, carried out then, as now, through the office of the
parish priest, *pastorsämbetet*; a law on freedom of the press
was enacted in 1766; the Swedish Royal Academy of Science was
founded in 1739, and the Royal Academy of Arts in 1786;
Linneus published his *Species Plantarum* in 1753; Celsius
invented the 100° thermometer; Swedenborg published his "True
Christian Religion" in 1771. Not surprisingly, there were calls
for educational reform of the grammar schools, especially to
introduce a wider and more modern curriculum acceptable to a
growing middle class. Geography had been introduced by the
Statutes of 1721 and in 1745 a great educational commission
was set up, composed entirely of laymen in order to avoid
excessive influence of traditional academic and clerical points
of view. Many believed that the dead hand of Latin needed to
be removed and that parallel to the *gymnasium*, there should be
schools specialising in technical skills, commerce, navigation,
mining and the sciences. Ultimately, proposals were published
and debated at length, but in 1760 were rejected. The
Commission was re-established in 1770 but in the final report
in 1778 recommended a return to the Statutes of 1724. It was
left to private initiative in the towns to open schools for
boys which offered a modern commercial and technical curriculum,
and for girls which offered an education appropriate for the
daughters of the middle-class merchants and professional men.
Meanwhile, in 1779 the clergy in parliament had called for compulsory schooling for all.

In 1792, Gustav III was assassinated. His successor Gustav IV
lost Finland in the Napoleonic War and was deposed in 1809. A
new constitution was drawn up and the French Napoleonic Marshal,
Jean Baptiste Bernadotte, was invited to be the constitutional
monarch. He took the name of Carl XIV Johan. The treaty of
Viennain 1815 compensated Sweden for the loss of Finland by
creating a new union with Norway. Industrialisation continued
to advance and towns grew large: 10% of the population were in
urban areas by 1800; 20% by 1900. Communications improved, by
road, rail, water and by the printed word. It was increasingly
argued that such developments required an educational system in
which the grammar school was made much more liberal both in its
curriculum and in its social composition: there should be a
common school for all children with links between the traditions
of popular and selective schooling, as well as links between
both of these and the technical and vocational school world. An
increasingly complex society looked for a literate, skilled and
morally sound population.

1800-1950

The democratisingof school in Sweden is not simply a phenomenon
of the twentieth century, nor merely a product of the radical
intellectualism of theperiod of the French Revolution. It has
its roots deep in Swedish tradition, perhaps even as far back as
the Viking village law, the idea of the moot where all freemen
would discuss their common problems. It is, of course, true
that until 1866 when an elected assembly was introduced, parliament had been restricted to the four estates of the nobles, the
clergy, the burghers and the farmers, with the nobles and clergy
enjoying privileges denied to the rest of the population. In
Sweden, as elsewhere in Europe, universal adult suffrage for
men, and later for women, has been achieved only within the last
hundred years. It is true, too, that the medieval system of
apprenticeships, *skråväsendet*, with its pupil journeymen and
master craftsmen, was not abolished until 1846. But up to the
middle of the eighteenth century at least, before urbanisation
and industrialisation, there was no significant employee pro-
letariat. The farmers were certainly poor, indeed desperately
poor, and they lived very isolated lives in small, scattered
farmsteads. But these were free men. They knew the power of
local nobility, the prestige of the clergy, but they had never
been serfs and the 1809 constitution was designed to see that no
all-powerful monarch could make them so. In the parliamentary
debate on that constitution Rektor Silverstolpe commented "The
new basic law must be protected. The most certain protection

lies in a nation made capable by education. That education
must be made available through the support of the state and it
must be available to all".[6] This support for the common school
was even then associated in the eyes of men such as Silverstolpe
with the need to reform the traditional grammar school. "A
properly organised official education is needed to defend the
newly won freedom. The classical school did not encourage the
free development of its pupils, instead it hindered free
development and as such was a kind of political tool, working
in the wrong direction; therefore, it must be reformed".[7]

In 1812 an education committee led by Silverstolpe attempted to
find ways of implementing proposals for compulsory schooling.
Its report in 1825 was less than encouraging. There would be
no compulsion to attend the popular schools and they would continue to be financed by parishes with no state grant. At the
same time, in 1820, a new statute expanded the town grammar
schools and also proposed three-yearly revisions which, in
fact, took place in 1824, 1832 and 1847 - the idea of rolling
reform in the 1960s and 1970s is not wholly new - and a new
commission began in 1825 to revise the curriculum of the
gymnasium. Its report in 1828 recommended two lines, Latin and
Modern, *Real*, which were in fact introduced by the statute of
1849.

It would be simple, and wrong, to suppose that all conservative
and clerical opinion was opposed to reform of the grammar school
and to limiting the growth of popular education. Professor
Ågardh, theologian at Lund and later Bishop of Karlstad, and a
member of the 1825 Commission, had deplored the encyclopaedic
nature of the classical curriculum: "The main fault which
seems to be inherent in the present Swedish school is super-
ficiality, or the many-sidedness of knowledge, at the expense
of thoroughness".[8]

Such views found favour in the minds of leading conservatives
such as Geijer and Wallin in the 1830s and paved the way for
the establishment in 1840 of the Ministry of Education and
Church Affairs, *ecklesiastikdepartmentet*, the statutes of 1842
which provided for the establishment of a compulsory elementary
school, *Folkskola*, supported by state grants, together with
teacher training colleges called Normal Schools in Stockholm
and in each of the other twelve bishoprics.

To pass legislation is one thing: to implement it is another.
The story of this development is treated in great detail and

clarity by Paulston in the only major study in English of
Swedish educational history from 1842 to 1950.[9] Briefly to
summarise his analysis, he divides the period into four phases:
a) 1842-1918, characterised by early demands by liberal
idealists and social utopians for educational unity in an era
of conservative dominance; b) 1918-1932, a period of "conflict
and compromise in partial reforms with universal suffrage and
political stalemate"; c) 1932-1946, when there was "priority
for social and economic welfare state reforms with social
democratic predominance"; and d) 1946-1950, with "reformula-
tion and parliamentary acceptance of comprehensive school
reform, with continued social democratic leadership for socio-
political reconstruction".

The Swedish elementary school, with its counter-parts in other
countries where formal legislation had been passed earlier
(Prussia 1963, Denmark 1814) or was delayed until later (England,
France, USA, in the 1870s and 1880s) took a generation or
more to become part of the normal life of a child. In Sweden,
especially in the rural areas, much depended on the attitudes
and energies of the local clergy.[10] In the towns the growing
need to keep children off the streets and the more obvious
need for formal schooling for the future employee made provision more likely. Additional grants were given in 1856 to
help set up "small schools", småskolor, especially in the more
remote rural areas, for children aged 7 to 9. But the school
inspectors of the 1850s and 1860s were likely to find at the
time of their visits only half of the pupils on roll actually
present.[11] By 1849 there were nearly ten thousand elementary
teachers, half of them men and half of them women, and they
felt themselves sufficiently identified to form their own
teachers' association. Virtually all 7-13 year olds were now
enrolled in school, some 650,000 children, and in 1882 new
regulations formally divided the elementary school into a
two year 'small school', followed by a four year 'big school',
at the end of which a continuation school offered the equivalent
of about six weeks full-time schooling. These schools were
essentially parish schools, with the local vicar as ex-officio
chairman of the school board, a situation which existed right
up until the 1950s. From 1875, however, there were state
grants towards teachers salaries, thus increasing the extent
of state control and influence. Parallel with the establishment of the elementary school, there were three other lines of
development. First, the grammar school reform continued; the
regulations of 1856 instituted what were called läroverk, the
secondary grammar school of nine years duration, with a common

curriculum for the first three years before dividing into Latin
and Modern Lines. In 1862, what was known as the maturity
examination, the *studentexamen*, signifying the satisfactory
completion of the full grammar school course, was taken in the
school itself rather than at the university, and if passed gave
right of entry into the university. In 1878, the designation
Higher General Secondary School, *Högre Allmänna Läroverk*, was
introduced for those state schools offering classes up to
studentexamen. There also began a half classical line, where
Greek was replaced by English and more mathematics. Secondly,
commercial and technical schools were appearing, Göteborg, for
example, having had a technical grammar school since 1816.
These were to lead either directly to employment or, as the
century progressed, to the institutions of applied technology
such as the Stockholm Technical High School (1878) or similar
high schools for veterinary, pharmaceutical, agricultural,
commercial, mining or art studies. Significantly, studies of
theology, law or medicine, all of which had vocational application, had all the status of the medieval university, but
applied studies in other fields were rejected by the traditional
academic world. Stockholm and Göteborg however, in 1878 and
1891 respectively, by virtue of private donations, set up their
own high schools for mathematics, science, and some of the
humanities. Thirdly, the education of girls had become
generally accepted by the middle of the nineteenth century,
private schools such as Wallinska in Stockholm (1831) and
Kjellbergska in Göteborg (1835) having achieved widespread
support, and by the 1880s virtually any town with a population
of over 3,000 had six-or eight-year girls' schools, *flickskolor*.
Girls were also allowed in 1870 to take *studentexamen* and go
to university. These three strands began to come together and
to find intellectual expression in the movement of the Young
Swedes of the 1870s and 1880s. This was a group of radical
social critics of whom the dramatist August Strindberg is the
best known figure today, but which then included nonconformist
ministers, trade unionists, political socialists, teachers and
some liberal members of parliament. 1883 saw the publication
of two highly significant tracts; first, there was the attack
by Adolf Hedin on the dominance of Latin[12] in which he
lambasted the vanity of the classically educated and their
contempt for knowledge of a more obviously utilitarian character.
In Hedin's eyes, those who supported the place of Latin as a
compulsory subject in the grammar school were aristocratic,
anti-democratic and thus in opposition to the national interest.
In his view, the school for citizenship for which he strove was
not to be found merely by a modern line with its greater emphasis

on mathematics and modern languages. This attack led to bitter
controversy in both press and parliament. Hedin's critics
argued that he was damaging the cultural heritage, that Latin
was the essential basis for subsequent scientific enquiry, that
the grammar school needed above all peace and quiet, its work
as little disturbed as possible.[13] The clergy especially spoke
loud and clear in the defence of classical learning.

But while Hedin attacked Latin, Fridtjuv Berg, an elementary
school teacher who became a liberal MP, argued persuasively for
an extension of the common school and its establishment as the
basic school for all.[14] Together with some, but by no means
all, of his liberal parliamentary colleagues, he argued for
radical changes and a more simple approach to the organisation
and content of schooling, especially in the years of childhood.
The common school should be a national institution for all,
Nordic in character and understandable by all. Depth of knowledge "for its own sake" was less important. There was no
necessity, for example, to lay so much stress in language on the
niceties of grammar and syntax. What was especially dangerous
in the eyes of such liberals was the long held demand of the
burghers for a more vocationally and practically orientated
lower secondary school – a six year lower secondary school,
realskola, followed by a three or four year upper secondary
school, *gymnasium*; such reforms were mere palliatives, designed
to meet the needs of one particular social group and to keep out
the masses.

The views of Hedin and Berg had much in common with those of
the late nineteenth century social democrats. The first workers'
meetings in 1879 and 1882 had included discussions on the content of schooling and had especially criticised the dominance
of learning the catechism. At the third meeting in 1886, Berg's
friend, fellow elementary school teacher and later MP, Emil
Hammarlund, accepted Berg's proposition for "improved and free
schooling, with a general citizenship school as the common
school, from which students could pass directly to schools of
higher education".[15] The Social Democratic Workers Party (SAP)
was founded in 1889 and at its fourth congress in 1897 adopted
ideas based on those developed by the German Social Democrats
to formulate two goals: to encourage the development of a
common citizenship school and to work for the separation of the
school from the church. The formal propositions were the work
of Axel Danielsson, who had published in 1891 a utopian novel
in which an emigrant son described for his father his impressions of a visit to Sweden in the middle of the twentieth century:

"We are all educated to a greater or less degree and the
treasures of knowledge are available to all. There is no longer
a special upper class school and a special lower class school.
Recently you wondered about that massive temple out in the lake.
In golden letters there is the simple inscription 'Common
School'. On that site there used to be a dressage institution
for the sons of the bourgeoisie, with the motto 'The fear of
the Lord is the beginning of wisdom'. We have got rid of that
dual education system. It had to go when social classes went.
We have a general common school, not only open for all, but
compulsory for all. That is where we get the education you
marvel at. From the age of 8-18 we do nothing else but study.
Poverty does not take us away from our teachers at the age of
12 or 13, as it did for our fathers and grandfathers. Education is a necessity for all of us, and when we leave the
Citizens School at 18 to start to serve society, we know more
than the student of old used to know and we have learned to
regard the school rather than the church as the holy temple".[16]
But as Egidius rightly points out, while school had become more
important than at any time in history and while significant
social groups such as employees and women sought to change
existing power relationships, school questions did not loom all
that large in the social and political debate. "It is always
easier to argue for the rights of innocent small children ...
than to argue for equality between adults of different sexes
and different social backgrounds ... The privileged have been
on their guard and, as far as the rules of the political game
allowed, strongly resisted all changes in schools which they
suspected would lead to changes in the system of social hierarchies and the balance of power in the different occupational
groups".[17]

In 1894 the first formal link was made between the elementary
and secondary school systems, whereby the first three years of
the elementary school or its equivalent in the private schools
was required as an entry qualification to the *läroverk*. In
principle, this was an important change, but in practise, it
had little immediate effect; economic and psychological
obstacles remained effective barriers to transfer from the
elementary to the grammar school. Furthermore, it was an
opportunity which was in the main limited to those living in
or near towns of some size. The mass of the population were
still in rural areas, where even to get to school was a major
achievement. This was the experience of many of today's grandparents. Imagine children from little crofts deep in the
forests; in mid-winter, the father would put on his big boots

to stamp out a path for the little ones to follow in the deep
snow down a track to and from the farm to the road or the
village. Once at school kindly teachers would perhaps need to
find dry socks for sodden feet, and in any case the school room,
lit by oil lamps and candles, would be open for only five or
six hours of the day.

In 1899 a Grammar School Committee was set up under the chair-
manship of Karl von Friesen, Rektor of *Södra Latin Gymnasium*
in Stockholm, and discovered that under a third of the pupils
completed the full grammar school course. This led, on the
one hand, to the establishment in 1904 of a Grammar School
Board in place of the Cathedral Chapters which had previously,
within the framework agreed by parliament, been responsible for
curriculum matters, and on the other hand, by the Statute of
1905, to the division of the grammar school into a four or
five year lower secondary school, *realskolan*, with its own
leaving examination, *realexamen*, and with a curriculum which
did not include Latin, and a three or four year upper secondary
school, *Gymnasium*. Some of these lower secondary schools also
became co-educational, though the teachers remained all male
until 1918 when women were first allowed to be *Adjunkter* or
Lektorer. But the common school notion was rejected, as was
any idea of a selective school which had any of the burghers'
desire for a curriculum which had overt, utilitarian value for
commerce or industry. A further development in 1909 was the
introduction of four year municipal lower secondary schools
which took pupils who had completed six years in the elementary
school and by 1918 there were forty of these schools with
4,400 pupils and having the same status as the state lower
secondary schools. Thus the elementary school was no longer
wholly a blind alley: depending on the facilities available
in a given locality, transfer could take place after three or
six years in the elementary school to a selective school.

Paulston's examination of the period from 1918-1932, together
with the more recent study by Bergstrand,[18] show clearly both
the complexity and the bitterness of the educational debate in
the 1920s. This dealt essentially with the same issues which
had been at the centre of the post-1945 debate and which are
still live issues in the 1980s: the democratisation of the
educational provision, its quantative as well as its qualitative nature, the feelings of stress within the schools and
especially by the teachers related to the seemingly unending
changes of direction and emphasis.

Politically, the period begins with the coalition government of
1917, the first time the social democrats had achieved power in
association with the liberals. In 1920 the National Board of
Education, *Skolöverstyrelsen* or *SÖ*, was established, with
separate departments for grammar and elementary schools. It
was the social democrat, Värner Rydén, who became Minister of
Education and one of his first acts was to set up a great
educational commission designed to resolve the conflict between
three major groups. One group comprised the political right
wing and traditional academics who wanted the selective grammar
school course to start as early as possible. A second group
was the growing middle class who were content to see increased
opportunities for transfer to the growing number of municipal
lower secondary schools and there to follow curricula which
would lead either to traditional academic upper secondary
schooling, or to lines of study with more overtly commercial or
technical orientations. Thirdly, there were those radicals
who looked back to the ideas of Berg and the basic school, as
well as sideways to the early ideas in France and Germany of
Ecoles Uniques or *Gesamtschulen*, the polytechnic ideas of
Marxism-Leninism in the USSR, or the pragmatic melting-pot
tradition of the USA, to which so many Swedes had emigrated to
escape the hardships and poverty of the turn of the century,
and which were so realistically portrayed in the 1960s in the
historical quartet of Wilhelm Moberg's novels of emigrants,
immigrants and settlers.[19]

Rydén succeeded in introducing in 1919 a three year technical
gymnasium and a two year technical school, and a vocational
school department was added to the National Board. In 1922 his
commission proposed a six year basic school to be followed by
a four year lower secondary school with its own leaving examination, giving entrance to a three year *gymnasium* with its own
traditional leaving examination. Parallel with these could be
either a seven year *läroverk*, grammar school, or a six year
girls school, *flickskola*. Such a proposal reflected increasing
demands. The municipal lower secondary school had in the mid-
1920s nearly 9,000 pupils, six times their enrolment in the
1911–1915 period, and over 3,000 pupils a year were taking
realexamen in these schools, double the pre-war number. During
the same period between 1911 and 1925 the numbers of pupils in
state lower secondary schools had increased from 17,500 to
nearly 22,000. The liberal press, for example *Dagens Nyheter*,
supported these ideas, but not surprisingly they were bitterly
opposed by the conservatives as well as by the grammar school
teachers' association and university professors.

Massive debate followed in the press and parliament, with
proposals and counter proposals all taking place within a very
fluid political situation with frequent changes of government
and a period when Rydén himself had to leave office because of
a political scandal. Education was now a real political issue.
In 1924 the then conservative government rejected the
Commission's proposals and set up an expert committee of five
to produce an alternative scheme. The supposed importance of
school systems for the maintenance of social structure was
clearly to be seen. Bergstrand suggests that Swedish education
in 1927 was at a cross roads; it could have gone to the radical
left, or to the reactionary right. In fact, it sought the
middle way, under the direction of the then social democratic
Minister of Education, Jon Almqvist, a man who had himself been
an elementary school teacher and then an Inspector of Schools,
together with the support of important social democrats such as
Ernst Wigfors and Ivan Pauli, who were the products of an
academic tradition. The six year elementary school/four year
selective school system proposed by the Rydén Commission was
introduced alongside a four-plus-five system proposed by the
conservatives. No foreign language would be taught in the
elementary school, but the lower secondary school would be
co-educational. The object of this decision was to bring peace
and quiet to the schools and at the same time provide an
educational structure which would suit both the needs of society
for more education for a larger section of the population and
also the need of higher studies: a sound common school,
together with an opportunity to achieve real academic knowledge
and understanding through the lower and upper secondary school.

That there was no peace and quiet has little to do with educational politics. The 1930s in Sweden, as elsewhere in Europe,
were hard times: the Wall Street Crash, the Kruger crisis
which destroyed the financial empire associated with Sweden's
very important match-making industry, the decline in trade
which led to massive unemployment and the virtual death of many
small towns dependant, as so many of them are, on only one or
two major employers, all gave rise not only to poverty and
social unrest, but to a political situation in which problems
of work, food and housing were of more immediate importance
than educational reform. The social democrats achieved power
in 1932 but their socialism then had to be of the "knife and
fork, bread and butter" kind. School photographs, log books,
local newspapers, personal memories of people now approaching
retirement and asked to recall their school days, all bring
home very forcibly not only how recent is Sweden's present

affluence, but also how hard conditions were for the mass of
people within living memory. Ancillary services for school
meals, clothing grants, transport, medical inspections were
not yet statutory duties, and assistance varied from area to
area;   one would provide clogs and meal vouchers, another
would provide meals and have access to well developed urban
public health services, a third was too poor to do anything
at all of note. In these contexts, it is easy to understand
why the social democratic party held office without a break
for 44 years until 1976. To some extent political response
became a habit.

An increasing proportion of the population were living in towns
where they might well have enjoyed better social services than
in the country areas but where they would also experience
greater unemployment and the strains of living in overcrowded
housing of one room and a kitchen for a family. Very large
numbers, however, still lived in relatively sparsely populated
areas where children had long distances to travel to school.
Children born on a farm, even as little as 10 or 15 kilometers
from the town, might well have had a couple of kilometers or
more to walk through the dark forests and in the snow to go to
the small school at the age of seven, and at that age there
are trolls in the forests. At the age of nine they might have
to go and live with grandparents or an aunt, to attend the big
elementary school until the age of eleven or thirteen, when
they might pass the selective transfer examination to a lower
secondary school, which would probably mean having to get
lodgings with a family in the local town. At sixteen or seven-
teen, they might gain entry to a *gymnasium* but these would be
found only in the largest towns, and thus more travel or lodging:
boarding, or even hostels, has always been a rarity in Sweden.
The social limitations of class were thus compounded by the
geographical limitations of remoteness, and the 1930s were
hardly the time to provide educational grants for extensive
travel facilities. Besides, the social democratic Education
Minister of the period, Arthur Engberg, was not very interested
in education.[20] Sufficient for the government, supported by
the Farmer's Party, in 1935 to increase state grants for
capital and recurrent expenditure, including salaries, and in
1936 to make provision for the extension of all other elementary schools to age 14 by 1946 in order to give greater
equality between rural and urban areas and to restructure the
system of teacher training for the elementary schools in
order to reflect the increasing educational expectations of
those who sought to be transferred to the selective school

from which an increasing number of posts in commerce and public
service were recruited. Numbers going to the selective schools
steadily increased despite hardship and economic stringency.
In the mid 1920's nearly 6,000 a year went to the lower secondary school, whether state of municipal: this rose to 8,000 in
the first half of the 1930's and 10,000 by 1940. About half
of those entering the lower secondary school ultimately achieved
realexamen. For the upper secondary school there were some
2,500 entrants annually in the mid 1920's, 2,700 in the early
1930's, 3,500 in the late 1930's: of these, 1,600, 1,800 and
2,750 respectively reached *studentexamen*. While these
opportunities were undoubtedly greater in the urban areas, the
social aspirations of those in the countryside were significant.
In the area that formed the basis of the Moberg quartet on
emigration to the United States, there are case histories
readily available of persons born as late as 1940 who lived on
farms three kilometers from the village school and who could
attend only on alternate days of the week; yet some of those
children achieved entry to the lower secondary school in the
town 25 kilometers away, after which some continued their
education, often by correspondence, until they had achieved
degrees or professional qualifications.

Provision of school places, of course, also requires teachers,
and Sweden appears always to have had a high regard for teachers
and teaching and by international standards, a relatively
favourable pupil/teacher ratio. Teacher training had first
started in the Stockholm normal school and in the training
college in Lund in the 19th Century. By the 1880's there
were eight colleges, two for women and six for men, offering
a three year course based on the six year elementary school,
and qualifying some 300 candidates a year, 40% of them being
women. Output rose steadily to 800 a year by the mid 1920's,
though then declined to about 300 by 1940. From 1916 there
were sufficient applicants with *studentexamen* to warrant a
one year elementary teacher course for such candidates.
Parallel with this was training in a two year course for
infant teachers in small schools, a responsibility of the
counties which qualified between 600 and 700 candidates a year
until the mid 1920's when there was a rapid decline. Responsibility for these training colleges in 1931 was taken over by
the central government. In 1936 it was possible to envisage
a three year infant teachers course, though only 536 teachers
were qualified during the period 1931-1945, and for full
elementary school teachers a four year course for those entering with *realexamen* from the lower secondary school, or a two

year course for those with *studentexamen* from the upper
secondary school. The four year elementary teacher course has
been called the Poor Man's University of the 1940's and 50's.
It was not, however, the only alternative route by which the
aspirant working classes and the children of those in sparsely
populated areas could advance. Sweden has a long tradition of
adult education, much of it owing its stimulus to private
philanthropy, the nonconformist churches, temperance movements
and trade unions. The best known is probably the Folk High
School movement organised originally in Denmark, spreading to
Sweden from the late 1860's. Originally a dozen or so of them,
within half a century there were over a hundred run by the
state church, as well as by the free churches, and movements
such as the Blue Band Temperance Order. Another movement was
the Public Lecture, originated by lecturers from the University
of Lund going to Hvilan Folk High School and leading in 1898 to
the Central Bureau for Lecturers in Popular Science. These
served much the same function as the Workers' Educational
Societies, of which there were about 140 in the later part of
the nineteenth century, together with 15 Workers' Institutes,
known as Lecture Societies. "They were orientated towards
radicalism and science and stood in the centre of opposition
to the orientation of the elementary school towards God and
Country".[21] A third strand of popular education was the Study
Circle which was first set up around 1900 by the IOGT. In the
winter evenings, small groups would meet weekly to discuss
books or study material on chosen theoretical and practical
subjects. This became a very popular activity and was used,
for example, by ABF (The Workers' Educational Society) which
was set up in 1912, the Swedish Church Study Scoiety and the
Swedish Rural Study Society in 1930, TBV (The Employees'
Educational Association) in 1935, and by *Folkuniversitet*, the
Extra Mural People's University in 1943. By the 1940's, there
were thirteen such societies, all receiving grants from the
state, the counties or the towns. A fourth element of non-
formal education is particularly interesting, the use of the
correspondence school. Several such schools developed, run
by the co-operative societies, *Brevskolan*, established in
1919, the Armed Services, and the trade union movements. By
far the best known school, however, was the original one,
Hermods, founded in Malmö in 1898 especially to give courses
in commercial skills. It was not long before it was offering
courses in school subjects as well, and preparing its students
as private entrants for *realexamen* and *studentexamen*, as well
as for examinations of technical, commercial and professional

bodies. In the 1940's its activities at school level extended
to the systematic teaching of lower secondary school courses
by means of tutor-led correspondence programmes for ordinary
pupils in several schools in sparsely populated areas of the
north, which were suffering the additional problems of teacher
shortage when the men teachers were called up for military
service during the Second World War. While this correspondence
provision in schools declined as educational opportunities
expanded in the post war years, the technique itself extended
in the 50's and 60's to first and second year university
courses, and the principles as well as the practice of distance
teaching has had a not insignificant influence in recent years,
though Hermods itself has now largely reverted to its traditional
adult education role.

By 1940, then, Swedish society and politics were still significantly divided into at least three strands, which in
occupational terms could be classified as administrators,
technicians and skilled workers, and manual unskilled workers.
There still remained deep suspicions of attempts to alter this
social structure, especially when the Second World War was
such an apparent threat to democracy and what was regarded as
the natural order. Nevertheless there was a growing consensus
for change, set in a complex of shared values rooted in common
traditions, even though the population remained relatively
scattered, except for the three major conurbations. There were
traditions of freedom; of an identity to be defended at all
costs - a nineteenth century slogan at the time when attempts
at greater unity of Scandinavia failed and neutrality became
a political holy cow was "we must defend ourselves like hedge-
hogs", and ever since a very high proportion of Sweden's public
expenditure has been on defence and the maintenance of conscript
services; of public participation in debate; of that slightly
puritanical nonconformist earnestness in social questions; of
self-help. In education, too, there were deeply rooted traditions: of scholarship, in the Teutonic tradition whereby
almost every statement justifies a foot note at least as long
as the statement itself, or where every word or phrase in a
foreign language would have a series of rules of usage; of
the authority of the teacher; of the dominance of the printed
word. Knowledge was power and for most children even well into
the 1950's in the rural areas knowledge was achieved at the
lowest level in the little red schoolhouse in the village, with,
for so many, its two teachers (known administratively as the
'b' school) or at best, one teacher for every two classes (the
'B' school).[22] The major question of 1940 was not whether there

should be a "ladder" to which one could transfer rather than one which could itself be extended in an end-on educational system, but at what point the transfer should take place, and how many transfers could be accepted.

It is wholly understandable that the social needs of stable employment and a decent standard of living for all should dominate the 1930's. It is also understandable that the government in 1940 could direct an expert body, the 1940 School Committee, to look at the dimensions of the problems of school reform and to suggest ways to proceed. The title of the main report of that body in 1944 is not without significance, "School in the Service of Society".[23]

CHAPTER 2

A Generation of Change: 1950-80

"Practically nothing remains today of the school system Sweden
had in the 1940s. In the span of thirty-five years change
has been almost total, both in terms of school structure and
content of education. Certainly, teaching/learning processes
have changed to a lesser extent, but even in this respect the
school of today is considerably different from the school of
the 1940s".[1]

Structural Changes

The structural changes are relatively easy to identify. (See
Fig. 1). The parallel system of non-selective elementary schools,

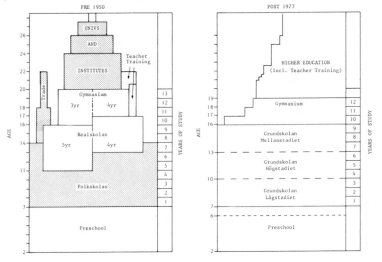

Fig. 1.   The Swedish Educational System.

21

folkskolor, and progressively increasingly selective and diver-
sified schools, *realskolor*, and post compulsory academic and
vocational provision in *gymnasium* and *yrkeskolor*, has been
replaced by an integrated series of end-on institutions. The
basic compulsory sector, *grundskolan*, has been extended to the
age of 16 and divided into the three stages of 7-10, 10-13,
13-16. The post-compulsory sector has been integrated into a
common *gymnasieskolan*, and instead of catering for some 10% in
the selective upper secondary school, now caters for virtually
all 16 year olds. Access to an integrated system of higher
education is possible on a quota system from all lines of study
in *gymnasieskolan*, together with quotas from adult education or
simply work experience. In sum, the system has been made wholly
comprehensive, with a simple structure of schools and an increase
in educational opportunities for all. In content, student
diversification has largely been postponed until the end of the
compulsory sector and while in recent years there has been an
increasing emphasis on the means to satisfy the needs of differential abilities, the structure makes no provision for streaming
or tracking within the compulsory sector. In terms of process
the school is infinitely more democratic in its way of working
and school is increasingly seen as part of the society within
which it is located. Marklund has also said "In no other
country with comparable cultural and economic standards have
reforms of education been preceded by such thorough going preparatory work as in Sweden".[2] Almost every year since 1944
either a major report or an appendix to a major report has been
published, and each of these has been accompanied by extensive
coverage in the press, on the radio, on television and in the
professional journals. It is not surprising that there are
many who look back on the "good old days" when they felt they
knew where they were and what the schools were supposed to do,
who are inclined to reject new notions teacher role and an
emphasis on learning rather than teaching.

The basic purpose of these organisational changes have been to
provide flexibility, a flexibility which could not be achieved
merely by changes within the old types of school. Without
wishing to imply that reform in Sweden has followed a consistent
and unaltered line over the last thirty or forty years, it is
nevertheless true that the directives to the 1940 Committee
which covered both primary and secondary school, have a contemporary ring: "The different school forms should be seen
as part of a whole and the solution of their multi-various
problems should be sought in a direction which is applicable
not only to the particular type of school concerned, but which

also furthers our total culture; the end goal should be to suit our educational system to our national needs and the demands of modern life, and to structure it so that each citizen has the possibility, by the simplest and most effective way, and without excessive economic outlay, to obtain that education which he needs for the good of society and for his own future work".

The report of the 1940 School Committee (SOU 1944:20) was the last of the reports to deal with the structure of the parallel elementary/selective system which in one form or another was the traditional pattern in all Western European countries. This body of experts drew upon many academic studies of a wide range of issues and produced over 4,000 printed sides between 1943 and 1947. In a recent study of this period Richardson[3] has argued that ideological perspectives on the maintenance of a dual system and the introduction of a unity school were far from the only major issues confronting the Committee. Its members were especially concerned with the consequences for the existing structure of schools of the increase in proportions of each age group who were seeking and obtaining transfer to the selective system. As economic conditions improved, as the move from the countryside to the towns increased, as social aspirations could be realised, so the lower secondary schools became increasingly crowded. Nationally, in the 1930's, they had accepted about 10% of an age group: by 1944, it was 25%: by 1948, it was 30%, and in the towns the transfer rate was twice as great as in the rural areas. A rising birth rate from 80-90,000 a year in the 1930's to a peak of 130-140,000 in the late 1940's aggravated this pressure. But as Marklund has argued,[4] the impulses for change were firmly rooted in all political parties and, perhaps more important, in popular movements such as the trade unions, employer associations, the co-operative movement, the Land and School movement, and many similar groups. The impact of this socio-political progression, with its long tradition in Swedish politics and above all in the liberal party, was ultimately decisive when, after 1945, it was incorporated into the general welfare programme of the Social Democratic Party.

While there was agreement both in the 1940 committee and politically on the need for longer schooling, there was dis-agreement about how to organise it. The Committee itself retained the idea of a four year basic school, followed by four years of differentiated lines, one theoretical, one technical and one practical. Furthermore, during 1944-45 the Committee shifted from a clearly socially orientated view to one more focused on the individual personality; for example, as

Richardson noted,[5] in 1944 it said in its first report "The
school is wholly in the service of society, acts under its
direction, works for its purposes ..."; but by 1945 it was
saying in a subsequent report "It must ... not be forgotten
that people do not live wholly for society and the state but
also for themselves, for the development of their own person-
alities, for their families and homes". Paulston[6] has also
shown that political consensus had not yet been achieved at
the level of detail. Social democrats had divided views on
how to make schooling more democratic and egalitarian;
liberals were worried whether the financial and teacher resources would be available to extend schooling; conservatives
wanted to retain a differentiated curriculum from as earlier
an age as possible; the Farmers' Party, *Bondeförbundet*, later
to become *Centrepartiet*, wanted later differentiation but
were afraid of the cost; Communists sought late differentiation and a school which was democratic in its texts, its
curriculum and its methods of work. By 1946 the term "Unity
School" had at least four meanings:[7] either a totally unified
system with a common basic school; or a system unified to the
end of the lower secondary stage, delaying classical studies
until the upper secondary school; or a system of six years of
common schooling, followed by differentiation; or a compulsory school for 8-9 years, followed by separate post-
compulsory schools.

While nothing specific came of the 1944 proposals, the debate
no doubt contributed to that change of political climate which
enabled the post-war government to set up the 1946 School
Commission to make the necessary political decisions to implement reform. As its report in 1948 put it:[8] "The time now
seems ripe for the abolition of dualism and the realisation of
the Unity School idea ...". In 560 sides it proposed the
"general lines of development for the democratisation of the
Swedish school system". In summary, it looked for

a)   a nine year Unity School divided into three stages;

b)   one school to replace all existing schools up to the
     age of 16, except those for the severely handicapped;

c)   the school to be undifferentiated for the first eight
     years and then divided into three streams called "g"
     (*gymnasium*, i.e. academic), "a" (*allmänn*, i.e. general)
     and "y" (*yrkes*, i.e. vocational);

d)   no terminal examination, i.e. the abolition of *realexamen*,
      the old lower secondary school examination, and selection
      to be replaced by election of alternative courses;

e)   reorganisation of teacher education, with class teachers
      up to grade 6 and then subject teachers;

f)   a child centred/activity pedagogy approach.

Such a school would meet the needs of individuals, would recognise that most pupils would leave school at 16 for the world of
work - "one must however realise that the nine year school will,
for many, be their only formal education" - and which would
accept that school is an agent of society and cannot ignore the
needs of that society. It was recognised, of course, that these
perspectives may well conflict one with another and especially
that social and technological change constantly made new demands
on the content of education. Indeed, the 1940 Committee had
emphasised that "the school cannot accept the task of equipping
the pupils with all the knowledge they will need ... The goal
of the school must essentially be limited to putting into the
hands of its pupils those tools with which they can themselves
widen their knowledge after the end of schooling".

The 1946 Commission also said "In on-going school reform goals
must not be regarded as determined once and for all time". The
main reason for reform was essentially to democratise schooling:
"The most important purpose of the school will be to educate
democratic pupils". But this sentence should not be mis-
understood - "(This) does not imply uniformity ... a democratic
school must be an environment for the free development of
children ... for whom co-operation is a need and a pleasure ...
(This) presupposes an alteration of teaching methods ... (from
those which) develop dependence and belief in authority and
passivity ... (to those which) develop independence and critical
attitudes in the pupils ... A democratic school has to accept
this programme ... (and) has to be many sided, offering to
each young person that educative process best suited to his
aptitudes and appropriate for this future life".

It was inevitably precisely the way in which the school could
provide for individual needs that caused in the late 1940's,
and still causes, the most intense debate. Figure 2, in
retrospect, makes clear that in the period since 1945, the
period of compulsory schooling has been extended, and the level
of organised differentiation of students delayed from age 11 to

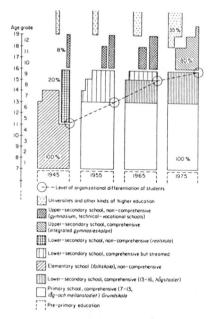

Age grade

— Level of organizational differentiation of students

Universities and other kinds of higher education

Upper-secondary school, non-comprehensive (gymnasium, technical-vocational schools)

Upper-secondary school, comprehensive (integrated gymnasieskolan)

Lower-secondary school, non-comprehensive (realskola)

Lower-secondary school, comprehensive but streamed

Elementary school (folkskola), non-comprehensive

Lower-secondary school, comprehensive (13-16, högstadiet)

Primary school, comprehensive (7-13, låg-och mellanstadiet) Grundskola

Pre-primary education

1945
The diagram describes—in a simplified way—the old Swedish school system with primary and secondary schools totally separated and partly parallel to each other, and with few students in secondary education.
1955
Experiments with the comprehensive school started in 1950, and the compulsory school leaving age was gradually raised. Classes in grades 7-9 were mostly streamed, usually with an academic stream, a pre-vocational stream and a general stream. The introduction of technical-vocational schools at the upper-secondary level was started.
1965
Parliament decided in 1962 that the comprehensive school should be introduced in the whole country during a ten-year period 1962-1972. The level of organizational diversification of students was set at grade nine, student age 15. New kinds of upper-secondary schools were started.
1975
The introduction of the comprehensive school is now complete. Even grade nine is now non-streamed, according to a revision from 1969 of the national curriculum. Schools on the upper-secondary level are reorganized from 1970 into an integrated system with 22 academic, vocational and general streams in the same school, within which there is a gradual differentiation.

Fig. 2.   Development of the School System 1945–75.

Source: Marklund, S and Boucher, L, The Curriculum for 13–16 year olds in Sweden: a review of changes, 1950–1980, *Compare*, 10, 2, 1980, pp.161–177.

16. The 1946 commission rejected the ideas of differentiation
by lines of study as early as age 11 and argued that such was
not appropriate until age 15. Instead, teaching should be
individualised within the framework of a mixed ability class.
It also recognised that this approach was made more complicated
by the broader and more specialised curriculum appropriate for
13-16 year olds; there was a need on the one hand for practical
work and on the other for the study of a second foreign language
(German) and for the separate sciences of physics and chemistry.
In these circumstances a certain choice was inevitable, which,
it was argued, should be made by the pupils and the parents and
not by the school. The final year was seen as having a special
character, with strict division into lines which could be
related to vocational goals, but which, above all, would be
able to provide a special course for those who continue in
academic studies after the age of 16.

A system of this kind was especially advantageous to those in
rural areas. It was proposed to establish a nine year school
in every commune, with a centralised 13-16 stage in large communities and 7-10 or 7-13 stages in the smaller villages.
Clearly it would be expensive and it would be difficult to get
competent teachers, but these reasons should not prevent its
introduction, not only in the interests of democracy, but also
because in the long run a technological society needed educated
manpower: it was argued that "If our forefathers a hundred
years ago were prepared to pay for a six year school, should
we not be able to create a nine year school"? Furthermore,
a democratic school needed to free itself from the fetters of
beureaucracy teachers needed to be free from the constraints
of excessively specific curriculum requirements, and lay
opinion should be heard at all levels, with decision making
more decentralised. While these plans were not formally published until the summer of 1948, they had in fact been widely
discussed before that, notably following a speech in 1947 by
the Commission's secretary, Stellan Arvidson. A summary of
the official comments on the report, the *remiss* by significant
groups and individuals, were also the subject of much discussion, as was the government bill for a new school law put
to parliament in February 1950 in a 600 page document.[9] The
minister, Josef Weijne, did not deny the virtual unanimous
opposition of the grammar school and university staffs to the
idea of delayed differentiation until the final year of the
compulsory school. He believed, however, that discussion of
the question of differentiation has now gone so far that "it
does not seem to me possible to resolve it by inquiry; the

decision must now be sought in practical experiments ... The
ten years ahead of us before the school reform can be implemented
on a large scale should be well used to determine the methodo-
logical resources, to test the strength of various types of
organisation and to draw definite conclusions on the structure
of the Unity School on these debatable points".

The opening section of the original bill (p.48) stated that
"measures shall be taken to introduce within a period to be
determined later, a nine year compulsory Unity School designed
to replace the elementary, continuation, lower secondary, vocational, municipal middle, and girls schools". The parliamentary
committee to which the bill was referred inserted after the word
'designed' the words "insofar as the proposed experiments demon-
strate its suitability".[10] Thus began that period of experimentation and research which led to the total reform of compulsory
schooling in the Act of 1962.

Experiment and Research

Throughout the 1950's these experiments were conducted in an
increasing number of areas of the country. Their results were
summarised annually, and then collectively in 1959.[11] Led by a
division of the National Board of Education and supported locally
by elementary school inspectors and from 1958, the county boards
set up that year, they covered a variety of issues concerning
the length of compulsory schooling; different syllabus patterns;
problems of differentiation such as the maturity of children on
starting school and growing differences between children at the
outset of puberty; different patterns of organising the 13-16
stage in terms of choice of subject and lines of study; alternative courses; issues of study and work guidance; problems concerning practical work experience; problems of the ways in which
schools operate as social institutions; problems of assessment and
marking; problems of teachers and their competence at various
levels. Many useful lessons were learnt: English could be fitted
into the timetable from the fifth year onwards, largely at the
expense of time for Swedish; the limitations of the experimental final year course for non-academic pupils based on a mass
of vocationally orientated subjects became clearer; differentiation on the basis of parental choice did work; better structured
courses, text books, diagnostic and attainment tests and other
teaching aids made possible "individualisation within the framework of the ordinary class". Above all it was seen that "the
core of the school reform and its ultimate purpose lies in the

internal school organisation",[12] in which context stress was
laid on better guidance to teachers by means of counsellors
and in-service training and above all better initial training.
But the experimental period was fraught with difficulties:
the programme was based on voluntary participation by the
local authorities, and even by the end of the 1950's, only 14%
of the authorities were involved covering less than a quarter
of the population. Only 1% of an age group went right through
all the nine years in an experimental school and a quarter of
those at the experimental schools left the 13-16 stage to take
places in the existing selective schools. Only 14% of the
teachers at the 13-16 stage had formal competence to teach at
that level in academic subjects, and 30% of teachers of practical subjects were untrained. It was recognised, too, that
a period of ten years was all too short to give definite
conclusions.

The idea that research and experimentation should determine
whether of not to introduce the nine year Unity School was
dispelled by a parliamentary decision in 1956[13] when it was
stated that the experiments would lead to the introduction
of a "compulsory organisationally integrated nine year Unity
School". This statement was reinforced by a ministerial
statement in 1956,[14] and in that year a school preparatory
commission was set up to draw up the guidelines and detailed
structures for the new school form, published in 1961[15] and
leading to the 1962 School Act. It is sometimes believed
that these decisions were the outcome of research. Along with
the experiments led by the Board of Education and the local
authorities there were ordinary developmental projects conducted by teachers in schools, as well as a very large number
of academic studies, such as the hundred or more listed by
Bjerstedt[16] and those summarised by Husén and Boalt.[17] Some
of these studies were commissioned by the official committees
of enquiry, some arose in the ordinary process of academic
study. One of the best known is that by Svensson.[18] This
derived from the situation which existed in Stockholm in 1955,
when the city authorities had kept the northern half of the
city with traditional parallel school forms and had set up
three different kinds of experimental school, under the 1950
programme, in the southern half. The city thus had seven
different patterns of schooling for children aged between 13-
16. The Teacher High School in Stockholm took this opportunity
with official approval and help to look at some aspects of
this organisation. In terms of the data collected and statistical analyses of experiences, Svensson could certainly suggest

that organisational differentiation did not have the great
influence on academic achievement that was frequently maintained
in debate. On the other hand, Svensson's study did not seek to
take into account aspects of school work such as discipline or
teachers working conditions; furthermore, the mode of analysis
itself tended to dictate the results achieved, and Dahllöf,[19]
in subsequent re-analysis, came to somewhat different conclusions about the school results obtained by the pupils
concerned.

Other academic researches which were of significance included
those by Bromsjo and Dahllöf on content analysis in civics,
mathematics, and Swedish curricula; Johansson on curriculum in
physics and chemistry, Härnqvist and Grahm on reserves for
higher education and on the progress of students through the
gymnasium; Orring on progress of students through the
gymnasium and Johannesson on sociometric patterns of pupil
behaviour.[20]

It is clear, however, from the OECD reports[21] that in the inter-
play between politicians and social scientists, the dialogue
was often inconclusive and the policy in the end was based on
political decisions aided but not determined by research. Those
decisions recognised, as had the researchers themselves, the
difficulty of evaluating organisational changes because of the
complexity of processes involved and the number of variables
which require to be considered. "The scientific contribution
to experimental work on the 13-16 stage of the compulsory
school ... can be seen to have given scanty answers. The
results are often unclear and are strongly dependent on certain
pre-suppositions; strictly controlled experiments are hard to
bring about and where, nevertheless, they are achieved they
tend to lead to situations and questions of application which
hardly square with reality. The greatest importance of the
investigations should be seen in the contributions they make
to the dispersion of a number of pre-conceptions and how they
show that the questions concern values rather than facts.
School reform is in the last resort a political question".[22]

One of the most explicit confirmations of this was the decision
arrived at by the 1956 Preparatory Commission on the structure
of the 13-16 stage. This fundamental question of the proposed
new school, so closely related to beliefs about the desirability
of early differentiation and the retention even in a common
school of those programmes of study previously associated with
the selective lower secondary school, *realskolan*, defied

answer in terms of research evidence. It was resolved by the
so-called Visby agreement, a political compromise arrived at
from a conference on that island in 1960.

Compulsory Schooling Since 1962

The compulsory school, then, became *Grundskolan* by the 1962
Act.[23] It was progressively to be introduced throughout the
whole of the country and the last two local authorities were reorganised in 1969. In the twenty years of its existence perhaps
four characteristics are particularly worthy of attention. First,
it takes time for a new school form to settle down, and undoubtedly
its major problem lay in the 1960's in the establishment of the
13-16 stage. Most of the staff at that stage inevitably had to
be drawn from the old elementary schools and most of those teachers who opted to teach at this stage had to spend time obtaining formal academic qualifications to qualify for a permanent
appointment. At the same time, all of the teachers of the 13-
16 stage were having to come to terms with new groups of pupils,
more able than those normally experienced by the ex-elementary
teachers, less able by those normally met by the old grammar
school teachers, and with new syllabus content. Secondly, this
syllabus content itself was undergoing change. The process by
which these changes are made is discussed in Chapter 3: suffice
here to note that curriculum plans drawn up for the 1962 school,
Lgr 62, were the subject of reform by working parties that com-
menced the process of rolling reform in 1965; new plans produced
in 1967 led to the parliamentary acceptance of new syllabuses in
1969, Lgr 69. These in turn began to be the subject of new
experimentation and evaluation in the early 70's, leading to
proposals by the Board of Education in 1978 for a new compulsory
school syllabus and in 1979 to a parliamentary approval of yet
again a revised version of those proposals introduced in Lgr 80.
Thirdly, the organisational structure within which these teachers
and these curricula were to operate was subject to change. In
1962 the scheme provided for nine separate lines of study in
the final year of the school. Progressively, this differentiation has been simplified until there is now no formal differentiation. Fourthly, whilst it was still true in 1962 that
nearly half of the school population would leave the school at
the age of 16, by 1980 it had become apparent that practically
all pupils were going to continue schooling in the post compulsory
school sector. The idea, therefore, that the final year of
school could in one way be a preparation for work in the autumn
following the end of the school year, became less and less a
reality.

It is without doubt true that at the end of the 1960's and in
the early 1970's, the situation in the 13-16 stage was causing
considerable disquiet amongst teachers. The non-graduate
teachers' association, *Sveriges Lärarförbundet*, SL, conducted a
large scale enquiry of its own called "Insight into School",
Insyn i skolan, and found singularly distressing evidence of
unrest. For example,[24] the following is a description of an
actual lesson:

1207:   the lesson was due to start;   there were six pupils in
         the room;

1209:   two more arrived;

1210:   four more arrived, noisily;

1211:   two more arrived, with no excuse given and noisily
         climbed over desks to find their places;

1213:   two more arrived;

1217:   four more, saying that they had been to the school nurse
         - one of them was sent for a note of confirmation;

1221:   one more arrived, who, when asked where he had been,
         replied "what's it got to do with you?":   the teacher
         insisted and when the boy replied "I was out with my
         dog", another boy in the class was heard to say "he
         hasn't got a dog".

Of the lesson itself:-

1210:   the teacher began by asking questions;

1213:   a boy who did not belong to the class came in, walked
         around and went out again;

1220:   a boy was noticed reading a comic, was told to stop, did
         so, then started reading again when the teacher's back
         was turned;

1225:   somebody was whistling, three boys were noticed chewing
         gum, which was not allowed, the teacher noticed the comic
         and the boy reading it gave it to another boy who threw
         it on the floor and the teacher picked it up;

1227:   the boy who had been sent to the school nurse returned
        with a note covering three of them, but not the fourth;

1230:   two boys started fighting and the teacher carried on;
        four boys were discussing the television programme of the
        night before and the teacher went over to set work and
        then somebody threw a rubber across the room, and got up
        to collect it;   one boy who had had his hand up for ten
        minutes was seen by the teacher;

1232:   one boy got up and left the room;

1238:   two boys started whistling;

1243:   three boys were flipping coins and the boy who left at
        1232 returned;

1245:   two boys were noticed by the teacher for not working, one
        was told to move his place;   he refused;   the other was
        told to move;   he also refused;   two boys were writing
        in each other's notebooks and it became increasingly noisy
        and the teacher's voice rose to a shout;   one boy was sent
        out and the noise level dropped;

1250:   the bell rang for the end of the lesson.

The comment was made - "this picture can possibly be thought to
describe a very bad situation, but it can also be said that there
are teacher weaknesses. The enquiry group insist, however, that
in the light of other visits made it is not a special case.
This is supported by the comments of the teacher afterwards;
asked how he thought the lesson went, he said "today the class
was quite good, but that perhaps depends in part on the fact
that there was a visitor in the room".

To suggest that this situation was universally true throughout
Sweden is a travesty of the truth. In large numbers of schools,
and especially those in the smaller country towns, the 13-16 stage
presented difficulties but was settling down. Nevertheless, it
must also be recognised that "blackboard jungle" conditions did
prevail in certain of the less salubrious newly established,
concrete high-rise suburbs of the larger conurbations. It also
gave rise to considerable teacher stress. Asked whether they
would, themselves, enter the teaching profession if they had
the opportunity all over again, half of those in the 13-16 stage
said "no". It was conditions such as this that led in 1971 to

the establishment with the authority of parliament of a committee of enquiry chaired by the Director General of the National
Board of Education and concerned with co-operation in the
school, a commission which ultimately reported on the inner
working of school, *SIA*, aspects of which will be discussed in
Chapters 3 and 4.

Post-compulsory Changes

But while debate in the 1950's and early 1960's had tended to
concentrate on the compulsory school, the other sectors of the
system were also in the process of change. Initially in the 1950's
changes at the post-compulsory stage did not cause much discussion.   The only major development was in 1953 when a third
line, for general studies, was introduced into the academic
gymnasium, along with the existing Latin and Modern lines. By
1960, however, it was recognised that the new basic school would
lead to demands for a new post-compulsory provision and a
gymnasium enquiry was established, together with an enquiry into
the possible development of a new form of continuation school.
These committees reported in 1964[25] and proposed a new form of
academic gymnasium and the establishment of a new type of school,
the *fackskola*, the para-professional continuation school analagous
to the German *Fachschule*.   The overtly vocational schools,
Yrkesskolor, were also the subject of a committee of enquiry in
1963.[26] From 1966 a new post-compulsory system of the new
gymnasium, the para-professional continuation school and a
revised form of vocational schools was introduced.   The
gymnasium would have five lines of study, four of them of three
years in liberal arts, social sciences, economics and natural
sciences, and one of four years in technical studies. But a
process of continuous assessment, similar to that introduced in
the 13-16 stage, would replace the traditional school leaving
examination, *studentexamen*.   The para-professional school would
have two year courses in three groups of socially orientated
studies, economics orientated studies and technical studies. By
1963, however, it was already agreed in parliament that these
three elements of post-compulsory schooling were to be brought
together into an integrated school, especially to cater for the
increasing numbers of children who were continuing in full-time
education, direct from the basic school, and this integrated
school was introduced as from 1971, with the name *gymnasieskolan*,
i.e. retaining the traditional and honoured academic title.
Integration was far from achieved, even by 1980; but the
principle of rolling reform, together with changing social,
economic and political conditions, led in 1976 to a committee

of enquiry being set up to propose a reform of the organisational
pattern. Along with the structural changes, and the rapid
increase of 'retention rate' in the post-16 school, however, it
is highly significant to note that some 15% of pupils now take
'time out' from school after the age 16, and return after an
absence of a year or two. (See Chapter 5).

Secondly, teacher education which had been noted in the 1946
commission as a fundamental aspect of any school reform was not
totally ignored. A report in 1952[27] had recommended the establishment of teacher high schools, institutions of full university
standing, and declared that for comparability between the teacher
high schools, it would be desirable if they were concentrated in
the main university towns. Four such high schools were established between 1956 and 1968 (see Chapter 7). In the 1950's
teacher education for the elementary school had consisted of a
four year course for elementary teachers, *folkskollärare*, for
those entering with *realexamen*, or a two year course entering
with *studentexamen*. Infant teachers, known as 'small school'
teachers, *småskollärarinnor*, followed a two year course based
on *realexamen*. An expert teacher education committee in 1962,
known as LUS, reported in 1965[28] and its basic proposal for
teachers to be trained specifically for the three stages of the
basic school, 7-10, 10-13, 13-16 was introduced in 1967. An
official committee of the Board of Education, known as LUR
worked out details of courses for class and subject teachers in
two massive volumes, the 'Red' and 'Green' books of 1968.
Another Committee, known as LUK, was also set up in 1968 to look
at the training of teachers of practical subjects, and reported
five years later.[29] It was recognised, however, that the new
school needed a new category of teacher, that the traditional
division between the subject-orientated graduate and the class
teacher orientated non-graduate remained, and a further teacher
education committee (LUT) was set up in 1974 and reported four
years later.[30] (See Chapter 7).

Thirdly, the whole pattern of higher education began to be
called into question. Traditionally this had been divided into
the University sector, open only to those who had completed the
full academic secondary education leading to *studentexamen* and
the non-university sector, with lower entry requirements and
leading to courses of study of less than degree standard. Progressively, however, with more and more people achieving a full
secondary education and with increasing desire to make more
opportunities available to the adult population in an increasing-

ly egalitarian and democratic society, it became recognised
that reforms in higher education were necessary. The universities had received an increasing number of lecturing staff in the
1950's but in the 1960's the structure, scale, and location of
higher education became issues of political concern. In 1968,
therefore, a committee of enquiry was established (U68) which
conducted large numbers of studies and ultimately proposed a
radical reorganisation of higher education;[31] its proposals
were, in the main, introduced as from 1977 and will be discussed in Chapter 6 below.

Finally, once the main structures for the compulsory, post-
compulsory and higher education were defined or were in the
process of reorganisation in the 1970's, there was widespread
socio-political consensus that various disadvantaged sectors of
the community should be aided. One was pre-school provision,
the scale of which was limited in the 1960's compared with the
rest of the developed world. A committee of enquiry was set up
in 1968, known as the "Wendy House Enquiry", *Barnstugeutredningen*. This reported four years later,[32] and its proposals
for doubling provision and making pre-school places available
for all six year olds as soon as possible after 1975, were
accepted. The implications for pre-school teacher training are
obvious. This is discussed in Chapter 4 below. A second thrust
was to extend facilities for adults. If no further developments
were to take place, it would be well into the twenty-first
century before adults in general could be expected to have
experienced as much formal schooling as their children: indeed,
in the early 1970's it was quite likely that while 80% of
children continued in school to age 18, 80% of the adult population would have left school no later than age 15. As will
be discussed in Chapter 6 below, there developed a network of
provision for adults, in part to make available to them opportunities to take school level courses comparable with those
offered to 13-16 year olds or to 16-19 year olds; secondly
to make it possible for adults who had no more than elementary
or, at best, *Grundskola* education, but who were aged over 24
and had at least four years work experience (which could include
being responsible for the care of one's own children) to gain
access to higher education; and thirdly to encourage by liberal
grant aid that popular education offered by the study circle
movement.

The third educational thrust was to seek to improve opportunities for all in society, of whatever age, who suffered from
handicaps, whether these were intellectual, social, emotional,

or geographical. Even when demand for newly qualified class
and subject teachers began to decline in the 1970's, the
numbers of teachers able to attend full or part-time courses
in special education continued to rise, a trend which has only
partially been halted by the economies of 1980. As far as
possible, all handicapped persons should share the life of
ordinary people. At the same time, a national campaign to
disseminate what has become conventional wisdom at the intellectual level stresses equality between the sexes, even though
its effects have been less than desired.

A time chart since 1944 of major developments in the education
system might include the following:

1944   Report of the 1940 Committee of Enquiry, School in the
          Service of Society

1948   Report of the 1946 School Commission, proposing the
          9-year unity school

1950   Unity School Act: period of formal experimentation
          begun

1952   Teacher Education Report (from 1946 School Commission)
          recommending Teacher High Schools

1953   Academic Gymnasium divided into Latin, Modern and new
          General Line after Lower Secondary School leaving
          examination, *Realexamen*

1956a   No further entry to lower secondary school at age 11
          (i.e. 13+ entry only);

    b   Parliamentary confirmation of decision to establish
          9-year school

1958a   Ministry of Church Affairs renamed Ministry of Education;

    b   County School Boards established

1959   Publication of summary of reports of experiments
          since 1950

1960   The "Visby Agreement" on the proposed organisation of
          the 13-16 stage

1962a   School Law establishing 9-year basic *Grundskola*, with its curriculum, Lgr 62;

    b   Teacher Education Reform Committee (LUS) set up.

1964   Proposals for reorganisation of academic Gymnasium and for setting up new Continuation Schools, *Fackskolor*.

1965a   Board of Education's formal review of Lgr 62 begun;

    b   Teacher Education reform proposals made by LUS.

1966   New Gymnasium and Continuation Schools begun.

1967a   Reorganisation of Teacher Education into Class Teachers for (i) 7-10's and (ii) 10-13's; and subject teachers for 13-16's;

    b   Committee for reorganisation of pre-school set up;

    c   Committee on Reform of Teacher Education for Practical Subjects set up. (LUK)

1968   Enquiry into Higher Education (U68) set up.

1969a   *Studentexamen*, final examination from old Academic Gymnasium, taken for last time;

    b   Revised curriculum for *Grundskolan*, Lgr 69.

1971a   Local Government reformed: establishment of 278 local authorities, *kommun*.

    b   Integrated *Gymnasieskolan* begun, incorporating Gymnasium, Continuation School and Vocational School;

    c   Report, Insight into the School, by Elementary Teachers' Association (SL);

    d   Establishment of commission on co-operation in schools (SISK), leading with Parliamentary support to enquiry into Inner Workings of the School (SIA).

1972   Report of pre-school enquiry.

1973a   Report of Committee on Teacher Education for practical subjects (LUK);

b   Report of U68 on Higher Education.

1974a New Teacher Education Reform Committee for all stages
       of schooling set up (LUT);

b   Report on Inner Workings of School (SIA).

1975   Pre-School Act: provision for all 6 year olds a
       local authority requirement.

1976a Board of Education begins review of Lgr 69 on instruc-
       tions of Social Democrat Government;

b   Review committee for *Gymnasieskolan* set up;

c   Social Democrat government fell from office after 44
       years at General Election, replaced by Centre-Liberal-
       Conservative coalition under Centre leadership.

1977a Legislation for reform of Higher Education;

b   Law on Joint Participation in Decision-Making (MBL)
       for all employees, through their trade unions.

1978a Revised grant regulations giving more autonomy to local
       authorities;

b   Board of Education's proposals for review of Lgr 69
       published;

c   Teacher Education Committee LUT report published;

d   Centre Party leadership in Parliament replaced by
       Liberal leader.

1979a Non-socialist coalition government amendments to Lgr 69
       revision proposals agreed by parliament;

b   General Election - Centre-Liberal-Conservative govern-
       ment re-elected under Centre-Conservative leadership.

1980a Financial cut-backs introduced on all government spend-
       ing at time of economic recession;

b   Lgr 80 introduced by Conservative Minister, to begin
       1982.

Summary

The reform of the structure of education in Sweden thus seems to be complete. There is no realistic suggestion that the basic structure of the school system as it has developed in the last thirty years will be radically altered in the immediate future, despite changing political and economic climates.

The following chapters seek to describe the current scene, suggest why it is as it is, and in so far as an uncertain world permits, draw tentative conclusions for the future. But Sweden as it enters the 1980s is a very different country than it was even twenty years ago. It is no longer quite so affluent, no longer quite so self-confident. Earlier emphasis on equality of opportunity and democratising the school system has given way to notions of equity and justice in life conditions, with compensatory provision for those in need, for whatever reason. Earlier acceptance of central direction of changes sought and won in parliament has been giving way to methods of decentralised and, where appropriate, participatory rather than representative decision-making within frameworks agreed for the country as a whole. Patterns of employment, too, have changed, as Table 1 shows:

TABLE 1:   Employment 1960-1980

| | % Age of Employees | | |
	1960	1970	1980
Agriculture, Forestry, Fisheries	13.8	8.1	5.7
Industry, Mining	34.8	30.5	25.2
Building	9.1	9.7	7.0
Commerce, Banking, Insurance	14.7	17.7	19.1
Communications	7.5	7.2	6.9
Official Administration	11.0	18.5	28.2
Others	9.2	8.3	7.9

As Marklund noted[32] previous trends "shift in emphasis, change
direction, ebb away, hit a ceiling, make way for new trends".
The "front-loading" model of schooling, complete in itself
throughout a continuous period of time, and compulsorily for so
many years, appears to be giving way to a recurrent model, with
optional and not necessarily continuous participation during
the pre- and post-compulsory phases. Especially, it no longer
seems clear that there will be an ever-increasing period of
compulsory schooling after the age of 16. It would follow from
this view that the organisation of the pre- and post-compulsory
sectors will be more flexible than at present, and that the
teacher education required to meet the needs of the various
sectors of the total educational scene will need to be more
flexible, too, to meet not only changing demographic needs as
birth rates change and affect year-groups but also to meet
changing professional roles in relation to pupils, parents,
employers and local political interests in a less directive,
more participatory society. These issues will be the more
complex in a static economy, and will no doubt call for changes
in the financing and administration of education. The next
chapter therefore seeks to outline how the present system is
administered.

CHAPTER 3

Administering the School System

There is little doubt that education is the biggest "industry" in Sweden, and its schools and colleges the biggest places of work. No country, whatever its political system, can fail to devise means whereby an enterprise on this scale is kept under public scrutiny. Furthermore, in a country where there is positive encouragement, by education, tradition, law and experience, of ready access to information, and of active participation in that public dialogue which is the characteristic of a liberal social democracy, there is keen interest in matters educational: how the system is run; whether the decisions are, or should be, made in the local community or more remotely - and probably by more bureaucratic procedures - in the offices of the local authorities or central government; whether the seemingly endless process of change, so often presented as a "reform" and therefore an improvement, has in fact been worthwhile in personal, social and qualitative terms as well as in quantitative and financial terms. The most casual observation of Swedish schools and education offices make it clear that the changes of the last generation have cost a great deal of money (see Table 2). The school themselves are spacious, by international standards lavishly equipped with both staff and facilities, and are beginning to cease to look so obviously like schools both in their external appearance and internal design and furnishings. The proportion of the GNP devoted to education has risen from 2.3% to 7.2% from 1950/51 to 1979/80, a 6-fold increase compared to the $2\frac{1}{2}$-fold increase in the GNP itself, but conditions of work for all persons have changed out of all recognition compared with those depressing days of the earlier years of the century, and especially since 1950. Furthermore, public expenditure is far from all that is necessary successfully to achieve school reform. No government, however, can safely assume continued increases, or even maintained expenditure, especially as the affluent sixties have moved through the inflationary seventies to the uncertainties

and declining rolls during the compulsory years of schooling of
the remaining decades of the twentieth century.

TABLE 2:   Expenditure for School Purposes 1950-80 in Constant
           Terms (1950/51 = 100)

Year	Expenditure for School Purposes		GNP	Expenditure as a Percentage of GNP		
	Total	Per Student		State	Local Authority	Total
1950/51	100	100	100	1.3	1.0	2.3
1954/55	147	121	112	1.7	1.4	3.1
1958/59	185	140	124	2.0	1.6	3.6
1962/63	226	173	148	2.0	1.6	3.6
1966/67	301	227	180	2.5	1.7	4.2
1970/71	352	250	213	3.0	2.0	5.0
1974/75	432	278	238	2.8	2.5	5.3
1978/79	562	361	236	3.5	3.2	6.7
1979/80	640	411	246	3.6	3.6	7.2

Approximate working costs (excluding capital costs), Swedish
Kronor per student, 1979/80

Type of School	State	Local Authorities	Total Costs
9-Year Compulsory School	8,500	8,400	16,900
Upper Secondary School	10,500	8,000	18,500
Folk High School	15,000	6,500	21,500

(Assume 10 Swedish Kronor = £1.00)

(Source: Marklund, 1979)

Central and Local Authorities

As befits a country in which "rationalisation" has been a key
word in the recent past, the administrative structure of Sweden
has been reorganised and simplified in the post-war years. The
monarchy is now wholly "constitutional" the last remnants of
formal participation in decision making being removed in 1975
when the King ceased to preside over cabinet meetings. The
government is formed by those party groups which can command a
majority in the one-chamber Parliament, *Riksdag*, of 350 members
elected by proportional representation every three years: each
party which gets at least 2% of the votes in a constituency is
entitled to a seat, and the 28 constituencies thus elect 310
members chosen from the list of candidates in proportion to the
votes cast. The remaining 39 seats (i.e. excluding the speaker)
are, if necessary, shared between those parties receiving under
4% of the votes cast. This single chamber has existed since
1971, and replaced the "first chamber" of 150 members elected for
eight years by the town and county councils and the "second
chamber" of 233 members elected by popular proportional votes
for four years. There are five main parties which tend to get
seats. The largest single party for many years has been the
Social Democrats, with 40-45% of the votes: only rarely in
their long period of office from 1932 to 1976 did they achieve
more than 50% of the votes. The smallest is the "Communist
Party of the Left" (*Vänsterpartiet kommunist* – *VPK*), who tend
to obtain about 5% of the votes, but who have a solid majority
in the mining constituencies of the far north. The other three
parties are collectively known as the "bourgeois" group – conservatives, who used to be called the party of the right,
Högern, but who are now called "Moderates"; the Center Party –
up to the 1960's known as the Farmers Union Party, *Bonderför-
bundet*, and still essentially a party of the rural communities;
and the liberal "People's Party", *Folkpartiet*: these tend to
obtain, respectively, 10-15%, 20-25% and 10-15% of the votes.
From 1976 to 1980 there have been three "bourgeois" coalitions;
the first foundered in 1978 on policy regarding the development
of nuclear energy, which led to a national referendum largely on
party lines in 1979; the second sat out the term of the parliament elected in 1976; the third took office after the elections
of 1979, with a majority of one.

Each parliament establishes sixteen standing committees,
utskott, with membership proportionate to the party balance in
the House, and these are responsible for considering the detail

of government proposals, *propositioner*, or private member
proposals, *motioner*, and for making recommendations accordingly
to the whole House for debate and decision. It does not,
however, necessarily follow that agreement in committee means
acceptance by the House. The committees are for constitutional
affairs, finance, taxation, justice, law, foreign affairs,
defence, social welfare, social insurance, cultural affairs,
communications, agriculture, home affairs, commerce and industry,
employment and education. When necessary, ad hoc committees are
also established.

The Government, under the Prime Minister, constitutionally has
thirteen departments, each headed by a Minister, *statsråd:* for
justice, foreign affairs, defence, health and social welfare,
communications, finance, industry, agriculture, commerce, labour,
housing, local government and education. These ministries are
essentially responsible for political policy decisions: preparing bills, issuing general directives or making certain senior
appointments in the name of the Crown.

Government policy is carried out be separate central administrative agencies, variously called "office", *ämbetet*, "institution",
verk, or "board", *styrelse*. The four main agencies to which the
Ministry of Education, *Utbildningsdepartmentet*, relates deal with
ancient monuments and national museums, *Riksantikvarieämbetet*;
official archives, *Riksarkivet*; the National Board of Education,
NBE, for compulsory and post-compulsory schooling, *Skolöverstyrelsen* - widely known as *SÖ*; and the Universities and Colleges
Office, *Universitetets-och Högskoleämbetet*, known as UHÄ. Such
agencies enjoy a high degree of autonomy. Subordinate in matters
of political policy making, they are independent in matters of
executive decision-making and are responsible to "the Crown", in
effect the Government as a whole, and not to any particular
minister.

At the level of central government, clearly there must be co-
operation between all concerned with education other than the
Ministry and the executive agencies. Those most obviously
involved are the Department of Finance, which has overall
responsibility for public expenditure; the Department of Health
and Social Welfare, which with its associated Board of Social
Welfare, *Socialstyrelsen*, is responsible for pre-school provision, though not the training of pre-school teachers, and
for health services in the schools; the Department of Labour
and the Labour Market Board, *Arbetmarknadsstryrelsen*, or AMS,
which is responsible for employment exchanges and for vocational

guidance and whose Immigration Office administers the conditions
of entry for non-Swedish citizens who, since 1930, have outnumbered emigrants more or less every year and who now form 5%
of the total population and 8% of the children aged 7-16 in the
basic school; and finally with the Department of Local Government in its relations with the 24 counties, *län*, and 278 local
authorities, *kommuner*, which, since 1971, have replaced the
towns, market towns, *köping*, and rural communes into which the
country was then divided. The word "town" no longer has any
administrative meaning, but to translate *"kommun"* as "municipality" is perhaps a little misleading, except that each
"kommun" will have a "town" or at least a "township" in its
boundaries. To avoid confusion, the phrase "local authorities"
is used in this text for *"kommun"*.

The line between "policy" to be decided by central government
departments or, where so specified, by the local authorities,
and what is "administration" and thus the responsibility of an
appropriate executive board, is, of course, difficult to draw.
The issue tends to be resolved in terms of where ultimate
decision-making authority is vested.[1]

The 'Bible' for the administration of the school system is the
Handbook of Educational Administration, *Utbildningsför-
fattningsbok* - *UFB*, published annually in two volumes over
2,000 sides. Here are to be found the School Law, with its
current amendments, together with the decrees, *förordningar*,
regulations, *stadga*, and instructions, *bestämmelser*, made
under these laws. Notice of amendments is published throughout
the year in Bulletins, *Aktuellt*, which are then codified into
the next edition of *UFB*. There are similar Handbooks issued
by other offices and boards dealing with other aspects of
education - pre-school provision, higher education, labour
market laws and so on.

Without doubt, much is decided centrally. Education is one of
the issues of national politics to be finally determined in
Parliament in at least four respects: the structure of the
system; its main aims; the laws necessary to establish the
system; and the allocation of monies necessary to maintain
and develop the system. These decisions are normally made on
the basis of governmental propositions drawn up by the Ministry
of Education, the final votes following detailed debate in the
relevant parliamentary committees and in the whole Chamber. It
is, of course, highly unlikely that any issue of consequence
could reach the stage of parliamentary consideration without it

first having gone through widespread discussion not only in the
offices of the relevant ministries and boards of central and
local government, but also with all interested parties in the
country at large. Furthermore, in a country with a very large
measure of open access to information and laws which freely
permit publication and provide protection to journalists of their
sources of information, issues also receive widespread public
debate. Any major reform is almost certain to be preceded by
investigations carried out by a Commission appointed by either
Parliament or Government. Some commissions are deliberately
"expert" bodies, *sakkunniga*, and some are deliberately political,
usually with MP representation. They will be aided by representatives of the interests involved, which in educational commissions, will usually be teacher union members and administrators.
Many of these commissions will carry out research projects with
the help, as appropriate, of academic and governmental bodies.
They are likely, too, to make public discussion documents on a
large scale, to seek as wide a response as possible to the principles and proposals they are generating.

It is common practice for sub-reports and working papers to be
published, and the final report, known if it is an official commission as The State's Official Enquiry, *Statens Offentliga
Utredningen*, and referred to on publication as SOU: dates of
publication: number (e.g. SOU 1944:20, for the Main report of
the 1940 enquiry), is then subject to official and public comment
in what are known as *remiss*, reviews. By a given date, all
directly concerned and any group or individual who wishes to, may
submit their observation. The Minister to whom the committee
reported thenmakes publically available the sources of such
comments and a summary of the views expressed. For example, in
1971 in response to an enquiry into the system of marking results
in schools, there were over 900 sets of comments. Obviously
this is a time-consuming process, and it is not uncommon for
five or six years to elapse between the setting up of a committee
of enquiry and the final decision on its recommendations; and
it does result in a great deal of paper to read. On the other
hand, it also means that all shades of opinion have a chance to
make themselves heard and for their views not to be hidden,
especially as interest groups such as teacher unions make a
point of publicising in their own journals the views presented
in their *remiss*, and it is regarded as an important element
of democracy in Sweden.

The current school law sets out such items as the main goals
of the system; the legal rights and duties of individuals to
receive schooling; the powers and duties of the 278 local
authorities to provide the schooling; the necessity for each
authority to appoint a school board, *skolstyrelse*, and professional administrator, *skolchef*; the regional supervisory
role of the 24 county school boards, *länsskolnämnden*; and
the bases for determining the catchment area for schools,
elevområden. Similarly, laws and regulations giving the range
and size of parliamentary grants areas are set out, as are
details of such matters as the number of contact hours (periods
of 40 minutes per week) for different categories of teacher
and the minimum and maximum size of school class at different
levels and in different circumstances - for example, when it
is legally possible or required to sub-divide a class. Something over 50% of all costs of the school system comes directly from central government - the proportion being slightly
higher for the upper secondary school; the remainder forms by
far the largest item in local authority expenditure.

Parliamentary decisions are implemented by "the Crown", *Kungl.
Maj:t*, through the regulations or circulars, *kungl. brev*,
issued by the Ministry of Education. The Crown is also
formally responsible for making certain senior appointments -
The Director and Deputy Director General of the NBE, together
with members of the Board, and the School and Teaching Advisers,
skolråd and undervisningsråd, who head divisions and departments of the Board; the 55 Upper Secondary School Inspectors,
gymnasieinspektörerna, employed by the NBE and the county
inspectors, *länsskolinspektörerna*, employed by the counties;
directors of education in the local authorities, *skolchef*;
and the Heads, *rektorerna*, of the upper secondary schools. In
each case, the "lower level" of the administrative hierarchy -
the local school board, the local authority, the county, the
national board - will make its own recommendations as to the
person(s) it prefers to have appointed from qualified applicants, and the Crown will seldom reject such recommendations
if they are unequivocal and are legally justified, especially
in terms of the prescribed criteria. For all public appointments, there are detailed and published procedures whereby the
merits of each applicant are calculated, *meritvärdering*
these are negotiated by the unions, who have a right to ensure
themselves that the criteria have been correctly applied, and
it is open to an applicant to appeal, *överklaga*, if there is
reason to believe that a less well merited person has been
appointed. There is no appeal beyond decisions vested in the

Crown.

The officers of the National Board of Education are not
political appointments, and the members of the Board itself
are required to represent different sectors of society:
employers of graduates, employers in industry and commerce,
employers in the public sector and the welfare sector, employee
interests and, experimentally since 1968 and permanently since
1978, a student representative. In practice, these members
are drawn from organisations - national administration from
the Labour Market Board and the Universities and Colleges Board;
local government from the Swedish Association of Municipal
Councils; private employers through the Confederation of
Employers (SAF), employees through the main union groups - LO
for manual workers, TCO for salaried workers and SACO for
graduates; and the student from the Central Organisation for
School Students, SECO. Since 1974, there have also been three
NBE staff members on the Board. A simplified organisational
structure of the Board is given in Fig. 3. Proposals to restructure the Board and decentralise the power are, however,
shortly to occur (see Appendix IV).

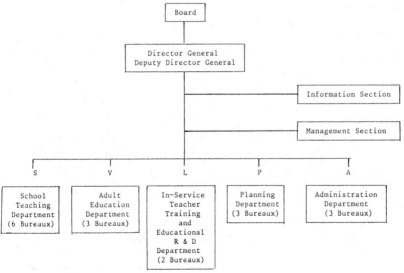

Fig. 3.   Structure of National Board of Education,
          Skolöverstyrelsen.

Source: Marklund, 1979.

In plenary sessions, with the Heads of the Board's divisions
and bureaux present, the Board decides all major issues and
especially those which are to be recommended to the Crown and
Parliament - budgetary issues, changes in the structure of
schools, forms of teacher education, major curriculum changes.
Authority to decide lesser issues is delegated to the Director
General, who in turn may delegate to senior officials. Normally,
the Heads of divisions and bureaux are appointed for six years,
though these are generally renewed. The expert advisers,
however, the inspectors for the upper secondary school and the
advisers for stages or subjects of specialised fields of school
activity, *konsulenter*, normally serve for shorter periods and
then return to their schools: these persons have a major role
in the on-going process of curriculum and school organisational
reform which forms part of the Swedish model of "rolling reform".
One major responsibility of the Board is to appoint, on the
recommendation of the County School Board, the Head of the basic
school; and it also acts as an appeal body from the county
and local school boards.

The 24 County Boards are composed of lay members constituted on
the same lines as the National Board. The senior officer is
the county school inspector, who is generally assisted by one
or two inspectors, and has the expert services of an in-
service-adviser and about a dozen part-time advisers, together
with the staff of the county school pyschological service.
Besides making its own recommendations for appointments to be
made by the National Board or the Minister, the County formally
appoints teachers in the region; approves applications for
grants from central funds, or for leave of absence by teaching
staff; agrees the dates of the school year for the county;
plans detailed changes in catchment areas; agrees curriculum
provision in the compulsory, post-compulsory and local
authority adult education schools; makes recommendations to
the National Board regarding additional post-compulsory provision in the local authorities such as the introduction of a
new line of study; approves building projects; organises in-
service courses for the county; and acts as an appeal body
from the local authority school board.

The precise function of a regional body at country level is
itself a matter of discussion; some argue that it is important
for planned development and for in-service training which is
not expressly local in nature; others argue that since the
Education Act of 1962 made each local authority the legal
authority for school provision at both the compulsory and post-

compulsory level, there is no real need for an intermediate
county or regional tier of administration. This issue is still
(1980) the subject of a government commission on the structure
and role of school administration centrally and regionally.[2]

The school board, *skolstyrelse*, of each local authority has the
formal, legal responsibility for the school system in its area,
to survey the general state of provision and to take those
steps necessary to ensure satisfactory facilities for children
and young persons. It is also required to administer the
schools inasmuch as the duties are not stated elsewhere;
ensure that the schools comply with current regulations;
encourage experimentation and in-service training; and promote co-operation between schools and homes. Members of the
school board, which must number at least 7, are in proportion
to the local political balance elected by the local council.
Its chairman is a local councillor, and the chief administrative officer is required to attend its meetings. It recommends
to the county those it prefers for appointment to established
posts, and to some extent local needs can be taken into account
alongside the more objective measures of academic qualification
and professional experience, but cannot override them. It is
free to make temporary appointments on its own authority. It
is, therefore, a very meaningful body at the local level, and
especially so when its members are likely to be known personally to those concerned: of all local authorities only 71
represent areas with a population of over 30,000; 140 have
populations between 10-30,000; and 66 have under 10,000.

In summary, then, Parliament decides goals and allocates funds;
the Ministry of Education implement these policy decisions on
behalf of Government. They are then carried out by the
National Board which is largely autonomous in developing
curricula, planning the main outlines of teaching, allocating
the government grants and inspecting upper secondary schools.
The National Board is assisted by the County Boards, who
inspect the compulsory school, plan and co-ordinate regionally,
and allocate grants to each local authority which, through its
school board subject to local political control, is responsible
for the schools of the area. This responsibility is carried
out within each School Management Area, *rektorsområde*, led by
a headmaster or headmistress. In most countries it is possible
to ask "where is the elementary, or primary, or secondary
school?" and be directed to a building, or perhaps a campus.
In Sweden, the term *"Grundskola"* or *"Gymnasieskola"* for ages
7-16 or 16-19 is a concept rather than a building; each may

be made up of a number of "school units", "*skolenheter*", and
a School Management Area may embrace a number of such units –
perhaps two or three units each containing provision for 7-10's
and 10-13's; perhaps a number of units which also include one
for the 13-16 stage. Similarly at the post-compulsory level,
there may be a "*Gymnasieskola*" for a district which includes
several local authority areas – provision of *gymnasieskolor* is
at present organised in 130 regions throughout the country;
but each school unit may well contain only a section of the
whole *gymnasieskola* – perhaps only the practical lines of study;
or only the theoretical lines: in fact less than a third of
the *gymnasieskolor* units have both academic and practical
lines in the same buildings or on the same campus (see Chapter
5 below).

The number of senior posts in each local authority area is
determined by a point count. Every group of 25 pupils aged
7-10 and 30 pupils aged 10-16 counts 1 point; every 30 pupils
aged over 16 count $1\frac{1}{2}$ points. An authority with a population
of between 10-15,000 is likely to have sufficient points to
justify at least a part-time, and possibly a full-time chief
officer as *skolchef* and perhaps three School Management Areas,
two for the basic school and one for the post-compulsory
school, each with a Head, *Rektor*, responsible for two or more
school units. The senior *Rektor* could serve as part-time Chief
Officer. Each of these areas, according to its point count,
is then entitled to one or more Directors of Studies,
Studierektor, who will be responsible for matters such as time-
tabling and staff deployment, or perhaps the administration
of school travel arrangements (which can be a complicated and
expensive activity in rural areas). Each school unit will also
have an Equipments Teacher, *tillsynslärare*, who is responsible
for ordering text books and all the teaching equipment for the
school unit and for the maintenance staff. These positions –
Chief Officer, Head, Director of Studies and Equipment Teacher
– form the team of "school leaders", and will all have reduced
teaching loads defined by regulation. Within each school,
there will also be other senior positions: Heads of subject
areas, the number of which depends on the size of the school
and hence the group of subjects involved; and for units with
pupils over the age of 13, there will be a careers teacher,
yrkesvalslärare, and a study and careers consultant, *syokonsulent*. Within a school unit there will also be a school
nurse, perhaps part-time or peripetetic between a number of
units; access through the county to the schools psychological
service; and of course, clerical, catering and cleaning staff,

and that most important of all school personnel, the caretaker,
who probably has a house or flat nearby. The school health
service gives regular annual medical checks and children at the
compulsory school are entitled to free dental treatment; school
meals are provided free of charge; there is free school transport for those travelling long distances or from remote farms;
all teaching materials are provided free; local authorities
insure all pupils against accidents during school hours; there
is provision - not always enough to meet demand - for leisure
activities outside school hours, either at the school or by youth
organisations; all instruction is free - including higher education for overseas students who can prove their ability to maintain
themselves if a place is offered; and there is a widespread
system of financial assistance in the form of study grants,
studiebidrag, and loans, *studielån* (see below, Appendix V).

Participation

Politicians, administrators, teachers and other school staff are
not, however, the only people concerned with how schools are run:
students and parents are undoubtedly interested parties, and if
the school is to be run as a democratic institution and is to
teach its pupils to become participants in a social democracy,
then scope has to be found to include them in the decision-
making processes. Without doubt one of the most obvious and
important changes in Swedish schools in the last generation is
the way in which the voice of the parent and the pupil can be
heard.

In the compulsory school, two organisations are compulsory for
teachers: first, the class conference, which includes all the
teachers who take a particular class, and secondly the subject
conference of all teachers taking a particular subject, irrespective of level. Where these concern individual pupils, they
and their parents have a right to be present. More immediately,
every school class in the compulsory school has, since 1977, had
a "class council" of the class teacher and representative pupils.
In the upper secondary school, it is a statutory requirement for
every school unit to have a joint advisory committee consisting
of the head, two teachers appointed by the staff, two students
appointed by the student body, and two others appointed by
the local authority. Its task is to promote effective co-
operation, good order, and a pleasing atmosphere, and should
discuss, inter alia, matters of comfort, rules and discipline,
the head's draft rules for his area, and efforts to relate
more effectively with parents, welfare authorities, and the

various specialist non-teaching staff in the school. The
committee is required to assist in the investigation of any
case which involves possible suspension or expulsion of a
student.

While perhaps inevitably the value of such councils and
advisory committees will vary from school to school, it is probably generally true that pupils themselves see their influence
to be limited because they are only advisory. On the other
hand, there is evidence that issues of consequence have been
profitably discused. Class councils can agree with the teacher
the approach to be adopted in a subject or the themes to be
taken up; and the discussion of common values in all schools
in 1979-80 has led to agreed school rules: one example for a
unit for 7-13s, posted in every classroom, reads:

1.   Show regard and be polite to each other.

2.   Help, and not disturb, each other during lessons.

3.   Contribute to enjoyable meals by being quiet and peaceful
      in the dining room.

4.   Take care of the school buildings and materials, each
      others'valuables and clothes.

5.   Don't throw rubbish about!

6.   Be punctual!

7.   Use acceptable language!

8.   All traffic in the school grounds is forbidden between
      7.30 a.m. and 3.30 p.m.

9.   Do not take school satchels into the classrooms before
      morning school begins.

10.   Be outside in the grounds during breaks but do not leave
      the school area without permission during the school day.

11.   It is forbidden to eat sweets during the school day.

12.   Ball games and throwing snowballs are allowed only in
      places where it is shown to be permitted.

13. Pupils from the junior and middle stages may mix in the
     school grounds, and should show respect for each other.

14. Be responsible for what you do and say!

These were the outcome of meetings of teachers, other adults
and all classes.

For parental involvement, there is a national Home and School
Society, *Hem- och Skola Föreningen*, formally recognised as a
consultative body, and this has branches in every school area,
and has meetings with each school unit, represented by the
Head and Director of Studies. At the level of the school
board, representatives may attend as observers, and if proposals in the 1970's for school management committees are
ever implemented, parents would be included on them, represented through the Society. But as is noted at the end of this
chapter, these kinds of activities are at the level of representative decision-making, and as is common in all such
situations, tend to involve those who are active in public
life and be as successful as the representatives are themselves active. They tend not necessarily to involve those
directly concerned with the pupils as a whole. Attempts are
made to overcome this by having, in each class of the compulsory school, two representative parents - desirably a
"class mamma" and a "class papa" - who are encouraged to call
together all parents in the class and to meet with the teachers
involved. Individuals, however, still appear to prefer informal contacts, by telephone or by meetings arranged at the
school; there is still some hesitancy of parents to approach
teachers, rather as there is in approaches to doctors or
lawyers; and in any case, contact is much more likely at the
7-10 and 10-13 stages than at the senior level, when it tends
to be more formal and spasmodic, and linked with specific
occasions when significant choices are being made or school
grades awarded.

Who, then, decides what? The range of powers and duties of
the various boards, central, regional and local, the pattern
of which is not dissimilar for other social services, might
well suggest that there is little scope for local initiative.
It is certainly true that the overriding issues - the framework of the system, the goals of the curriculum and the allocation of time between its different activities, the main items
of curriculum content, the conditions of service for teachers,
the manner by which the economic support for local authorities

is calculated and administered – these are decided centrally
and administered locally. But this tends to ignore two facts.
First, there has been a significant move in recent years in all
facets of public administration formally to increase the scope
for decentralised participatory decision-making within nationally agreed frameworks which ensure equality across the country.
Secondly, there are both formal and informal processes by which
influences other than those of the central determining bodies
themselves are able to make themselves felt, and to encourage
what Marklund called "progressive administration".[3]

The most important controlling force in ensuring equality of
provision is no doubt finance: and "he who pays the piper"
inevitably tends to "call the tune". To this extent, in any
system where salaries are paid on nationally agreed scales and
where standards of staffing in terms of both number and qualification are the subject of national agreements between unions
and employers, a very large measure of public expenditure is
pre-determined: over half the cost of the school system is
accounted for by salaries, mainly of teachers. Similarly,
there are statutory requirements to provide materials, meals,
transport, welfare services and basic administrative costs for
the compulsory school, and in effect for all 16-18 year olds
and a third of 18-19 year olds in the upper secondary school.
The local authority also has certain responsibilities for
adult education, especially to provide courses at school level;
and the payment of grants and loans, while financed by central
government monies, is all at nationally agreed scales. The
authorities responsible for financing nearly half the costs of
the school system and those aspects of adult education within
their purview have limited opportunity to meet deficits of
government grants by their own levels of taxation: their
estimates are subject to government guidelines and control can
be, and is, exercised by altering the amounts and the kinds of
activities which attract grant aid – for example, in 1980 the
possibility was raised of ceasing statutory grants for school
building, partly in terms of giving greater freedom to the
local authorities, but partly undoubtedly to limit local
authority expenditure. There is, of course, a form of "equal-
isation grant" to ensure that the less wealthy authorities are
not too obviously disadvantaged. Economy comes, then, at the
local level by perhaps reducing the standard of provision and
by limiting expenditure on those activities which are discretionary – the kind of pre-school provision (day-mothers sent
to ordinary homes are cheaper than places at pre-schools);
some kinds of "enrichment" services at the compulsory school

are cheaper than others; some of the adult courses are more
for leisure and pleasure than necessity.

In order to increase scope for local decision making, there
were important changes in the grant system in 1978. Instead
of fixed sums being applied to specific provisions, the new
system provides for a total resource to be available to a
local authority, 75% of which is a base sum calculated on a
pupil capita formula, and 25% is a strengthening resource
derived from previous specific grants for special education,
elective courses, activities linking school with employment,
and monies reserved for special purposes. This total sum may
now be allocated as the local area sees fit, within the limits
of statutory obligations: school unit A with large problems
of immigrant children might want to devote extra resources to
language teaching; school unit B might have a widely dis-
persed catchment area with several children travelling from
outlying villages and needing leisure time facilities related
to the school; school unit C might have particular problems
calling for enrichment teaching because of the demographic
changes in the catchment areas - the closure of a factory,
perhaps, and thus increased youth unemployment. In this way,
the absolute dominance of central financial control is
lessened. At the same time, local decision making does
encourage differences of opportunity in different areas as a
consequence.

These moves are closely related in origin and effect to the
introduction in January 1977 of the new law on The Joint
Regulation of Working Life (MBL). This gives the employee the
right to interpret the meaning of negotiated agreements. This
law has helped to strengthen the influence of teachers and
other staff on decision-making within the school system, and
has led to many more meetings and committees. Whereas a
chief officer or head could once act on his own, there now has
to be a series of information-giving and negotiating procedures, which can delay action, but which can help to ensure
that a measure, once agreed, will be implemented with the
full approval of all concerned. Significantly, too, it is a
procedure which involves others than just teachers: the
clerical, domestic and maintenance staff are also involved
and have a right to participate in general discussions and
decisions which affect them.

The significance of this law as it applies to teachers was at
once seen in relation to the acceptance by Parliament in 1976

of the proposals which derived from the massive enquiry into
the inner workings of the school, SIA, in 1976.[4] This recommended, inter alia, a more flexible use of resources of staff,
time, money and space; a broader concept of the school day
with a mixture of required, elective and optional activities;
the abolition of the concept of the school class, replacing it
by the concept of a working group of pupils served by a working
team of teachers; greater contact between school and the
society it serves; and greater scope for local decision-making
by a local committee with representatives of management, school
leaders, staff, parents and pupils – the latter three all chosen
through their respective unions. Clearly the fullest implementation of these ideas would lead to significant differences
between schools in the ways in which they carry out their
required tasks. Equally clearly, in the context of the joint
decision-making law and the nationally agreed conditions of
service for teachers, won after long years of pressure, the
teacher unions are anxious to ensure that the flexibility and
local individual initiative which SIA encourages and which
teachers themselves support in principle does not and cannot
lead to a worsening of conditions for their members in areas
where local influences might be damaging to them.   In
particular, the SIA proposal for a school management committee
has yet to be implemented: when unions become part of management, the whole basis of employer-employee relationships
change. [5]

There is, too, a third change in the law which affects
employees: since 1974, all are protected against arbitrary
and unfair dismissal. Sacking an administrator or teacher
has always been difficult, especially within the public service
with its system of "established", *ordinarie* and "non
established", *extra-ordinarie*, or "temporary", *extra*, posts
(see Chapter 7 below). Appointments as Chief Officers or as
Heads are in the first instance for a limited period, generally
six years, and are then renewable. An applicant probably has
an established post already, and on taking up the new one in
a non-established capacity can himself leave to return to his
original post or can be relieved of the new post and placed in
an established post or can be relieved of the new post and
placed in an established post within the school area: this
indeed happened in 1980 to a headmaster who simply did not
get on with his new staff, though it was the subject of much
discussion and enquiry before the final decision was reached.
But the law ensures that a person who has been retained for
six months in a post for which no time limit was initially

specified is then permanently appointed (albeit to a non-established or temporary vacancy); and only for extreme dereliction of duty can a public servant be removed. In normal circumstances, of course, this causes little problem. It does do so, however, when persons other than the school board and the teacher unions are involved: for example, those cases where parents refuse to have their children in a class where the teacher is a chronic alcoholic. In days of participatory decision-making, the teacher unions have yet to define adequately in legal terms precisely those conditions where dismissal is justified. They will, too, be required in the 1980's to think through and negotiate those conditions for redeployment which will surely result from falling rolls at different age-levels, circumstances which are certain to vary from area to area.

Administrative Progressivism

It is at this point that Marklund's identification of "administrative progressivism" is particularly important.[6] He sees this as the third driving force behind educational development since 1950. It is consequent upon the other two, namely the socio-political progressivism which dates back into the liberalism of the nineteenth century and the social democratic ideas of the twentieth, noted in Chapter 1, together with the tradition of pedagogical progressivism which had its Swedish exponents as well as influences from Germany and USA; and it is created by the fusion of these traditions. But "it is precisely this fusion of mutually independent if not actually conflicting theses that is the necessary condition for realisation of the reform. The reform will succeed, if the third type of progressivism is achieved. This applies at all levels in the education machinery, the local and the central and to both teaching and administrative staff". Administration, in itself, is simply static, implementing principles without innovation; progressivism implies an advance - and it must be possible to administer the changes which are agreed. "Progressive administration" is called on to interpret the aims of educational policy, which are often expressed in very general terms; to take up a stance when aims conflict, rather than merely refer back those issues and situations where there is incompatibility; and to set priorities between different aims, not to thwart the political process but to implement its goals in ways which both money and circumstances permit. Money alone does not alter the ways in which school systems operate, any more than does a mere verbal expression of will in an act of parliament: "an implemented reform is always an administrative reform. Implementation is a responsibility for both the central and local administration. Communication between these two levels is of major importance. Local education committees, school managers and teachers are surrounded by conservative forces and will often fail to implement what is new unless they receive support from the central administration".

In these terms, "the reforms (since 1950) would not have been possible without fairly firm central direction. Central direction, however, should not be confused with authoritarian direction".7 The central educational policy could be decided only by Parliament, and the administration to implement those broad lines of policy contained in legislation could only be centralised. There was, and is, no real way in which any central government even in the most dictatorial of states can ensure that every local authority, let alone every school, every head, every class, every teacher puts policy immediately into practice or in the precise way intended by the new law or regulation. To exemplify in the context of curriculum change: there have been official curricula in Sweden for centuries, but there have always been arguments about what they should contain, and even when official requirements are quite precise, there is no doubt that there are differences in emphasis and ethos in schools around the country.

Furthermore, the formal processes of decision-making illustrate how a wide spectrum of opinion is able to be involved. The revision of the 1969 curriculum for the compulsory school may serve as an example. The NBE was formally instructed by the last social democrat government in 1976 to propose a revision as part of the normal process of 'rolling reform'. At the Board, a group of seven experts worked with three "reference groups" - an "interest group" with representatives from the local authorities, employers' trade unions, white collared workers, the academic world, teachers, parents and pupils; a parliamentary group with representatives from the five main parties; a co-ordinating group of the chairmen of the major teacher unions. Alongside their general work, these groups also considered three specific issues - alternative courses at the 13-16 stage; the freer use of resources; and syllabus content - using material prepared for them by the teacher unions and the NBE and involving teacher groups and experimental projects around the country. Within the NBE there was also a professional committee of MP's, academics, students and others which considered all working papers. A further special commit-

tee of the NBE and local authority members worked out the
economic implications of proposed changes. To generate public
debate, several special issues of the NBE's journal
Educational News were sent periodically in large numbers free
to all school districts for discussion among teachers, others
in the school, pupils, parent associations and local branches
of teacher unions. These discussion papers also posed questions to which the NBE requested answers, 900 of which were
received. In the autumn of 1947 all committees met for a residential conference prior to drafting the report. The final
proposal was published in April 1978 and in accordance with
Swedish practice, was sent to all relevant bodies for review,
remiss. There were nearly 300 replies, those of the teacher
unions based on replies from all branches - and all of these
responses are public documents. The Minister (by that time a
liberal member of the caretaker government formed when the
bourgeois coalition collapsed after two years of office) con-
cluded, no doubt correctly, that the proposals had not taken
sufficient account of the opposition to the idea of a more
integrated and common curriculum which it proposed, and
announced that a revised version would be the basis of the
government proposition in the spring of 1979, and which subsequently became Lgr 80.

But throughout the period of formal consultation and discussion,
there were the usual public debates in the press, on radio,
and on television at peak viewing times. The change in the
political climate reflected in parliament was mirrored in the
change in the public climate. A whole series of informal
processes was taking place, both at the level of central government and parliament and at the local levels. In a country with
a small population, it is inevitable that civil servants and
academics, at all levels, have close and on-going contact with
their friends from school days now in the worlds of commerce
and industry. The kinds of questions asked at local and informal levels reflect popular interests. There has indeed in
Sweden been much comment that the NBE has had too much
influence on the school system, and this has encouraged demands
for decentralisation of decision-making. But to believe that
central government takes no account of local opinion is just
as naive as to believe that local opinion alone is going to
determine central government decisions.

What in the end is perhaps more important is the extent to
which the mechanisms of open government and open decision-
making really operate rather than the formal structures deter-

mining the levels at which decisions are made. Furthermore,
parliamentary decisions are, by their very nature, political
decisions made by political parties: the instructions to the
NBE for its curriculum revision in 1976 were those of a social
democrat government, not the caretaker liberal government which
received their recommendations. But the implementation of
these broad decisions at the level of the school is a matter
of decision-making between interest groups, not political
parties, between parents and pupils as well as teachers and
chief officers. At this level, it is kinds of participatory
rather than representative democracy which are beginning to
show in Sweden, with decisions reached by agreement rather than
the majority vote in a council chamber of parliament, let alone
the decision of an individual. How far this trend will develop
is a matter for conjecture. It is, however, a matter under
discussion in Sweden and one which, together with other trends
to be noted in the ways in which schools are now beginning to
operate as living institutions, could have important consequences for the very concepts of school and school class,
teacher and pupil, to which we have been traditionally
accustomed. It is, then, an issue which will be considered
in relation to other trends in the concluding chapter.

CHAPTER 4

The School System

Pre-school

For a country which has devoted so much attention to formal schooling, it is perhaps surprising the Sweden starts formal schooling so late at the age of 7, and has, in international perspective, relatively few pre-school facilities. Of the 765,000 children aged under 6, approximately 80% are wholly outside the care of society and are the responsibility solely of their families;[1] 438,000 children are in the care of a parent who is at home the whole day; a further 152,000 are looked after privately, either by relatives or by a *dag mamma*, a woman coming to the home; about 8,000 children have the father at home while the mother is working; about 3,000 children appear to be at home without anybody taking care of them. Provision for the remaining 20% of pre-school children is the responsibility of the Board of Social Welfare, not the Board of Education, a division of responsibility which was criticised by the OECD Examiners in 1979.[2]

Clearly, these figures will vary considerably according to the age of the child and to the part of the country in which the child is living. In terms of age, approximately 5% of children under the age of 3 are registered in some pre-school facility and about 15% of children aged between 3 and 6; only at the age of 6 are there places for virtually all children. In terms of the different parts of the country, while Stockholm has over 30% in the care of the local authorities, Göteborg and Malmö about 25%, and the larger towns about 20%, in the sparsely populated areas the proportion drops to less than 15%. The same regional differences appear in the proportions of those who have a parent at home all day. While in the large towns this may be true for half of the children, in the sparsely populated areas, especially in the north, over two-thirds will have a parent at home. In the rural areas it is also very much more

common for grandmother or grandfather to live in the same place
as the grandchildren, and contact with neighbours is also
greater;   in the large towns, anonymity and loneliness, both
for children and for families, is much more common and many
have their relations and friends in different parts of the
country.

Access to work in different parts of the country is another
factor which influences how children are taken care of during
the day.   In the larger towns, it is relatively easier to
find work and therefore much more likely that the children do
not have any parent at home.   Conversely, in the remote areas
it is difficult to find work and at least one of the parents is
more often at home.   As children become older, these regional
differences remain.   From the age of 3, over 40% of children
in the Stockholm area will attend some communal pre-school
provision, whereas in the remotely populated areas this is true
for only 22%.   In Stockholm, less than half of the children
have a parent at home the whole day between 3 and 6, whereas
in the north over 60% have one parent at home.

It was only after the basic school system had been reformed
that Sweden began to pay serious attention to pre-school
provision.   In 1968 a commission of enquiry into child care,
Barnstugeutredningen, was set up to determine the goals for
the workings of play schools and day care homes, especially
for children of the ages 5-6;   to advise how the activities
should be organised to see if different aspects of the work
of the basic school in the first year could be prepared for
in a play school;   to identify the consequences of this for
the compulsory school;   and to discuss how a general pre-school
could be organised in relation to other child care facilities.
In particular, attention was to be given to the possibilities
of providing pre-school facilities in the remotely populated
areas and for the handicapped.   In part, too, the establishment of the commission reflected the growing proportions of
women who were in gainful employment.   Of all women between
the ages of 16 and 74 in 1965, only 49% were in employment;
by 1970 this rose to 53% and by 1976 to 60%.   For women with
children under the age of 7, 35% were at work in 1965;   this
rose to 50% in 1970 and 63% by 1976.   For women with children
in the ages of 7 to 16, 58% were at work in 1965;   this rose
to 60% in 1970 and 79% by 1976.   "Our wish to create a child
orientated society and our efforts towards equality for men
and women are closely related.   The family policy reform work
is characterised by this comprehensive view.   More and more

women wish to continue gainful employment outside the home, even
when the children are small. Already the most commonly occurr-
ing situation in young families is that both parents are gainfully employed outside the home. Everything indicates too, that
the frequency of gainful employment among women with children
will continue to increase. Society must then accept greater
responsibility for the satisfactory organisation of care of
these children during the parents' working hours. If society
does not accept this responsibility, experience has shown that
this affects the children, since women nevertheless go back into
the labour market. The parents are then forced to solve the
problem of child care without access to the security society
can provide".[3] The recommendations of the Child Care Enquiry
in 1972 were largely implemented in the Pre-school Activities
Act of December 1973. In Article 2, these activities were
defined as those "pursued in the form of a pre-school, a family
day nursery, or other complementary pre-school". Tables 3 and
4 show the then existing and the planned provision. From 1975
all local authorities were to provide a place for all 6 year
olds for at least 15 hours a week or 525 hours a year; in
sparsely populated areas for 700 hours for 5 or 6 year olds.
Local authorities were also given the responsibility as soon
as possible to provide places for all 4 and 5 year olds who
had special need for help and stimulus and, if possible, to
provide places for younger children with such needs. Each
local authority was also required to produce a 5 year plan

TABLE 3: Pre-school Provision in Relation to Mothers
          Gainfully Employed

YEAR	A	B	C	D	E	%
1955	11,900	11,700	23,600	265,300	139,400	16.9
1966	34,900	36,600	71,500	387,300	212,800	33.6
1971	40,600	37,400	78,000	399,700	217,000	35.9
1972	49,000	35,500	84,500	401,000	219,000	38.4
1973	55,500	36,800	92,300	389,700	210,900	43.8
1974	61,900	43,500	105,400	417,300	225,800	46.1

A   Children of pre-school years in day nurseries.

B   Children in local authority family nurseries.

C   Total A + B.

D   Children aged 0-7 whose mothers are gainfully employed.

E   Children aged 0-7 whose mothers work 20 hours or more per week.

%   Of children in child care of all those with mothers who work 20 hours or more per week.

Source: SOU 1975:62

TABLE 4:   Proposed Pre-school Expansion 1975-80

YEAR	A	B	C	D	E	F
1976	241,000	77,500	32	61,200	25	43
1977	248,000	87,500	35	62,100	25	40
1978	254,000	96,300	38	63,700	25	37
1979	261,000	104,000	40	65,400	25	35
1980	-	111,800	-	66,400	-	-

A   No. children needing places in day nurseries

B   Planned day nursery places.

C   % of children who can be offered a place in a day nursery.

D   Planned local authority day nursery places.

E   % of children who are offered a place in a municipal family day nursery.

F   % of children lacking municipal supervision.

Source: SOU 1975:62

assessing the need of day homes places for children with parents
who were at work. The purpose of these facilities was said to
be four-fold: to help the children to become open and caring
persons with the ability to co-operate with each other; to
help them develop a stable understanding of themselves as
individuals with the ability to co-operate with their environment; to help the development of understanding certain basic
concepts; and to promote suitable physical and social development. The primary emphasis is not to communicate knowledge,
but to promote personal development. "Children's development
is enriched by early participation in a living culture, not
simply as passive listeners or watchers but as active members
of that culture, preserving and developing the art of express-
ing themselves in speech, song, music, movement, colour and
form... One of the most important areas for personal development is the ability to communicate with other people, not only
through speech but through pictures and movement... Furthermore, the pre-school should give many opportunities to contribute to children's social development. Drama, music,
rhythm and different forms of physical activity are examples
of activities which naturally lead from individual activity
to co-operation in a group and at the same time have great
importance for the child's communication skills. The personnel
in the pre-school, who are in close contact with the children,
can also help to answer the children's questions in matters of
ethics and religion".[4]

The organisation of pre-school facilities continues to be in
one of two kinds, either what is called a Day Home, colloquially
called 'Dagis', or in a play school, 'Lekis'. The day home is
essentially for children aged 6 months to 6 years whose parents
are at work, and is open on week days from 6.30 a.m. to
7.00 p.m. The play school is essentially for children aged 4
to 7, providing a child minding facility for three hours a day
on weekdays. Currently, however, the trend is to integrate
the part-time groups in the play school with the full-time
groups in the day home. The babies, up to about 18 months old,
are likely to be in groups of four in one room; those up to
about $2\frac{1}{2}$, in groups of eight, tend to have their own self contained facilities, including a separate sleeping area and
access to a 'wet' area for play with water; those over $2\frac{1}{2}$
tend to be in groups of up to 20, again with their own 'home
rooms' for both play and rest.

The general guide lines for running these schools traditionally
emphasise a developmental, play-way approach, as the following

citations[5] suggest. 'There should be a large playroom common
to all groups, with different kinds of playing material, where
the children can take care of small animals and plants, read,
look at pictures, play with water, play with music and sounds
and make their simple "natural science" experiments. There
should also be screens where they can withdraw from others and
be on their own. They should be allowed to help in the kitchen
and those who want to could eat in the big dining room alongside
the kitchen. Outside there should be equipment for movement
games, slides, climbing frames, sand and earth in which to dig
and plant. The outdoor play area should not be too carefully
tidied and organised with ready made plants, so that the children can themselves engage in simple biological and botanical
discoveries. Children should also be taken to the woods and
countryside, to collect leaves, branches and berries and examine
these when they come back. In every pre-school there should
also be a rest room, partly for those who are ill, partly for
those who need therapy or handicap training. All attempts to
individual initiative and independence should be encouraged,
the old rule of 'look but don't touch' giving way to allowing
children to look, to see, to touch and to do. Small children
need a lot of bodily contact with adults and should be cuddled,
allowed to climb up and sit on the knee; adults should talk a
lot with the little children, not in children's speech but with
correct words, at the same time as they are dressing them or
helping them to feed. Little ones should, as far as possible,
have the opportunity to look in drawers and cupboards, take
things apart and put them away; they ought to have large
numbers of the same objects available so that the children
should not need to fight over them; finger painting and foot
painting should be permitted, along with rhythmical games and
dramatic exercises; conflicts between the children should not
simply be quietened down, but where possible played out in
dramatic form; and there should be books in the pre-school and
record players, radio and tv and ordinary daily newspapers.
All the personnel ought to be engaged in planning what should
be done in the pre-school, both during the day and over a
longer period of time, and to some extent, the children could
take part in such discussions. The teachers should make
observations of the children for two or three minutes at a time
and make notes on how they are developing'.

The appropriateness of this method has been the particular
concern of research led by Stukát at the Teacher High School
in Göteborg. It was expected that the experimental group of
children receiving a child centred curriculum, with emphasis

on social and emotional development, would show significantly
greater development than the control group. They did not. The
experimental group had higher attainments in terms of social
knowledge, in vocabulary and verbal expression, in daily life
routines and manual construction tasks. In measures of social
and emotional adjustment and of 'mental health', there was no
significant difference, and follow up tests showed that the
cognitive advantages were not permanent. The results suggested
that the pre-school should develop areas where some degree of
teaching is included, and this is reflected in current pre-
school pedagogical guidelines. This kind of approach is essentially related to what is known in Sweden as "dialogue pedagogy",
in essence an interaction between the older notions of "communication pedagogy", where the teacher alone initiates and the
pupils react, and of extreme "child centered pedagogy" where the
child alone initiates and the teacher reacts, the model which
has until recently been the most commonly to be found in the
Swedish play schools. In "dialogue pedagogy" the children and
the teacher both initiate and there is interaction, a give and
take between teacher and child. New emphasis is being placed
on teaching as well as enrichment programmes, where intellectual
and linguistic development is now accredited the same degree of
importance as social and emotional development. "The teachers'
role was defined as one of active educational intervention and
not limited to vaguely defined 'stimulation' and 'enrichment'".[6]

The extent to which the 1973 Pre-school Act has been implemented may be seen in the statistics in Tables 5 and 6 below. The

TABLE 5:   Day-home Registrations at Pre-schools 1971-1978

	Day Homes		Registrations by Age				
	No	Places	>2	2	3-4	5-6	7
1971	1,124	36,761	6,345	5,744	14,610	13,906	40,605
1973	1,534	52,324	8,748	8,015	19,112	19,609	55,484
1975	1,867	63,005	9,466	9,532	24,332	22,632	65,962
1978	2,990	106,675	25,101		38,267	37,945	101,393

Source: Statistisk Årsbok, 1979, Table 304

TABLE 6:   Play-school Registrations 1971-78

		Part-time Nursery Registrations		
	No Institutions	3-4	5-6	7
1971	2,019	2,401	80,492	82,893
1973	2,695	3,518	98,804	102,322
1975	3,327	3,916	108,114	112,030
1978	3,922	2,864	114,700	117,564

Source: Statistisk Årsbok, 1979, Table 305

increased day home provision between 1971 and 1978 is clear;
double the number of registrations of those under 3;   about
three times as many aged 3-4 and 5-6 has increased nearly three-
fold.   At the same time, part-time registrations at the play
schools have increased by some 50%.   Parallel with these
developments has been a significant increase in the number of
students being trained as pre-school teachers and in various
forms of child care courses and the visitor to Sweden will
readily see the increasing number of pre-school buildings being
put up in and around the towns.   In the 1960's and 1970's it
was quite common to see pre-schools operating on a small scale,
perhaps in the basement areas of flats.   Now a substantial
spacious single-storeyed building is likely to be found in
most residential areas, with parents delivering the little
ones at the school at some time after 6.30 a.m. and collecting
them again before 7.00 p.m.   The children lack for nothing in
equipment, and the child:adult ratio (including all domestic
staff, who are expected to be in contact with the children) is
likely to be 1:4 or 5.   It should be noted, however, that only
for 6-7 year olds, for those attending for three hours a day,
or those placed in pre-school facilities for reasons of special
need, are the opportunities provided free of charge;   for the
rest, a daily charge is made, related to income and the number
of children attending the school every day.   In 1980, the
range was between 2 and 24 kronor a day for one child (average
11 kronor);   1 and 8 kronor a day for those children (average

4 kronor). (Assume 10 kronor = £1). The cost of further pre-
school provision is, however, causing problems as the expensive
seventies give way to retrenchment in the eighties. A government statistical survey in 1980[7] showed that 137,000 new *dagis*
places were needed, and 59,000 new *lekis* places. While 75% of
those with children were satisfied with the *dagmamma* they had,
72% would have preferred a place in *dagis* if one were available.
Essentially it is a problem of money. A *dagis* place costs
65,000 kronor;[8] yet only 60% of those enrolled actually attend
every day, possibly because so many parents work only part-
time.

The most significant, and from the point of view of the formal
school system perhaps the most important, development in
recent years, however, has been the establishment of a pre-
school place for all 6 year olds; virtually all such children
now attend at this stage. While it was not the intention that
this provision should formally take over the teaching and
learning responsibilities of the first year of the pre-school,
nevertheless a number of experiments have been conducted whereby the pre-school and the first school work can be integrated.

Three such experiments may illustrate this trend. The first,
in the early 70's took place in Strömsunds, a local authority
in Jämtland, in the centre of Sweden, integrating the pre-
school with the first school, a study which was part of a larger
project on problems of sparsely populated areas. Here the
issue was essentially one of scale: there were simply not
sufficient children to justify separate pre-schools. Integration with the first school implies that for two days a week
5 and 6 year olds to, together with their older brothers and
sisters, to the ordinary school. Accommodation already existed
on a sufficient scale and the school buses were also available;
all that was needed was increased personnel. In each school
there was one pre-school teacher and an assistant, the assistant generally being a local housewife who had been given a
short training course. For the whole local authority there
was also a pre-school teacher to act as a consultant. Integration was not simply in terms of premises but was also pedagogical, but unlike an ordinary pre-school, which normally has
only a three hour session per child per day, and because the
children only came twice a week, here they were engaged for
five to six hours for each visit. They began with free play
for an hour, then discussions with the pre-school teacher
while the assistant took charge of the first school children.
As the pre-school consultant in the area pointed out, this

kind of co-operation was extremely valuable, creating a team of
teachers, psychologists, social assistants all working with
about 100 children in seven different schools. The alternative
would have been to close schools, and indeed, in that area some
twenty very small schools had been closed in the previous ten
years. Financially, too, the scheme was worthwhile since the
pre-school was able to use, in part, the resources of the
ordinary school.

A second experimental programme was carried out in Västerås, a
town with a long tradition of co-operation between pre-school
and the compulsory school. In 1971 a new complex was built in
an area of 7,000 people to accommodate all children up to age
13, and the main purposes[9] were to create more individualisation
and a smoother transition from stage to stage. The children
and teachers would know each other better, and there would be
no constraints of buildings or organisation to prevent children
of different ages and stages working and playing together, or
of personnel – class teachers, special education teachers
skilled in diagnosis, pre-school teachers, classroom assistants
and all others – to work together as a team. Pre-school children received "readiness teaching" in Swedish and Mathematics,
early developers had special instruction, contacts between staff
revealed shortcomings of mutual understanding, knowledge and of
methods. The evaluation of the project, however, suggested
that the early interest in integration declined and co-operation
did not become the norm. There appeared, too, some fundamental
differences of perception of the goals to be achieved, and there
was some suggestion that the traditionally directive organisation of the compulsory school, with explicit curriculum requirements, inhibited teacher experimentation. The evaluation con-
cluded that it would not be possible to achieve real integration between pre- and compulsory school "without changing the
operational goals which function within the respective systems".

A third experiment developed in Ludvika[10]. Here the original
emphasis in 1970 was on the identification at the pre-school
stage of those children likely to have language difficulties
when they entered the ordinary school, and to give them some
training in advance. Because in this town the school board was
exercising the local authority responsibility for pre-schools,
it was easy to arrange for pre-school teachers and the special
education staff to identify some 10-20% of the play-school
children deemed to be in need and for the special teachers to
run clinics for them. A three month training period was alloca-

ted from February to May, a programme of exercises in listening, observing and speaking was devised, and the clinic teachers made weekly visits to give a 20-minute exercise for 2-4 children in the company of the pre-school teacher, who subsequently carried out similar exercises for the remainder of the week. This approach began essentially as a local initiative, and one clearly directed towards facilitating the work of the ordinary school. Since then, there developed nationally an emphasis on the idea of co-operation between pre and compulsory school. There is, too, more talk of "compensation" and more recognition of the need for general social and emotional stimulus to which language training contributes. By 1979, Ludvika was providing a "contact teacher", generally a clinic teacher, for every pre-school, with the responsibility to get to know the children, identify those likely to have problems, participate in the child-care teams of pre-school teachers, welfare workers and psych-ologists, arrange visits to the compulsory school and above all to make contact with the parents. This preparatory work now runs from October to May, with the contact teacher making perhaps two visits to each class or group in the autumn term and three in the spring. Material for preparing for school is provided, but such training as is carried out depends on the pre-school staff. Further, this work now applies to all in the pre-school final year, and not just to a selected "remedial group", which could lead to a kind of streaming at age six. Attempts at statistical evaluation has also given way to more illumina-tive methods, to take up issues as perceived and to attempt to deal with them. For example, the pre-school staff have found the need for more help from the speech therapists and school psychologists; the idea of a team of adults who help the pre-school child is seen as perhaps better than relying on the one class teacher in the ordinary school; there is a value in small group-rooms in the ordinary school; parental contact is highly desirable; there is value in the co-operative council which brings together representatives from the school system and the social services department. Each school can devise its own ways of associating with its feeder pre-schools, within a general framework. In September-October, the contact teachers are named, first visits are made, and information is sent to pre-school staff. In November-December, the speech therapists and psychologists visit the pre-schools and the second contact visits made: in January-February, there is a third visit along with a child care conference and the plans for introducing the children to the ordinary school: in March-April, the fourth contact visit leads to the first of several visits of the pre-school children to the ordinary school: in May, the fifth

contact visit takes place, made, where possible, by the class
teacher the children are to have in August; In June, there is
a meeting for children and parents at the school, followed by
an evaluation of the experiences of the year.

In sum, Ludvika's experiences suggest that home and school
problems are often broader social problems, best discussed
locally, in concrete terms and in small groups of parents, teachers, officials and politicians. That typically Scandinavian
form of adult education, the study circle, is also highly valuable for parents of both pre-school children and of children in
the ordinary school to discuss issues such as what kind of
school is needed, how one can best build on pre-school experiences, what if any are the differences between pre-school and
compulsory school, how home and school can together provide a
secure environment for our children. The author of this report
noted that what started as a small end-of-year project to help
prepare some children for formal school in August had reached
the point where one might suggest a "school for parents" as a
way of achieving the original goal; but the question of how
to make the physical and psychological environment more friendly
for children is a social problem beyond merely parents and
teachers.

These experiments raise several issues beyond simply that of
closer links between the pre-school and the compulsory school;
perhaps thevery term 'pre-school' is becoming a misnomer in
the "educative society" and might in time be replaced with
"pre-compulsory", in much the same way as "post-compulsory"
can embrace traditional upper secondary schooling and other
provisions for what at present at least is the 16+ age group.
The "child-minding" role also gives way to a more pedagogically
oriented role, with all that this implies for the traditional
functions of pre-school and compulsory school teachers: it is
less and less easy to say that formal learning begins only at
a certain age and is led only by certain categories of person,
traditionally called 'teachers'. The question of who is
legitimately concerned with both the care and the education of
children also calls into question the relationships between
parents, teachers, other professionals, the representatives of
other public services, the politicians: and also questions,
the ways in which decisions are and might be reached in a social
democracy. Such ideas reappear in the ways in which the compulsory and post-compulsory school systems operate. Discussion
of them is therefore reserved for the concluding chapter.

The Compulsory School

It is the third week in August. About a million Swedish youngsters aged 7 to 16 are about to start the school year. They
will be at school for 39 weeks, Monday to Friday, throughout
the autumn term of some 18 weeks until mid-December, and the
spring term of some 21 weeks until about 10th June. There will
be the usual public holidays - All Saints Day in the Autumn,
May Day, Ascension Day and Whitsun Monday in the Spring,
together with two to three weeks over Christmas, and a week
over Easter; there is often a long weekend (Friday to Monday)
free in the Autumn; and in the last twenty to thirty years, it
has become common to provide a week in February so arranged
that three large regions of the country each take a different
week - a break which provides opportunities for winter sports
but is increasingly popular also for parents to fly to the
Mediterranean sunshine. There are also five extra days of duty
for the teachers, known as "study days" - one at the start of
the year for planning purposes, the others fixed throughout
the year, at dates whereby an occasional holiday for the children might be lengthened by a day, and used by the local,
county or national school boards for various aspects of in-
service training.

The normal school day begins at 8.00 a.m. or shortly afterwards,
and there will be lessons in 20, 40, 60 or 80 minute blocks
until about 11.00 a.m., when there is a break for lunch, where
a hot meal is available for the children free of charge, and
for the teachers who are there to supervise it; then lessons
again until about 3.00 p.m. Each 40-minute block is known as
an "hour", and the number of lessons in each subject area at
each age-range is laid down in "hours", what in England would
be called "periods". Similarly, the teachers' duties are also
expressed in so many 'hours' per week, 29 for class teachers
and 24 for subject teachers - and a teacher who has additional
"hours" of duty is paid overtime at set rates. For both pupils
and teachers, attendance at the school is required only for
those periods laid down for them on the time-table.

The aims of the basic comprehensive *Grundskola* are clearly
stated in the first section of the 1962 Education Act: they
are first, to impart knowledge; secondly to develop skills;
and thirdly, in collaboration with their families, to promote
the development of the pupils into happy individuals and competent and responsible members of society.[11] Legally, these
aims have not changed since they were agreed in the early 1960's,

nor has the basic organisational structure of three stages,
the junior level for 7-10's, *Lågstadiet*, the middle level for
10-13's, *Mellanstadiet*, and the senior level for 13-16's,
Högstadiet.

The curriculum, however, together with the general guide-lines
and working methods set out in the formal *Läröplan*, has under-
gone regular change: the original Lgr 62 with which the new
comprehensive school began was itself the subject of "rolling
reform" beginning in 1965, leading to a proposed revision in
1967, *Läroplansöversyn*; a new formal curriculum together with
some twenty slim volumes of suggestions in Lgr 69 (1969); a
further review in the 1970's led to a Board of Education
proposal in 1978 and, after prolonged debate in the changing
political climate which heralded the end of the forty year
Social Democrat parliamentary leadership in 1976, the emergence
of the current curriculum, Lgr 80, officially introduced in
August of 1982. Since only those pupils beginning school in
1969-1971 can possibly have completed all nine years without a
new curriculum being introduced, and even these pupils having
teachers in the final years of their schooling who were facing
the prospect of change in the coming year of two, it is perhaps
not surprising that the world of the compulsory school in
Sweden for the last twenty years has been somewhat unstable.

The official *Läroplan* covers the whole of the basic school.
The 1980 version, as in 1969 and 1962, emphasises that the
individual pupil is the centre of the school's activities, but
at the same time the responsibility for the development of that
individual is shared between the school, the home and society
at large. As Lgr 69, however, put it, "even during the years
at school the home has the primary and overriding responsibility
for the education and care of the child"; or in the words of
Lgr 80, "The school complements the influence and education
of the home. The main responsibility rests always on the
home".[12] It follows that the school has an ongoing responsibility to work with the home, to inform parents about its
activities and the child's responses not only intellectually
but also in terms of personality development. In particular,
the school also has a clear social purpose: in the words of
Lgr 69, "School is part of society ... (and) Co-operation in a
democratic society must be developed by free and independent
people. But freedom and independence must not be for selfish
ends: it must be the basis for co-operation. The school will
therefore stress and develop those characteristics of the
pupils which can support and strengthen democratic principles

of tolerance, co-operation and equality of rights between
people. A main purpose is to arouse respect for truth and
right, for the value of the individual human being, for the
sanctity of human life and thereby the right to personal
integrity". Lgr 80 uses similar phrases.[13] The ways in which
the school operates, therefore, should stress the need to
motivate the pupil to engage _actively_ in the life and work of
the class or group, in _concrete_ and meaningful situations,
encouraging the _individual_ to respond at his or her level, but
in an atmosphere of _co-operation_ where self discipline, a
sense of common responsibility and a feeling of togetherness
prevail - words which, in Swedish, give rise to the pedagogical
mnemonic of the 1960's and 1970's, MAKIS. Lgr 69 then followed
with eighty pages of suggestions for implementing these ideals,
followed by a further 120 pages setting out the aims, main
items of content and suggestions for implementation of the
subjects offered at all stages of the school. A further twenty
booklets on aspects of those subjects or of school organisation
were also produced. The new Lgr 80 is much shorter, less
wordy, less "poetic" in its language, more down to earth and
with greater stress on the basic skills and the essentially
intellectual function of schooling: "It is a main purpose of
the school to give the pupils good knowledge and skills ...
By emphasising basic knowledge and skills, the school gives
all pupils a good start" (p.15). At the same time, however,
the emphasis on active learning remains: "the need for active
participation by the pupil rejects a one-sided teacher-led
approach, that kind of teaching which consists only of the
teacher summarising material which the pupils then memorise
with the help of notes and a textbook and which they are
later asked to recall either orally or on paper". The positive
role of the teacher in the development of moral values is
also stressed in Lgr 80, not in an authoritarian manner but
so that "the values of the child are formed through contact
and co-operation with people whom the child trusts and wish to
emulate". Appendix VI summarises the contents of Lgr 80.

It is always hard to know how accurate are generalised state-
ments about the schools of any country. For almost every
statement made, there could be made a qualification in one
school or other. Visitors are often taken to "show places",
and in any case are more likely to pay visits in the neighbour-
hood or the major cities. The normal school throughout the
country is, by international standards, very well built,
spacious, well staffed both in terms of numbers and qualifications of teachers - the gross teacher pupil ratio of 10:1 is

clearly the highest in the world - and equipped with all the
material that most experts anywhere could think of - up-to-
date textbooks in ample supply, ancillary reading material, all
manner of audio-visual aids. The "materials room" of any
school is a veritable supermarket for the teacher, and the
tillsynslärare, the teacher who is responsible for ordering
equipment, seems at least prior to the 1980's to have had no
shortage of money to buy stocks of this or that. Each classroom, too, will have ample storage space, neatly in cupboards
or in trays stacked under working shelves - the walls well
covered with board and hessian for pinning up work; a slide
projector and tape recorder on a convenient trolley; a TV
monitor; a phone with connections to the main offices and
stores; ample black or white boards; and convenient racks
above to hang maps or pictures, with pointers and drawing
instruments hanging ready at the side. One seldom sees the
clutter of cardboard boxes so common in English primary
schools.

The staff rooms, too, reflect an affluent society, one which
has a high regard for schooling and all who work with it, and
one which in recent years has paid much attention to working
conditions. Such rooms are now called "personnel room" -
mainly used by teachers, but in fact open to all who work in
the school; it is likely to have a little kitchen where coffee
is available more or less all day, served either in proper cups
or in plastic beakers - none of the cracked mugs or shared
spoons so commonly found in England. The chairs and sofas,
tables, vases, curtains and pictures would do credit to many
a home or hotel lounge; and as far as possible the "working
areas" - notice boards, lockers, places to mark exercise
books - as well as racks for outdoor clothing and the public
telephone - are provided in partitioned corners or in adjacent
rooms. A separate 'non-smoking' area is now also commonplace.

The daily lives of teachers and pupils are without doubt now
much less formal than even a generation ago. Then it was
commonplace for the teacher's desk to be on a raised dais at
the front of the room; dress would be formal - business
suits for the men, dresses or costumes for the ladies; boys
would bow to the teacher, and girls make a little "bob" -
even in the street when riding their bicycles. The teachers
were addressed in the formal third person singular, as "sir",
magister, or "miss", *fröken*, and while the younger children
were addressed with the familiar second person singular, "you",
du, and the Christian name, use of the surname was not

uncommon for older teenagers. Today, teachers are likely to be
dressed more informally, and the pupils to wear the international uniform of jeans and tee-shirts;   teachers and pupils
alike use the *du* form of address, and Christian names.   The
class might well stand when a teacher or stranger enters the
room, but the little bows and curtsies are reserved for use by
"well-brought-up" children when introduced to important stran-
gers or really old people.

Of course there are schools in which there is much motivation,
activity, concretisation, individualisation and co-operation
amongst pupil work;   where schools and homes and local employers work closely together;   where teachers not only work one
with another but also in close contact with all the other
adults in the school.   There are, too, many new schools with
imaginative designs - open plan, carpeted areas, linked classrooms with rooms for small group work or spaces for individual
study.

The normal school, however, is still very likely to be the
traditional "egg crate" of separate classrooms to hold up to
30 pupils, and the normal pattern of teaching remains of the
"frontal" kind: teacher facing rows of pupils in desks,
determining content, controlling the method, and while setting
projects and differential assignments still nevertheless
retaining the class working more or less at a common pace over
common material.   There is no streaming at any stage: each
class is 'mixed ability';   and it is a fundamental principle
of the compulsory school that the children (or the parents) are
free to choose alternative courses offered by the school.
This is part of the school law and while the school may inform
the child or parent of the requirements and of the pupil's
school record, it cannot override any choices made.   The idea
of "dialogue pedagogy", while not wholly absent in the basic
school, can hardly be said to characterise it: observation
would suggest that "individualisation within the framework of
the class" remains a goal to be reached rather than an expression of daily experience.   Nevertheless, a National Board of
Education Survey in 1972 did show in social studies that teacher instruction accounted for only 24% of working methods in
the 13-16 stage, with 11% discussion;   17% group work;   6%
study visits;   8% miscellaneous and 34% individual work;   and
a further study in 1975 in social studies in Class 5 showed
about a third of the teachers using group work regularly,
several times a week, and in a further 20% using it once or
twice a week.[14]   Individual involvement in planning work is

also by no means infrequent.

Perhaps _Lågstadiet_, the junior level for the 7-10's, has been least affected by the changes of the last generation. The teaching of young children always has been less formal, and the growing links with the pre-school encourage this. It is at this stage that the visitor is most likely to see children behaving "naturally", spontaneously, working at different activities within the class, or even being allowed to work elsewhere within the school. Except for the teaching of craft, for which specialist teachers are appointed, the child in _Lågstadiet_ is still essentially in the charge of a class teacher, who takes the class for the next three years, the class size in law being limited to 25 and in practice averaging just over 20, especially in the late 1970's when the birth-rate began to fall, as has been the case throughout the developed world.[15] For the first two to four weeks, the newcomer to Class 1 is given a gentle introduction to the routines of school, attending for only a couple of periods a day in groups of ten to twelve, and at the same time enabling the teacher the better to get to know them. The length of this introductory period will vary, in part related to the extent to which preparation for school has already been a feature of the last year of the pre-school, in part dependent on the number of children and the extent to which they have clear problems of adjustment — about one in ten of all children in the basic school are immigrants, half of them Finnish-speaking and the remainder made up of Yugoslavs, Greeks, Turks, and thirty or more nationalities — and in part dependent on factors such as school transport needs in a country where so many pupils have to come to school not simply by a school bus but perhaps in twos and threes by taxi from remote farms. By mid-September, the children are expected to attend the full school week — 20 periods a week in the first year, 24 in the second, 30 in the third; though throughout the stage there are built-in opportunities for small group work, the so-called "resource periods" where the number of periods allocated for the teacher exceeds that allocated for the pupils, as indicated in Figure 4.

For the 7-10s, there has been little argument about what the children should be doing. The main purposes are clear: on the one hand to begin in a formal context to mix with others, and on the other to learn the basic skills of the 3R's together with knowledge of the locality and the opportunity to develop creative interests in music and craft. Debate has

Subject	Periods per Week						Total
	Year 1		Year 2		Year 3		Yrs 1-3
	Pupil	Teacher	Pupil	Teacher	Pupil	Teacher	Class
Swedish	9	15	11	14	9	10	29
Mathematics	4	7	4	6	5	6	13
English (i)					2	2	2
Music	1	1	1	1	2	2	4
Craft (ii)					2		2
Sport (iii)	1	1	2	2	3	3	6
Orientation Subjects (iv)	5	6	6	7	7	6	18
Total	20	30	24	30	30	30	74

(i)   For teaching English, it is recommended that the pupils have four 20 minute sessions.

(ii)   Both word and metal and textiles; groups of 10-17.

(iii) The Lgr 80 name for what was Gymnastics.

(iv)   Religion (2+ periods per week) and 'knowing the locality' (3 or 4 or 5 periods a week per pupil, 4 or 5 per teacher) .

Fig. 4: Curriculum Schedule, 7-10's (Lgr 69; unchanged in Lgr 80, except that there is no longer any division into years, and the subjects are listed in (Swedish) alphabetical order)[16]

tended to centre on four themes. The first concerns the extent to which the development of pre-schools and the advent of places for all six year olds will lead in fact if not in formal expectations to an increasing number of children reaching the

age of compulsory schooling already initiated into the pleasures
of reading and the practical skills of number bonds. A second
issue is whether it is worth allowing two periods a week in
Class 3 for the teaching of English. Thirdly, how far should
one move towards the ideas of 'open' education, open in the
sense not only of space and the absence of classroom walls but
also in the sense of a less specified curriculum, less structured
relationships between pupils and adults, less cut off from the
real world outside the school. Fourthly, how far might the
adults work together in teams, not only of two or three ordinary
teachers along with a special education teacher, but also with
the psychologist, school nurse, welfare worker and even 'unqualified' parents and other adults in the community.

The solid core of the work remains in the teaching of Swedish,
nearly half of the pupil's time being devoted to this, and in
a country where compulsory schooling starts so relatively late,
maturity alone makes it possible for the majority of the class
to have mastered reading at the end of the first term, leaving
the resource time and the increasingly ready availability of a
teacher allocated to special education to deal with those with
reading problems. The emphasis on language work is essentially
utilitarian, to make it possible for the school to communicate
knowledge, enrich personality, provide a basis for further
study and equip its products to meet different situations in
life: the main items of content at the 7-10 stage direct
attention to observation and expression, discussion, to use
reading for pleasure and as a source of information and
experience, and to write in order to communicate. In Mathematics, too, the approach tends to emphasise the four rules
and basic concepts. After a flurry of excitement in the 1960's
with 'modern mathematics' and set theory there is now something
of a reversion to more traditional content areas where basic
knowledge and knowing one's tables is again seen as fundamental.
Piggetian principles and the use of structural apparatus are
translated into traditional texts and methods. Perhaps the
liveliest aspects of work with the 7-10's is the social studies
course, when traditional Christian bible stories and church
services blend with the customs of other religions, relationships with others, and a wide range of practical issues in the
locality - elementary health education, with due emphasis on
the dangers of alcohol and tobacco; sex education; traffic
education - as well as learning about local history and geography, the weather, elementary economics in raw materials,
concepts of property, ideas of commerce and trade; something

of the wider world and the traditions of other countries;   and
above all a good deal on the living world of nature all around
them, in the gardens, the fields and the forests.   Swedish
children learn from an early age that they live in a land of
beauty, that pollution of all kinds is a human problem, that
fresh air and healthy living is worth striving for.   But Sweden
is not alone in having to recognise that the real world
presents pictures of human behaviour much in conflict with the
values and knowledge imparted in the schoolroom.

Throughout the 7-10 stage, the teachers maintain their own on-
going records of pupil development, and have regular contact
with the parents, and especially at the end of each term.   There
is no formal grading at this stage, though informally the
teachers may well use the 1, 2, 3, 4, 5 scale in which all
school marks in Sweden are expressed, both for their own records
of exercises set in class and in conversation with parents and
colleagues, though a 3-point scale is more likely.

The second big change in the life of the Swedish school child
comes at the age of 10+, the transfer to *Mellanstadiet*:   who
is going to be my class teacher, and will I have new classmates?
As class size can be 30 at this stage, it might well mean going
to a new building, too.   As the previous chapter explained,
Grundskolan is a concept rather than a specific school, the
stages of 7-10, 10-13, 13-16 tending to have more unity in
themselves than the whole period of 7-16.   The teachers at this
stage are normally in contact with their colleagues from the
7-10 stage, and may well have been given before the autumn
term the unofficial marks which the pupils had received in the
first school.   There will in any case almost certainly be a
meeting early in the autumn term, after the 10-13 teacher has
met the new class for a week or two, when the teachers from
the two stages share their impressions and information about
the children's backgrounds and general behaviour.   There is,
however, no formal school record card, and if a child moves to
another district it is left to the teachers concerned to make
such contact one with another as they feel desirable.

The atmosphere of the 10-13 stage tends to be more formal than
for the younger children, and with more scheduled periods per
week (see Fig. 5), the children are in the school more or less
all the time it is open.   The day normally begins in their
own classroom - there is no regular school assembly;   and it
is still not uncommon for the teacher to begin the day with
prayers and a hymn - each classroom has a small organ as part

Subject	Periods per Week						Total
	Year 4		Year 5		Year 6		Yrs 4-6
	Pupil	Teacher	Pupil	Teacher	Pupil	Teacher	Class
Swedish	9	10	8	8	9	9	26
Mathematics	5	5	5	5	5	5	15
English(i)	2	2	4	5	4	5	10
Music	2	2	2	2	1	1	5
Images(ii)	2	2	2	2	2	2	6
Craft(iii)	3		3		3		9
Sport (iv)	3	3	3	3	3	3	9
Orientation Subjects(v)	8	8	8	8	8	8	24(21)
Domestic Science	–		–		–		– (1)
Total	24		35		35		104(102)

(i)   English: 4 x 20 minutes was recommended in Lgr 69 in Year 4.

(ii)   The Lgr 80 name, *bild*, for what was Drawing.

(iii)   Craft: as in *Lågstadiet*, includes wood and metal and textiles; can be in two groups with 17 people, or must be with 24 or more.

(iv)   The Lgr 80 word for what was Gymnastics.

Fig. 5: Curriculum Schedule, 10-13's (Lgr 69; Lgr 80 unchanged except for totals in brackets and no longer divided into separate years, and the subjects are listed in (Swedish) alphabetical order).

(v)   Orientation subjects: Lgr 69 assumed 296 periods in a 37
      week year, divided into Religion - 70; Civics - 37;
      History - 52; Geography - 62; Natural Science - 75.
      Lgr 80 reduces the total to 21 periods per week over the
      three years.

of its normal furnishings, and class teachers are still expected
to learn to play at least chords to accompany singing. But
since the class teacher's normal commitment is for 29 teaching
periods per week, it is inevitable, too, that the class will
have other teachers as well, and also inevitable that each
school unit will tend to make it possible for the teachers to
offer those activities which most interest them, irrespective
of their formal qualifications (Chapter 7 on teacher education
discusses this point in greater detail). The subjects for
specialisation tend to be English, wood and metal as distinct
from the textile crafts, art - an activity which in Lgr 80 is
now formally seen as much broader than drawing and painting,
and is called *bild*, which might be translated as "images" or
"form" - and gymnastics, now renamed in Lgr 80 as sport. There
might, too, be some specilisation in the orientation subjects
between social studies and the natural sciences.

It is, then, all the more possible to envisage teams of teachers
working with groups of children rather than simply a class
teacher system, and since most school units for 7-10's and
10-13's tend each to have two to four classes per year, the
size of the school unit alone encourages such ideas of co-
operative teaching and a more personal atmosphere. There was
a tendency in the 1960's for schools to become larger and more
impersonal, but it is now policy to restrict any new school
unit to a maximum of 500 pupils.[17] These administrative and
organisational patterns fit conveniently the ideas which emerged
in the SIA deliberations of the early and mid 1970's on the
working environment of the school, and on the ideas for the
reform of teacher education. The idea of the "working team",
with access to welfare, medical and psychological personnel,
and to the services of the native-language teachers and teachers
of Swedish for immigrants, seeks to ensure that each pupil
receives the kind of schooling that will serve his individual
needs. The extent to which it succeeds in these respects is
inevitably a function of the social as well as the professional
skills of all the persons involved: those brought up in
earlier traditions of school organisation do not always find
it easy to adapt to new patterns, any more than student teachers
in initial training find it easy to adopt new ideas of co-

operative teaching which they themselves had not experienced at school and which they may not find exemplified in the schools in which they practice. Much depends, too, on individual perceptions of one's job. Teachers are accustomed to working alone with groups of twenty or more pupils in classrooms or workshops or laboratories, to deciding their own methods and selecting their own content. It is noticeable, however, that there is much more co-operation between teachers now than a generation ago; texts, teaching materials, tests, judgements are more readily shared, even though this sharing tends to take place more in the personnel room and at conference times (for which one period a week was allowed as from 1979, when the teaching commitment was reduced from 30 to 29 periods), rather than in opening the actual classroom teaching to each other.

For the pupils at the 10-13 stage, greater demands tend to be made both in class and in homework, though most work is done in school rather than at home. The pace of work increases, and differences in levels of attainment begin inevitably to become more noticeable. With the introduction of Lgr 80, teachers are formally required for record purposes only to grade the pupils in years 8 and 9. Informally, however, marking school work on the 1,2,3,4,5 scale becomes a regular feature of school life already at *Mellanstadiet*, and however much the formal grading requirement is removed from the basic school as a selective instrument, it is hard to see how some form of assessment and expression of pupil response can be totally removed. "Did I get it right?" and "How is Ann-Marie getting on?" are wholly understandable questions for both pupils and parents, just as "Did they understand what I had been teaching?" is something the teacher wants to know. The selective function of school marks is undoubtedly a major issue at those points when selection needs to take place, and the elimination of selection by the school at the age of 13 or later removes this official need for marks. It does not, however, remove the need for judgements of some kind, to give information or guidance: and for some, the judgement might also be a motivating carrot. So the regular "test", referred to in Swedish school life as a 'writing', *skrivning*, becomes more and more a feature of school life, the pile of exercise books to be marked, the sharing of results. It is in this context that the school normally makes most contact with the parents as it is required to do so twice a year. How this is done might vary. Each parent knows the home telephone number of the teacher, and every teacher makes clear to the parents how he or she may

best be contacted – either by a fixed appointment system at the
school or by phoning home. It is common for the teacher at
home to be phoned up in the morning about 7.00 or 7.30 to be
told that the child is ill or has to be absent for some reason;
and at the end of each term in December or June it is common,
too, for the class teachers to have two or three evenings
devoted to phone calls with parents, discussing their children's
development and results, or to have a series of meetings at the
school. This closer contact with the home, together with much
less formal relationships in the school, is perhaps the most
noticeable change in Swedish schools at all levels in the last
generation.

But the 10-13 stage is still essentially one of childhood:
school reform tended to extend 'primary' schooling at the expense
of early specialisation. The school day is short, and there is
much time left over. For those who live near the school, and
whose parents are at work, the phenomenon of the latchkey child
is commonplace. What such children do with their time depends
much on themselves and on the weather; and the winter provides
as much opportunity as does the summer. A mini ski-jump will
be made on this hill, a slope for sledges on that; and it is
common for a piece of ground to be swept clear of snow and then
flooded two or three times to be made into a little ice rink
for the boys from the flats around to put up a home-made ice-
hockey goal or the girls to try to be ice dancers. Outside
most towns and in the suburbs of the conurbations it is common,
too, to see a slalom slope where the youngsters try to emulate
Ingemar Stenmark; both this, and a short 2 kilometre track for
cross-country skiing through the forest is likely to be flood-
lit – important in a country where it is dark from about 4.00
p.m. for much of the winter; and there will also be longer 5
and 10 kilometre tracks through the forests, marked by red or
blue or yellow colours on the trees. Sport is a major activity:
and woe betide the teacher who makes is difficult for the class
to watch a major skiing event or the ice-hockey matches,
especially those with the USSR or the Czechs, with whom a draw is
a success and a win a matter for national rejoicing.

But there are many children who cannot go home after school:
they live too far away. For them, the local authority provides
other activities. For children up to 10, this might well take
place in the same building as the pre-school, and provide added
opportunity for younger and older children to be together. For
older ones it might be something arranged in the school – various
clubs, or indoor sports, or scope to develop interests such as

music: Sweden has a lively tradition of choirs and of string
or brass orchestras, and the local *Musikskola*, provided by the
authority either free or charging a small fee, is a popular
centre for children of all ages to learn to play guitars, piano,
violins and trumpets.

As the 10-13 stage draws to an end, the age of childhood gives
away to the teenage world. In terms of schooling, this means
going to *Hogstadiet*, the big school for the 13-16's. And here
really begins the process of choice in schooling. To an extent,
therefore, the way of working at the 7-10-13 stages seeks to
help the youngster to learn to make choices. This is one reason
why the teachers throughout the basic school are expected to
discuss with the pupils the details of the work they are to do,
what content might be emphasised and what approaches might ·be
adopted. It is a reason why, too, the official guidelines stress
active engagement by pupils in their learning. As was noted in
an article in a teacher journal, however, freedom can be an
uncomfortable matter: "Miss, why don't you tell us what we must
do, as you used to do?".[18] To make choices is hard; and when
it is your own choice, there is nobody else to blame.

One of the final responsibilities of parents and pupils at the
10-13 stage is, therefore, to make the choices necessary for
Class 7. As Chapter 2 indicated, when the new *Grundskola* began
in 1962 this was a complicated task, and one which had significant consequences for all schooling from the age of 13. In
any case, early diversification tended to imply a pass-fail concept which the 1962 Act had sought to abolish. The curriculum
changes in Lgr 69, which are set out in Fig. 6 below, introduced
a much simpler pattern of choice. The first decision was whether
to take the advanced or the basic course in either or both of
Maths and English. The next decision was to select between a
second foreign language, technology, art or economics. In foreign
languages, there was a choice of German or French, and in each
case, either an advanced or a basic course. The technology
course sought to give an overview of important technical processes, products and personnel, and to give pupils the opportunity
to practice motor skills, develop skills of analysis, planning
and construction, and to understand relationships between manual
and intellectual work tasks. The course in Art was to enable
pupils to experience and understand different forms of artistic
expression in pictures, words, music and movement. The Economics
course was to enable pupils to experience the importance of social
relationships, acquire knowledge of factors influencing consumption, distribution and production, and develop attitudes towards

personal, family and societal economics. The course dealt with
such matters as travel, office equipment, typing, leisure,
domestic equipment and personal spending.

Subject	Periods per Week						Total
	Year 7		Year 8		Year 9		
	Pupil	Teacher	Pupil	Teacher	Pupil	Teacher	
Compulsory							
Swedish	3	4	3	4	4	5	10
Mathematics	4	4	4	4	4	4	12
English	3	3	3	3	3	3	9
Music	2	2			1	1	3(2)
Drawing	2	2	2	2	1	1	5
Craft	2	2	2	2	1	1	5
Domestic Science			3	3	2	2	5(4)
Gymnastics	3	3	3	3	3	3	9
Orientation Subjects(i)	10	13	10	13	10	13	30(32)
Electives(ii)	4		3		4		11
Total	33		33		33		99(100)

PLUS Free choice (2 periods a week) and practical work
experience (*pryo*) - two weeks in Year 9

(i)   Approximately equally divided between social studies -
       religion, civics, history and geography; and natural
       science - biology, physics and chemistry.

(ii)   Second foreign language (advanced or basic course); or
       technology; or art; or economics.

Fig. 6: Curriculum Schedule, 13-16's (Lgr 69) (Numbers in
         brackets in Total column as in Lgr 80)

Little booklets have been made available for each child and his
parents, and the pupils in Class 6 probably make study visits to
the senior level school. The *Högstadiet* teachers also make
available such information as they can of what there will be on
offer in the coming year. The "free choice" activities depend
a great deal on local interests, and include a wide range of
indoor and outdoor sports, various crafts, and activities such
as animal care. The *Mellanstadiet* teacher discusses possibilities with the class, offering such guidance as it felt appropriate in the light of the knowledge acquired through teaching
the class for the past three years. Parents may also ask how
the child has performed and what are the consequences for further
study and future jobs in choosing this or that. The choice,
however, is indeed freely vested in the parent: even a child
with a "1" in Mathematics or English cannot be prevented from
taking the advanced course. In practice, most choices tend to
be realistic: and experience at the 13-16 stage soon brings
home clear errors of perception. Self motivation can also be
at least as indicative as school grades for future scholastic
success.

Table 7 below shows what choices have been made in recent years.
It is at once clear that there has been considerable sex bias
in the choices made. Boys were more likely to choose the basic
courses in Maths and English, but more boys than girls took
the advanced Maths and more girls than boys took the advanced
English. In the craft options, there was a massive orientation
by boys towards the wood and metal crafts, by girls towards the
textile crafts. Hardly any girls took technology, but they
outnumbered the boys three and four times in the economics and
art courses, and in the advanced French courses. It is also
noticeable that it is common for pupils to start with the
advanced course in Year 7 on the principle that it is easier to
drop to the general level that it is to rise to the advanced.
Initial choices in Class 7 are not in this sense finally deter-
minative. On the other hand, it is necessary to take the
advanced courses in both Maths and English to qualify for entry
to the theoretical, academic, lines of the post-compulsory
gymnasieskolan, and to take the advanced second language course
for entry to the humanities post-compulsory academic line.
Choices made at the end of *Mellanstadiet* have had far reaching
implications under Lgr 69.

Early in the autum term, the teachers who had taken the final
classes of *Mellanstadiet* will meet with their colleagues from
Högstadiet to discuss the pupils, much as they had done three

TABLE 7: Pupil choices at 13-16 stage - Percent

Subject Group	BOYS			GIRLS			TOTAL		
	Yr 7 1977	Yr 8 1978	Yr 9 1979	Yr 7 1977	Yr 8 1978	Yr 9 1979	Yr 7 1977	Yr 8 1978	Yr 9 1979
Group 1									
M(G)/E(G)	23.5	25.4	32.4	15.7	16.8	24.5	19.7	21.2	28.6
M(S)/E(G)	12.3	10.9	9.1	4.8	4.1	3.7	8.6	7.6	6.4
M(A)/E(S)	6.4	7.1	9.1	14.6	16.9	22.1	10.4	11.9	15.5
M(S)/E(S)	57.5	56.3	48.7	64.8	62.0	49.3	61.1	59.1	49.0
Other	0.2	0.2	0.6	0.2	0.2	0.3	0.2	0.2	0.4
Group 2									
Wood/Metal	93.9	93.8	94.2	14.3	16.0	13.0	54.9	55.7	54.4
Textiles	5.9	6.1	5.3	85.5	83.9	86.5	44.9	44.2	45.2
Other	0.2	0.1	0.4	0.2	0.1	0.4	0.2	0.1	0.4
Group 3									
Economics	5.2	7.0	6.6	21.9	23.9	22.5	13.4	15.3	15.9
Art	1.7	2.8	3.5	5.7	7.2	9.1	3.6	5.0	6.2
Technology	46.3	46.9	48.6	0.9	1.2	1.2	24.1	24.5	25.3
French(G)	0.8	1.0	1.7	2.4	3.2	5.3	1.6	2.1	3.5
French(S)	9.1	7.8	6.6	25.4	22.6	19.0	17.1	15.1	12.7
German(G)	5.9	6.6	10.1	7.8	9.1	12.9	6.8	7.8	11.5
German(S)	30.8	27.8	22.5	35.7	32.6	26.6	33.2	30.1	24.5
Other	0.2	0.2	0.4	0.2	0.2	0.4	0.2	0.2	0.4

M = Mathematics; E = English; (G) = General Course; (S) = Special Advanced Course; "Other" = special provision made for special cases.

Source: SCB, U1980:6 Table C, p.17.

years earlier with the 7-10 teachers; and for some weeks, it
will not be uncommon to find the 13 year olds returning to
their old class teachers to tell them how they are getting on,
and what it is like to be at the new school. Figure 7 sets out
the new Lgr 80 curriculum schedule, effective from 1982.

Subject	No. Periods per week Years 7-9
Child Care	1
Images	5
English	9
Home Economics	4
Sport	9
Mathematics	12
Music	2
Orientation Subjects:	32
(Social Studies – includes *pryo*)	(17)
(Natural Sciences)	(15)
Craft	5
Swedish	10
Electives	11
Total	100
PLUS Free activities	5

Note: Technology is now compulsory, within Natural
        Sciences

Source: *Läroplan för Grundskolan, Allman del*, p.157
(Subjects listed in Swedish alphabetical order)

Fig. 7: Curriculum Schedule 13-16's, Lgr 80

Lgr 80 starts from the assumption that all courses in *Grundskolan*
will give the same possibilities for study in *gymnasieskolan*
(Lgr 80, p.14). The main changes for those entering *Högstadiet*
in 1982 are in the area of electives and free-choice. The
school must offer 3-year courses in either French or German if
chosen by a minimum of 5 pupils, but these will be at one level
only, the "advanced" and "basic" distinction of Lgr 69 having
been abolished, and they cannot be taken in Class 9 unless taken
for at least a year beforehand. There must also be provision
for teaching the home language of minority immigrant pupils – in
which case they must also take Swedish as a foreign langugage.

Otherwise, it is for the local school board to decide what
electives to offer, in courses ranging from a term to three
years. The law ensures that parents may freely select from
what is offered, but the choice must operate for a year at a
time. Further, the courses offered must not be sex biased nor
must they emphasise any one subject and thus lead to ability
grouping.

There are also compulsory "free activities" for at least 5
periods a week for the three years. The guidelines in Lgr 80
(p.21) state that these acitivities should meet the needs of
social and cultural stimulus; encourage self-directed activity;
stimulate participation in decision making; wider contact with
adults outside the school; widen knowledge of cultural and
leisure time groups in the locality; bring together pupils of
different ages and sex; provide security for younger pupils;
especially seek to engage poorly motivated pupils and develop
a positive attitude towards school; and develop a natural and
unforced relationship between pupils and adults.

It is perhaps worth noting that Lgr 80 changes the name of
Gymnastics to Sport. The three periods a week are mainly concerned with skills of personal physical development: the main
headings of the syllabus for sport, which cover six well spaced
sides, are gymnastics; health; hygiene and ergonomics; ball
games; dance; athletics; orientering (which includes traffic
teaching); play; swimming and life saving; skiing; skating
(which includes life saving on ice). Competitions are normal
within the class, and sometimes with parallel classes, but the
idea of "school teams" as a normal part of school life is rare.
Those who want to take up particular sports are encouraged to
do so by joining the local sports club, for example the
Allmänna Idrottsklubb, AIK, of the town. This is likely to
have branches for a number of sports, and while the school
gymnastics teachers may well have a leading role in the clubs,
it is as likely that other adults will be involved. One of the
advantages of this emphasis on the club rather than the school
is that it facilitates continued participation in sports when
the youngster leaves school. The facilities of the school −
which of course belong to the local authority − may well be
used to some extent; equally the school may make use of public
facilities: there is hardly any community of any size which
does not have its sports hall, a cinder track, an ice-rink
(often doubling for an all-weather soccer pitch) and a slalom
hill.

The biggest changes the pupils will find at *högstadiet* are four-fold. First, the school is almost certain to have pupils from several 10-13 stages. This is inevitable in the country districts, and common enough in towns where the school units for younger children have been kept smaller and more local. Secondly, they will meet far more teachers in the course of a week. A study for the *SIA* commission revealed that the normal child would see a dozen teachers in Class 7 and between twenty and thirty before the end of Class 9: such is the consequence of teacher special-isation, and the difficulties of offering a wide range of choices. Its effect on the climate of schools is discussed below. Thirdly, it is a bigger unit, one where there are generally specialist teaching rooms, and to start with the newcomers may not know their way around and get lost. Finally, it has a reputation of being 'tough', with the newcomers being 'ragged', and, from Class 8, an increasing atmosphere of boredom and apathy.

The pace of work is also stepped up: this is, after all, the stage at which the selective grammar school of previous genera-tions began, and there remain expectations in the minds of some parents, some pupils and some teachers: even those teachers who, before 1962, were teaching at the top of the old non-selective elementary school have been required to obtain formal academic qualifications similar to those of the old selective school staffs to be able to be appointed to established posts at the 13-16 stage. The normal academic subject teacher will offer two, perhaps three, subjects, and indeed will be qualified to teach those subjects right up to age 19.

Teaching remains in unstreamed classes for most of the work, and the problems of differentiation become increasingly obvious. There is, however, no significant move to eliminate non-streaming at this stage, since this conflicts with the idea of a common school offering free choices: indeed, Lgr 80 expressly rejects ability grouping: "... the pupils are to be grouped so that as great a social mix as possible is achieved in the classes and working units". Small groups may be created as long as they do not remain together for more than a term and must not be identical in composition in more than one subject (Lgr 80, p.46); only to this extent has the desire of teachers[19] for smaller groups been recognised. One reason is the consequences it could have for studies after the age of 16, especially when linked with the choice of certain electives: those who take a second foreign language, as well as those who take the advanced courses in Mathematics and English, tend to be those who seek a three or four year *gymnasieskolan* course. Organisational links between

the compulsory and the post-compulsory school are, however,
progressively being broken, and as entry to the 16-19 school
becomes more or less open to all, without selection, the dangers
of early and irrevocable choice are removed.

This does not mean, however, that all students are, or should be,
treated alike. The Minister of Education, in presenting the
plan for Lgr 80 in April 1979, made much of the increased scope
for differentiation, and newspaper headlines at the time spoke
of as much as a third of the work being differentiated. Such
comment is hardly justified in terms of the structure of the
curriculum, but is justified in terms of the official emphasis
given to individualisation within the teaching group as opposed
to organisational differentiation. What are called *tema* -
roughly translated as assignments (not projects, which is a
different technique) - should occupy about a third of the time
in all subjects. These are studies in depth which the pupil
and teacher choose within the framework of the compulsory
curriculum. The content of such assignments is to be sought
within the main items of content set out as part of the official
curriculum requirements, and several such themes should be
covered in a year. About twelve periods a week should be allocated for such studies, and there is every reason why they should
spread over into the uncommitted parts of the school day, thus
combining both assignments and the so called "free activities".

It is this facet of curriculum change which is perhaps the most
important and the most difficult to analyse.[20] It is too easy
to look at curriculum structures and too easy to forget what
actually happens in schools in the process of teaching and
learning. Good teachers learn soon enough that there is little
point in asking pupils what they do not know, or to do what they
can not do - unless they deliberately want to "cool out" such
pupils. Instead, they set differential assignments for different situations, or readily accept differential levels of response.
To do this is progressively easier, too, when the content of
subjects is less specified in official syllabuses: indeed, the
National Board of Education in its curriculum reform proposals
in 1978 which ultimately led to Lgr 80, went so far as to suggest
only a content to cover a subject from age 7 to age 16, and not
to specify the requirements at each stage; but this was too
much to be accepted in a country accustomed to having main items
of content set out if not for each year then for each stage.
This kind of freedom for the individual school and teacher to
specify the annual content of learning is of course closely tied
to the increased decision making emphasised in *SIA*, the MBL pro-

cesses for participation in decision making, and the revised
grant regulations permitting local areas to give their own
emphases within the national framework. Lgr 80 has formalised
such expectations in curriculum terms by setting out the prescribed requirement in one brief General volume, written in
everyday language and not attempting to hide difficulties of
interpretation. The prescribed syllabus in each subject begins
with a brief statement on the reasons for including that subject,
the goals and the main items of content. It is then the responsibility of the pupils, teachers and head of each school to produce its own detailed plan of work, aided but not prescribed by
a volume of commentaries by the NBE on the official requirements.
"Planning ... implies that the teachers and pupils decide how
long to devote to different aspects, the order in which different
questions are taken up, the methods by which the questions should
be treated and which teaching aids should be used" (Lgr 80,
p.29). In these terms "completing the course" is not at all
the same as getting through a text book. Only time will tell
how far this new freedom to teachers will result in courses
which reflect the parliamentary proposition 1978/79:180 that
"central concepts" should determine the curriculum while at the
same time permitting decentralisation of decision making.[21]
Appendix VI gives some examples.

Inevitably, perhaps, the ways in which schools operate for pupils
and teacher will vary. It could be argued that the expressed
goal to help students to live and work together should result
in more group work and more assignments being assessed in terms
of group effort; it could be argued that the ability to work
responsibly, without overt supervision and co-operatively as a
member of a work team, is at least as important as grades in a
wide range of individual subjects: but the norm remains at the
13-16 stage as elsewhere of teaching the class with grades for
individual performance. An example from the teaching of Social
Studies in a school which was avowedly experimental and which
was used as an exemplar in the process by which the curriculum
changes from Lgr 69 to Lgr 80 were discussed showed how difficult
it is to change methods. Extensive facilities for staff planning
were available - the staff had used the freedom to deploy
resources according to locally perceived need to employ a part-
time clerical assistant rather than to buy more materials. A
large number of self-learning packages had been produced. The
school buildings were such that it presented no great difficulty
for students to work individually, or in small groups, or as a
class of 25-30, or in a large group of up to 100. In fact,
most of the work was done with the teachers in the traditional

position in the front of a normal class;   the teachers worked
normal contract hours with whole classes and not a team together
with the students;   and the leader of the team, who in discussion
suggested he was well aware of what "dialogue pedagogy" and
individualisation could mean and how it could be implemented,
felt that it was not so much a question of time or even of
resources that prevented a more open and flexible approach, nor
was it the need to revise those schemes which had been produced
in the first flush of enthusiasm when the school was newly opened
and the staff newly appointed: rather it was the feeling that
they lacked the energy, the drive to do it.

These must not be seen as critical, negative comments.   Much has
been achieved in individualisation.   But there is still much
teacher-talk in classrooms, passivity and dependence on the part
of the learner.   The idea of "rolling reform" is an essential
component of on-going curriculum development: but to change
the ways of working and constantly to revise what one is doing
and how one is doing it can be a very tiring practice at the
level of the classroom.

Such changes are not made any easier by the existence of groups
of pupils who are demonstrably "book-weary" as the Swedish
expression has it.   It is true that it remains possible for such
pupils to be given special leave to spend most of their school
time at places of work between the ages of 14 and 16.   But the
idea that a curriculum which is vocationally orientated would
solve the problems of the 13-16 stage is to seek salvation in
an age which no longer exists.   Time was when the majority left
school at 14, 15, 16 for the world of work: and they left school
for good. Even in the 1960's it was clearly desirable to ensure
that all students should receive practical work orientation, *pryo,*
within their civics course, and including brief spells of work
experience.   This aspect of the curriculum still remains, and
is indeed a most valuable orientation to the world of work.   In
an increasingly technological society, it is perhaps increasingly
necessary for all students to experience both theoretical,
academic, study and practical work-based experience, along with
effective study and work guidance.   But today, when hardly any
pupils leave school at 16 to begin work, there are many who
continue into the 16-19 school simply because there is nothing
else for them to do.   It leaves parents, teachers, the public at
large with a formidable problem: how to make school life meaningful for those who are bored by traditional schooling, and who
demonstrably react by passivity, apathy, nonchalance or simply
truancy.

There is little doubt that the daily life of some 13-16 schools is something of a battlefield, and reports of this are not uncommon in the large conurbations.   There are also areas of Stockholm and Göteborg in particular well known for this, and indeed in the late 1970's the Head Teachers of Göteborg schools carried out their own survey which revealed an unadulterated picture of dissatisfaction which they described as a travesty of true education.[22] Significantly, however, they recognised that the solutions to their problems involved society at large at least as much as the schools. The goals of the schools were not wrong: it is indeed right to stress respect for truth, the rights of man, tolerance of other's views and ways of life; and the official syllabuses are full of emphases on acceptable social values and Lgr 80 specifically emphasises the role of the school in value formation. The achievement of these goals in the schools needs the kind of working environment in which people - adults and teenagers - live and work co-operatively together: a return to the authoritarian schools of the past is no answer. But if schools are to achieve such ends, they need the co-operation of society, and especially of the home and of the employers. If it is right to see school as part of society, it cannot be right to expect schools as institutions and its teachers and other adults as people to behave differently from other institutions and people.

On the other hand, it is quite wrong to see all the 13-16 school units in such a negative light. First, to some extent it has become mere conventional wisdom to expect ragging, vandalism, truancy - to do what the others do, to dress in the extremes of fashion, whether it is long hair or crew cuts, pointed shoes and velvet jackets or sneakers, jeans and leather coats with studded "hell's angels" belts, ear-rings or anti-nuclear energy badges. Secondly, the vast majority of small towns simply do not have the problems on the scale of the large conurbations, and they remain quiet, their peaceful idyll disturbed now and again by a gang on mopeds or a few youngsters defiantly drinking forbidden alcohol. The extent of violence should not be exaggerated. There is much evidence, too, that pupils when asked a year or two after leaving the basic school freely say that not enough was demanded of them at *Grundskolan*, that teachers did care but that everybody is trapped in a depersonalised system dominated by theoretical studies which most of the pupils did not really understand, divorced from practical reality, and by a marking system which as ever favoured those from higher social class backgrounds and made the employment prospects of the less able and the less socially aspirant all the more difficult. *"Bort med betyg"*, or do away with marks, is seen by some as a solution in the sense that their selective function is exaggerated: but surveys agree that the vast major-ity of adults and pupils would keep marks for other purposes.

The great salvation of the school was seen in the 1970's to be the implementation of the *SIA* proposals, accepted by Parliament in 1976. The schools do now have control over about 25% of the monies available, to use as they see fit, whether for special education, teaching immigrants, the free activities offered, or resources to improve individualisation. The "new ways of working" are clearly seen in the elimination of the ideas of "help classes" or "special classes" and their replacement by integration of all except the very severely handicapped in the ordinary classrooms and providing individual and small group teaching for them as needed. The extent to which this was offered at the different stages is indicated in Table 8. This kind of integration is

TABLE 8:   Integrated Special Educational Provision 1976/77

% pupils in ordinary classes (n.b. one child can be in more than one category)

| Category | 1976 YEARS | | | | 1977 YEARS | | | |
	1-3	4-6	7-9	ALL	1-3	4-6	7-9	ALL
Reading & Writing	12.5	14.2	7.5	11.5	14.2	14.9	7.5	12.2
Mathematics	6.8	9.3	4.4	6.9	8.2	10.8	4.9	8.4
Observation	0.4	0.7	2.7	1.3	0.5	0.8	3.2	1.5
Special Help	1.7	2.5	3.8	2.6	2.2	2.7	4.5	3.1
Speech Difficulties	4.0	1.2	0.3	1.9	4.2	1.2	0.3	1.9
Hearing Difficulties	0.1	0.1	0.1	0.1	0.1	0.1	0.1	0.1
Special Gymnastics	0.2	0.2	0.4	0.1	0.2	0.2	0.5	0.3
Prep. for School	3.5			1.2	3.2			1.0

Source: Statistisk Årsbok, 1979, Table 374

TCSE - H

made possible by the concept of the "working unit" rather than
the school class, and indeed the idea of the class as necessarily
the teaching group is tending to disappear especially at the 13-
16 level: the class instead becomes the basis for child care,
for planning, for leisure-time activities, and is led by a
"work team" of teachers and others.   The emphasis in *SIA* on
greater contact between the school and the world of work is
found in what are called the *SSA-råd,* the committees in each
local authority for co-operation between school, the labour
market board and employers, which is important more at the post
compulsory stage in the context of vocational courses.   Meanwhile, the Board of Education is preparing new guidelines for
the practical work experience programme in the basic school,
and the current (1980) experiments in some 80 municipalities
is expected to lead to a new programme for all from 1982.   The
idea of an integrated school day, bringing together the formal
instructional activities of the school with the informal leisure
activities, means that the school has added responsibilities
for the pupils: clearly it is valuable for the pupils to have
meaningful activities to follow during "free periods" of the
normal school timetable and when there would be nobody at home,
and there is growing co-operation between schools and leaders
of non-school societies, especially in youth clubs, the libraries,
and the sports clubs;   and scope too for the pupils themselves
to be involved in deciding what programmes to offer.   By law,
the integrated school day (including normal lessons) must not
exceed 5 hours 20 minutes for children in classes 1-2 or 8
hours for classes 3-9:   and although there has been money for
these activities since 1978/79, in fact only half of it was
used in the first two years.

The new ways of making decisions envisaged by *SIA* are found in
the "class council" which plans the work of the class, under
the class teacher in concert with the "working unit conference".
The old "staff meeting", *kollegiet,* is replaced by the "personnel
conference" of all permanent staff, teachers and others;   and
there is a compulsory child care conference in all schools, led
by the head or his deputy, and including the class teacher, the
school nurse, the school curator and/or psychologist, the study
and work-guidance leader, any other relevant staff, together
with the pupil(s) and parent(s) concerned, and responsible for
deciding whether a pupil needs to be in a special class or for
reasons of adjustment needs to be excused from ordinary school
work.   If the parents do not agree with the recommendation,
they have the right of appeal to the local school board.
Finally, *SIA* envisaged in-service courses for school staffs, and

as will be considered in Chapter 7 below, there are series of
courses being offered both for the school management personnel –
heads, deputies, the teacher supervising materials, *tillsynslärare*,
heads of subjects – and other courses made up of 10-15 people in
each, and including all other members of the "working team",
teachers and others.

Perhaps the modern, complex technological society expects too
much of its compulsory schools; perhaps, indeed, the emphasis
on the wholeness of the educative process has led people to
equate school with education; perhaps Sweden is beginning a
process of rethinking the role of school at this basic level,
and beginning to suggest that the traditional concepts of
school, school class and school teacher are changing. If
teachers, pupils and society at large are not wholly satisfied
with the basic school as it has emerged from the reforms of the
last generation or so, the answers clearly do not lie in a
return to an age which no longer exists: that much was clear
in the almost unanimous viewpoint expressed in a wide range of
leading articles in the national and local press at the start
of the 1980-81 school year. At the same time, there was
unanimous regret that the enthusiasm of the 7 year old starting
out on nine years of compulsory schooling with its 10,000
lessons, gave way to the apathy and boredom of those in the
final year, especially in a situation when most were obliged to
transfer to the 16-19 stage in the absence of any practical
alternative.

CHAPTER 5

The Post-compulsory Upper Secondary School

The compulsory sector has the basis for development in the eighties. It has its new curriculum, Lgr 80, and proposals for a new pattern of teacher education and teacher deployment to provide a staff for the basic school as a whole (see Chapter 7 below), together with a revised grant system giving greater scope for local decision-making and the idea of *SIA* for making the working environment more acceptable to all concerned. At the same time, the structure of post-compulsory provision has been unaltered since 1971 and its future organisation is yet to be decided. That there would need to be change was recognised in 1976 when a committee of enquiry was set up. The Chairman of the Upper Secondary School Enquiry, Urban Dahllöf, announced in January 1981[1] that the main proposals would be:

(a) Courses to be offered annually in nine blocks, each of a month. This would facilitate links with adult education and with work experience training, though with a longer "school year" which would no doubt mean that teachers' conditions of service would have to be re-negotiated.

(b) At least two of the blocks would be required for practical work experience.

(c) Students would form groups of 8, with a tutor, and each group would negotiate a programme of study and work experience.

(d) Since Lgr 80 makes no subject differentiation in *Grund-skolan*, levels of achievement on entry to the upper secondary school must vary considerably. The new course structure should then be built up in relation to the knowledge and aspirations of entrants, structured within three broad sectors of science and technology, care and personal services, and economics.

(e)   The current grading system would be replaced by competency
      requirements specified for each course, and students could
      then end their studies at different levels within any pro-
      gramme of study.

These proposals, however, will certainly be the subject of
extensive public discussion, and parliamentary debtate. Changes
cannot be implemented before 1985 at the earliest. This
chapter, therefore describes and comments on the system established in 1971.

The Upper Secondary School 1971-81

Just as there is no real suggestion that the basic school should
revert to the old parallel elementary/selective grammar school
system, there is no suggestion that the integrated *gymnasieskola*,
established in 1971 following a parliamentary decision in 1968,
should be unscrambled again into separate, and selective, sectors.
Equally, however, just as the nine "lines" with their different
variants for the final year of the basic school in the 1962
scheme gave way to a virtually undifferentiated structure for
the final years of compulsory schooling, so too it is likely
that the present 23 lines, with their variants, in *gymnasieskolan*, structured within three broad fields of study, Arts and
Social Studies, Economics, and Science and Technology, (see
Appendix VII) might well become less differentiated. This
present structure emerged, as was noted in Chapter 2, from the
traditional academic *gymnasium*; the long-established vocational
schools, *yrkeskolor*; and the new continuation schools,
fackskolor, which had emerged in the 1960's. The courses in
the old vocational and continuation schools became the two-year
lines of the new *gymnasieskola* - indeed, the official statistics
still distinguish between these two strands; the courses of the
old academic gymnasium became the three or four-year lines, the
four-year course having a long tradition from the old 'technical
gymnasium'.

The idea was that these different educational traditions should
merge into an integrated school: and as with all such reforms,
this called for not only new curricula which would make inter-
change between the different lines relatively easy, but also
new buildings and new staff attitudes. Furthermore, this
development was taking place when important changes were beginning to be noted both in the expectations of those in their late

teens[2] and in the employment patterns of society,[3] both of
which had significant consequences for the numbers who would
stay within the school system after the age of 16, what kinds
of study they wanted them to take up, and when and how this
study should take place - whether end-on to compulsory school,
or on some kind of sandwich programme, or on the emerging
recurrent education model, known in its earlier days in Sweden
by the meaningful phrase "coming back education", "*återkommande
utbilding*".

The sheer scale of post-compulsory provision is perhaps the
most obvious sign of change since the early seventies. Then,
barely a half of an age-group might, at some time or other,
continue after the compulsory school - the proportion varying
regionally as well as in socio-economic and sex terms. By 1980
there was provision for 100% of 16 year olds and a further 10%
or so for those over 18 but under 20 who want to return.
Virtually all school leavers at 16 apply in the spring for a
place in *gymnasieskolan* the following August, and the guidance
staff at both levels of schooling are busy explaining possibilities, with the help of a clear and attractive booklet available
to all pupils, spelling out entry requirements for the different
lines, showing what job opportunities they may lead to, what
possibilities there are to change from one line to another after
the first year, or even the second year.

Ideally, of course, this should be the end product of a continuous process of guidance which began in Class 6 and which
influenced the choice of electives at the 13-16 stage, especially
when entry to all three and four-year lines of *gymnasieskolan*
require advanced English and Mathematics, all the two-year
lines for art, social sciences and economics require advanced
English, the two-year technical line requires advanced mathematics,
and certain specialised courses also have special entry conditions,
which might include previous vocational practice. Furthermore,
when there are more applicants than places, which tends now to
be true for most of the options, the grade point average in the
final marks at the end of class 9 is used for selection purposes.
Of all applicants, over 90% are offered places, and about 85%
take them up -though not always in the line they would have
preferred. Most, but by no means all, of those who do not apply
or who do not take the place offered, are those whose school
grades at the end of class 9, at age 16, were not very good -
a fact which is of course not unrelated to the non-scholastic
and apathetic atmosphere which can exist in the final year of
compulsory schooling.

The arguments for the elimination of school marks as a selective
device at this stage are also relevant: those who, on a relative
marking scale, have tended to be at the bottom end throughout
schooling, having been told in effect that they are "no good",
now find themselves being told they are not only "no good" but
"not wanted", whether in school or by employers. But there are
also those who could, in terms of school marks, easily stay at
school and quite possibly in the lines of their choice: but
they want to leave - either because a job is offered to them,
or because to leave school and go to work at the end of compulsory schooling is the normal social expectation in their
home and district, or simply because they want to take "time
out" and experience the big wide world, whether as "au pair" in
Germany, France or England, or just to feel more independent
and adult. Only 2% of boys with good marks in class 9 and from
higher social classes do not continue at school, but 66% of
girls with low marks and from working class homes leave school
(see Table 9).

TABLE 9:   School Leaving After Class 9

Father's Social Background	Boys Grade Level			Girls Grade Level		
	High	Average %	Low	High	Average %	Low
Academic etc.	2	12	35	4	17	48
Clerical	7	16	51	9	25	62
Workers	4	19	54	12	30	66

Source: Härnqvist K and Svensson A, for Gymnasieutredningen
(the Upper Secondary School Enquiry), quoted in
Lärartidningen/Svensk Skoltidning, 23/1980, p.5.

Whatever the reason for staying on, or not staying on, gymnasieskolan now has to cater for virtually all 16 year olds together
with a further 10-15% of under 18's who are returning. And for
them, courses have to be provided. In the optimistic sixties,
and in a country where faith in rational planning is a characteristic feature, the curriculum of the gymnasieskola was so
structured that while the content was still expressed largely
in terms of subjects, the framework was expressed in terms of
occupational fields. The economic functions of schooling were

much to the fore. The essential question to ask the 16 year
old was "what kind of job do you want?", and the essential purpose of the school, beyond the general social and political
purposes of developing independent but co-operative citizens,
was to see that the kind of courses it provided led to the kinds
of job society wanted. Even the traditional academic courses in
the arts and social sciences, economics, natural science and
technology are given this orientation: and this line of thinking
is reflected in the occupational basis of the revised patterns
of higher education which began to emerge in the discussions of
the U68 committee, set up in 1968 (see Chapter 6 below).

The subject requirements in these lines remain much as they have
been for a generation or more - an encyclopaedic survey of
twelve or more subjects. As may be seen in Fig. 8, there is a
substantial common core of Swedish, Mathematics, English, Science,
Religious Knowledge, the Creative Arts and Physical Education,
not just in the first year but throughout the whole course.
Only about a third, at most, of the time-tabled week is devoted
to studies specific to one of the five main academic programmes.
It has always been from these that the majority of the new
entrants to traditional academic fields of higher education are
expected to come, and the majority of those following these programmes would expect to go on to university or its equivalent.
Traditionally, and until the end of the 1960's, they had led to
studentexamen, the successful completion of which gave right of
entry to university; and even in the 1970's, a grade point
average of 2.3 on completing a full secondary education secured
a similar right. The moves to open access to higher education
in the 1970's to those who followed the two-year lines of
gymnasieskolan, or to those who were over the age of 24 and had
four (originally five) years of work experience, were not in
themselves seen as a challenge to the intellectual supremacy of
the traditional academic studies in the upper secondary school.

Nevertheless, all lines of study in *gymnasieskolan* have, since
1971, been presented as having a vocational end product. The
three-year Liberal Arts line was said to "provide a sound basis
in various sectors of the labour market ... requiring a good
general education and a knowledge of languages"; the three-year
Economics line "provides a basic vocational education for tasks
in wide fields of the economy and administration". When access
to all lines of study in a system of higher education structured
around five occupational sectors became selective in 1979, it
was bound to prevent some of those in the traditional academic

Subject	All	Arts		Soc. Sc.		Economics		Sciences		Technology		
	1	2	3	2	3	2	3	2	3	2	3	4
Swedish	3	3	4	3	4	3	3	3	3	3	2	
English	3	3	2	2	-/3	2	-/4	2	3	2	-/1	
German/French	-/3	3	2/4/6	3	-/4	3	3/4	-/3	-/3	-/3	-/1	
3rd Language	4/-	3	-/4	3	-/4	3	-/4	-/3	-/3	4/-	-/1	
History	2	4	2	4	2	2		4		2		
Civics	3		2/4½	3	4½	3	2½	5	2	5	2	
Mathematics	5	-/3		2	4	-/3	-/3	5	5	3	5	
P.E.	3	3	2	1	1	1	1	3	2	3	1	
Linguistics		3										
Latin		-/7	-/7									
Greek		-/4	-/4									
Religious Knowledge	-/3/5	3	3		3		2	2	2		2	
Philosophy		1/2	3		2				2			
General Science		2		4								
Physics	2½							4	4	4	4	
Chemistry	2½							2½	2	4		
Biology								1½	1½			
History of Art/Music	1	1		1				1				
Music or Drawing	1	1		1								
Psychology				2		8						3
Managerial Econ.	-/2						2					
Accounting							-/3					
Distribution							-/7					
Administration							-/7					
Law							2					
Typing	-/2					1	-/1					
Shorthand						-/3	-/3					
Ergonomics												2
Technology										6	5	2
Tech. Variants											11½	30

Fig. 8. Gymnasium Curriculum Schedule – Academic Three and Four Year Lines: Periods per Week.

lines of *gymnasieskolan* from proceeding to higher education
either directly or even after a year or two of employment.
Initially, 20% of places were reserved for applicants direct
from school. The consequence of this has been, since 1979, for
both staff and students in the three-year and four-year lines,
to be less certain about the opportunities for further study;
for some to chase higher grades – there was a suggestion in
1980 that the average grade in the final year had tended to
drift upwards from the expected norm of 3; and for demands to
be made to increase the proportion of places reserved for candidates direct from school – as has been done, to 30%, as from
Autumn 1981.

The original expectation for *gymnasieskolan* was that some 50%
would seek places in the more overtly practical and vocational
two-year lines – the old *yrkesskola* lines; some 20% in 'the
more theoretical two-year lines – "continuation school", the
old *fackskola*; and some 30% in the three and four-year
academic lines – the old *gymnasium*. There was, too, a temporary
drop in the proportion of an age-group applying for immediate
entry in the mid 1970's. As the decade ended, however, new
patterns seemed to be emerging. Table 10 shows enrolments for
the three years 1976, 1977 and 1978.

Of all enrolments, nearly 38% are in the academic lines; a
little over 30% are in the directly vocational lines, and these
proportions have been rising; and the proportion in the theoretical two-year lines is only 12-13%. If the "special course"
conditions are ignored (and when *gymnasieskolan* was set up,
there was no expectation that they should be anything like as
numerous as has in fact happened to date), the proportions
between vocational, continuation and academic lines in 1976-78
has been approximately 39%, 15-16%, 45-46% respectively. The
"special course" students, however, are a significant group
totalling 16-18% of candidates, nearly three-quarters of them
staying for over a year. These short courses tend to be more
overtly vocational, in the field of economics, ecology and
natural science, and tend to omit the general classes in
Swedish, English, or perhaps mathematics. They cannot, therefore, give the general competence required for entry into
higher education, though they may lead to specific vocational
courses at the level of higher education, one example of which
is the school for forestry studies in Karlstad, the only one
of its kind in the world. It is especially, but by no means
exclusively, such courses that appeal to those who left class 9

TABLE 10: Gymnasieskolan Enrolment 1976-78: Year of Study

	1976	%	1977	%	1978	%
2-Year lines						
Ex Continuation School Year 1	14,310		15,377		17,276	
2	13,402		13,034		14,256	
Total	27,712	12.5	28,411	12.5	31,532	13.3
Ex Vocational School Year 1	37,316		39,620		42,258	
2	31,034		33,183		35,376	
Total	68,350	30.9	72,803	32.1	77,634	32.7
3/4-Year lines Year 1	28,731		30,296		32,318	
2	26,273		26,488		27,902	
3	24,363		24,707		24,887	
4	4,229		4,396		4,667	
Total	83,596	37.8	85,887	37.9	89,774	37.9
Special Course under 1 Year	11,351		11,279		10,929	
over 1 Year	30,144		28,077		27,246	
Total	41,495	18.7	39,356	17.4	38,175	16.1
GRAND TOTAL	221,153		226,457		237,115	

Note: the figures include returners to school, in addition to the 16+ age cohort; in 1978, for example, there were 13% over age 18. The annual figures have not, therefore, been used to calculate drop-out rates.

Source: *Statistisk Årsbok* for relevant years

for the world of work and who returned to school after a year
or two. About 2% of entrants to upper secondary school did
this in 1960; by 1979, this had risen to 15%.

Tables 11 and 12 analyse *gymnasieskolan* enrolments between 1976
and 1978 in terms of fields of study and lines of study. Of
those taking arts and social studies, about a half are in the
two-year courses and nearly a fifth (though a declining proportion) are taking special short courses. Rather less than a
half of those in the economics field take two-year courses, and
just over 10% of them take special courses. Only just over 40%
of those in the natural science and technological fields take
two-year courses, but about a quarter take the four-year courses.

Gross totals, however, tend to hide significant variations.
There is, for example, a drop-out of around 5% after the first
year and a further 3% after the second year. Many of both sex
find the pace of work at *gymnasieskolan* much greater than they
had expected. The school day is still filled by required class
contact time amounting to 35 periods a week, there is more
private study to complete both at school and at home, and the
intellectual demands are greater than many envisaged. There is,
too, substantial change of course from year to year, both
within the various lines in the arts-social science-economics-
natural science-technology sectors and between these sectors.
This is quite normal after year 1, and is facilitated by the
fact that 80% of the first year courses is common to all lines
of study. The least likely to change tend to be girls in the
arts and social science fields.

Significantly, too, the figures hide a clear social differentiation, with students from the professional and managerial home
backgrounds overwhelmingly predominating in the three and four-
year lines, and those from unskilled home backgrounds dominat-
ing the overtly vocational courses. Furthermore, traditional
sex differences remain, as with the electives as the 13-16
stage, despite efforts both within schools and in society at
large to remove such stereotyping. The girls, on the whole,
avoid technology and the natural sciences; they share equally
with the boys in the three-year economics and two-year music
lines; and they dominate in the three-year social science line
and the two-year lines of office and distributive trades,
social work, arts, textiles, care services and consumer services.

Perhaps most significantly of all, the figures hide the difference between what the applicants initially sought and what they

TABLE 11:   Gymnasieskolan Enrolment 1976-1978:   Fields of Study

	1976		1977		1978	
	N	%	N	%	N	%
ARTS/SOCIAL STUDIES						
2 year	38,499	47.1	41,610	49.1	47,114	52.1
3 year	23,583	28.8	23,994	28.3	25,377	28.1
Special	19,649	24.1	19,064	22.5	17,920	19.8
Total	81,731		84,668		90,411	
ECONOMICS						
2 year	18,682	46.7	19,214	47.3	20,029	48.1
3 year	16,442	41.1	16,882	41.6	17,376	41.7
Special	4,902	12.2	4,500	11.1	4,265	10.2
Total	40,026		40,596		41,670	
TECHNICAL/SCIENTIFIC						
2 year	38,881	41.0	40,390	41.8	42,023	42.2
3 year	21,100	22.3	20,521	21.3	20,368	20.5
4 year	22,471	23.7	24,490	25.4	26,651	26.7
Special	12,343	13.0	11,086	11.5	10,552	10.6
Total	94,795		96,487		99,594	
INDEPENDENT SPECIAL	4,601		4,706		5,438	
ALL 2 YEAR LINES	96,062	43.4	101,214	44.7	109,166	46.0
ALL 3/4 YEAR LINES	83,596	37.8	85,887	37.9	89,772	37.9
ALL SPECIAL COURSES	41,495	18.8	39,356	17.4	38,175	16.1
Total	221,153		226,457		237,113	
ALL ARTS/SOCIAL STUDIES	81,731	37.0	84,668	37.4	90,411	38.1
ALL ECONOMICS	40,026	18.1	40,596	17.9	41,670	17.6
ALL TECHNICAL/SCIENTIFIC	94,795	42.8	96,487	42.6	99,594	42.0
ALL INDEPENDENT SPECIAL	4,601	2.1	4,706	2.1	5,438	2.3
Total	221,153		226,457		237,113	

Source: *Statistisk Årsbok* for relevant years.

TABLE 12:   Gymnasieskolan Enrolment 1976-78: Lines of Study

	Basic Lines			Special Courses		
	1976	1977	1978	1976	1977	1978
ARTS						
Consumer Goods	8,615	9,057	9,924	5,836	5,268	5,387
Nursing	12,656	13,694	14,701	13,706	13,493	12,231
Music	351	346	364	56	127	114
Social	16,877	18,513	22,135	–	–	–
Liberal Arts (3 yr)	8,225	8,185	8,753	–	–	–
Social Science (3 yr)	15,358	15,809	16,624	41	176	188
ECONOMICS						
Distribution	12,857	13,703	14,347	2,334	2,620	2,353
Economics	5,825	5,511	5,682	–	–	–
Economics (3 yr)	16,442	16,882	17,376	2,568	1,880	1,912
TECH./NAT.SCIENCE						
Clothing	712	651	709	974	667	615
Food	1,671	1,686	1,833	358	342	322
Workshop	8,740	8,904	9,091	4,629	3,754	3,102
Motor Engineering	5,082	5,626	6,201	667	780	865
Woodwork	998	1,023	1,053	345	354	348
Building & Construction	7,106	8,174	8,793	323	384	353
Elec. & Tele Comm.	6,463	6,664	6,839	2,477	2,062	1,979
Processing	611	687	708	207	350	354
Forestry	1,108	1,140	1,217	307	311	324
Agriculture	1,731	1,794	1,859	831	881	927
Technical (2 yr)	4,659	4,041	3,361	113	482	502
Maintenance Services			359			
Nat.Sciences (3 yr)	21,100	20,521	20,368	–	–	–
Technology (4 yr)	22,471	24,490	26,651	1,112	719	861

Source: *Statistisk Årsbok* for relevant years.

were in fact offered. The notion of rational planning with
manpower requirements in subsequent employment pre-supposes
that there would never be a wholly free choice. Matching the
desires of applicants with the number of places which the
country as a whole and individual towns and regions in particular decide is desirable and can make available is unlikely
ever to be perfect in a free society. The margins of error
indicated in Fig. 9, however, give support to those critics who

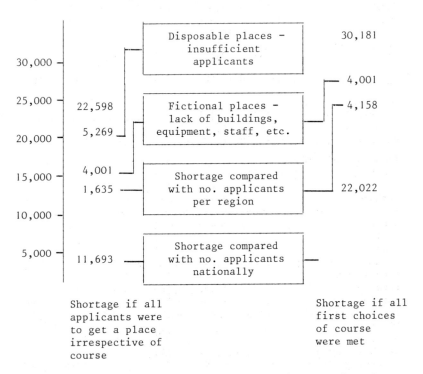

Fig. 9. Availability and demand for places in Gymnasieskolan
         1979/80

Source: *SÖ, Tillgång och efterfrågan på platser i gymnasie-
         skolan, läsåret 1979/80: en regional jämförelse*
         (Availability and demand for places in the Upper
         Secondary School, 1979/80: a regional comparison),
         1980:9, Dnr P 80:1167, dated 1980-05-05.

feel that modern technocratic Sweden, having attempted to develop
in its youth the ability to make choices as well as to be
socially responsible citizens, is in fact manipulating the
students by limiting their choice of course of study. As the
study quoted shows, in 1979, a year when the 16 year olds
numbered 114,188 and there were, in theory, 113,700 places
available in the *gymnasieskolan*, there were 125,399 applicants,
some 13% of whom were aged over 18 and were wishing to return
to school. Of these applicants, 18% did not get a place at all;
and had every applicant taken up only his first choice of course,
there would have been a 24% shortfall of places.

This study showed that there was some relationship, but by no
means an inevitable one, between the number of applicants and
the extent of unemployment in the region; and there was, too,
an absolute shortage of required places in certain of the 65
regions into which the country is divided for the purpose of
planning post-compulsory provision. The three regions which
include Stockholm, Göteborg and Malmö provided from some 25% of
all the places for 16 year olds, and eleven other regions which
all included larger towns provided a further 50% of the places.
Those who live in or near the larger towns, therefore, have a
clear advantage in seeing their wishes realised. For the
Autumn 1980 entry, a not dissimilar pattern prevailed. With an
age-group of 124,000 16 year olds, there were 133,000 applicants
(including 16-20's) and in June of the year, 122,000 places
allocated, but 28,000 were not offered their first choice.[4]

On the other hand, even if the availability of places in the
various lines does indeed have the effect of "steering" individual choice towards certain areas of study, and is thus somewhat in conflict with the expressed goal of educating free
citizens capable of exercising socially desirable choices,
"public demand" for the traditional academic fields of study
has clearly not been overridden by "social need" models of
manpower planning. As will be seen later, this is also true of
higher education. Traditions of a society of free people
remain very much in evidence.

The "Integrated" School

To what extent is *gymnasieskolan* integrated? It has already
been noted that there are regional differences in availability,
and different enrolments in terms of sex and of social background. The National Board, in an enquiry in 1975,[5] used four
criteria: courses in each of the sectors, arts and social

studies, economics, science and technology; a balance between
two-and three-four-year programmes; a balance of the sexes in
the whole school, within the range of between 40-60% for either
sex; and a school which offered both practical and theoretical
lines of study. It also argued that integration was possible
in a school which offered only 11 of the 23 lines and had in
all about 500 students, and that no fully integrated school
need have more than 1,200. In fact, the average school has
about 750 students, and it is now policy when the total number
of places being provided for exceeds 1,000 to have a prima
facia case for building two school units.

The School Regulations, however, require integration only on
two criteria, the practical-theoretical balance and the two-year/
three-year balance. In these terms, in 1979/80,[6] 206 of the 278
local authorities maintained 340 *gymnasieskola* units. Of these
143 were "integrated", 117 had practical lines only and 80 had
theoretical lines only. Analysed by local authority, 93 of
them had only "integrated" units; 67 had units which offered
only practical lines; 8 had units which offered only theoretical
lines; 10 had both "integrated" and "practical" units; 12 had
units which were either "integrated" or "theoretical"; 12 had
wholly separate "theoretical" and "practical" units; and 4 had
separate "integrated", "theoretical" and "practical" units. In
the country as a whole, there were also a further 140 *gymnasieskola* units administered by the counties rather than the local
authorities, providing courses in nursing, child care, forestry
and agriculture under pre-1970 regulations and which in time
will either become part of the normal local authority school or
part of the higher education provision in the region. There
were also 9 *gymnasieskolor* privately run but in receipt of state
grants in return for following the state regulations for staffing, curriculum and the usual building and health requirements.

Integration, however, is not simply a matter of organisational
provision. Even when administratively "integrated", the various
sections of the school are often quite separate. Timetables are
planned for each line of study, and except in travel to an from
school (which is even more likely than at the 13-16 stage in the
rural areas because of the need to centralise different kinds
of provision) students in different lines of study are unlikely
to have much opportunity to mix during the day. Furthermore,
there is as yet relatively little integration of staff. Just
as in *Grundskolan*, teacher training has yet wholly to adjust to
new patterns of school. The theoretical lines are still taught
by teachers qualified in the traditional academic programmes of

university study followed by a year of professional training:
the practical courses tend to be taught in the main by teachers
who have qualified by virtue of technical qualifications and
work experience, and for whom professional training is officially
required but has been taken by about only half the staff.
Students in the two-year practical lines are therefore unlikely,
even in an "integrated" school unit, to meet the traditional
upper secondary academic staff, just as those in the theoretical
lines are unlikely to meet staff whose background is essentially
in the "real world" rather than "academe".

In theory, too, the grades awarded in the different lines should
be comparable: though if that were the case, those with the
lower grades from class 9 and who tend to be found in the more
overtly practical lines would continue to get the 1's and 2's
on the 1-5 marking scale. In fact, the marks awarded are
relative essentially to the line of study rather than to the
age group as a whole. One of the most obvious problems that
has therefore required attention is the validity of *gymnasieskolor* marks in terms of access to higher education, for which
there are now separate quotas for those applicants who come
from the two-year lines on the one hand, and the three or four-
year lines on the other. A second problem, which has become
even more noticeable with the increased proportion staying on
at school, has been the low level of Swedish among those pupils
taking the most practical courses. A third problem has been
the lack of motivation of those who, were the employment market
more buoyant, would take the first opportunity to leave school
and take a job. A fourth has been the nature and efficiency of
the system of study and work guidance, *syo*, an essential component of a non-compulsory school in which there is a wide
range of choice open to the student, but in a society which tends
to seek formal qualifications for jobs and to match schooling
and employment.

It is, therefore, not surprising that the enquiry into *gymnasieskolan* was set up in 1976. There had been changes in society;
the integration of goals and organisation of post compulsory
schooling in 1968 had not really examined the problem of how
best to effect the integration of studies; the school as at
present organised is not designed to accommodate recurrent
educational provision other than in arranging special courses;
the studies made in the early 1970's for the reform of higher
education had shown the need both for more theoretical study at
school for entry to the more vocational higher studies as well
as more vocational study at school for the theoretical studies

at a higher level; those who did not continue at school were
becoming demonstrably more disadvantaged; and the traditional
distinction between post-compulsory schooling and adult education was becoming increasingly less tenable. The original
directive to the enquiry said that there should be vocational
and theoretical aspects in all lines of study; that there
should be more possibilities to interweave periods of study
with periods of work; that the organisation into lines should
be examined; and that while opportunities for recurrent study
should be provided, care should be exercised to ensure that
the less motivated are not simply "cooled out" at the end of
the first stage of a step-by-step structure.

On one point, the enquiry was soon agreed: it was possible to
have a more flexible *gymnasieskola* without having entry based
on school marks. That view was expressed early in 1978 in
response to a study on the school marks question.[7] Parliament
accepted that an experiment on these lines should start in
Örebro in the autumn of 1979, but there were unexpected delays.
In the era of participation in decision-making, all involved
had to agree how to operate such a scheme: the class teacher
association (*SL*) wanted teacher comment to be one of the
grounds for deciding a place; the subject teacher association
(*LR*) was opposed to moves towards a mark-free basic school.
Another possibility which the "Marks Enquiry" itself suggested
was entry criteria based on a combination of work experience,
expressed interest in a course of study, and special weight
attached to actual choice of a course in which the sex balance
was unduly skewed.

In 1980 it was finally agreed that criteria for making choices
would include the rank order of choices, repeated applications,
sex, previous study and work experience – but the National Board
expressly excluded any form of teacher judgement. The first
entrants on this scheme is in 1982, but a simulated "mark-free"
entry using the 1981 intake as a sample seeks to estimate how
far there would be a need for intensified guidance at the 13-16
stage, how such entry affects study possibilities if there were
no other changes in the 16-19 school, and how the school organisation might best change to meet the applicants' desire for
various courses.

At the same time, radical critics set up what was called the
Alternative *Gymnasieskola* Enquiry (*DAG*) which began its first
report with the comment "Every morning 450,000 Swedes stay home
and away from work ...", implying that something is very wrong

with the experience of work and wrong, too, with the school that prepares people for such work. One study was made of vocational courses, starting from the view that all courses should have a vocational bias; another was made of choice; and a third of pupil and other personnel influences within and outside the class-room, an issue seen as the most complex because it is considered possible to deal with the problems of the school only if all who live and work in it have the freedom together to plan, within broad frameworks, how it is to operate. The perceived short-comings from which this group began its thinking were the tradi-tional subject of divisions of school; the bittiness of a teacher's role in the school; the degree of directiveness exercised by national syllabuses; the influence of school marks on entry to higher studies; traditional teacher education; and inadequate premises in which to work. Even places of employment, towards which the pupils are ultimately directed, were seen to lack meaning, having become led by small groups of qualified technicians and administrators who control everybody else and where machines have so often replaced specific vocational skills: automation has removed 140,000 jobs since 1965 and can expect to remove a further 800,000 by the end of the century.

What *DAG* hopes to see is not more specialisation, but less – which implies a more highly educated work-force; participation by all in planning work; and a school which, interweaving work and study, prepares students for such a future, and in the process breaks the traditional monopoly of the products of purely theo-retical lines of study. One paperback on these themes[8] stressed how so much of the association between school, work and leisure concerns personal relationships, and that it is pointless to criticise the current school as either too theoretical or too practical: rather, the theory is inadequate and the practice is not educative. They argue that if "theory" is "a summary, an abstract simplification of how reality operates", then the hotch-potch of vague facts and data which school offers has nothing to do with theory.

Youth unemployment is the biggest problem for the 16-plus age-group: "It is not a lack of education among youth which creates unemployment – it is a lack of jobs"; and it is therefore argued that youngsters should not be offered more schooling merely as a surrogate for work. The programme which is suggested centres on ten themes – youth without work; work and schooling; practice; parenthood; a democratic school; the working environment of the school; the economy of the school; choice and evaluation;

youth outside school; why worry about the school in the local
authority? As a basic mode of study, it suggested the study
circle, whereby each participant himself enquires into the
situation which concerns him - not merely as a kind of fact-
finding situation, but starting from concrete experiences, re-
flecting and theorising about them, trying to put new ideas
into practice and using this as the basis for new experiences.
Theory without practice is pointless; but so is practice
without theory.

There is really nothing new in such ideas, nothing which could
not be implemented in any school, and indeed is so implemented
in some places. Further, it is not unlike the Experimental
Gymnasiet which operated in Göteborg in the early 1970s but
which gradually lost public support and has now disappeared.[9]
Emerging in the flush of enthusiasm which followed the student
unrest in 1968, this school provided admirable opportunities
for self-learning and participation - though it is not irrele-
vant to recall that its students tended to be able youngsters
from the higher social classes, and it is not surprising that
their ultimate academic results tended to be high. A dis-
proportionate amount of their time seemed to have been spent
discussing the official syllabus and deciding how to approach
this or that theme, so much so that they probably knew the
official curriculum guidelines better than many teachers; but
the act of doing so in itself required them to carry out much
of the intended field of study. By and large, however, it was
not these youngsters who, either then or later, could not find
work.

To some extent, the *Gymnasieskola* enquiry as established was
overtaken by events over which it had no control. Youth unemployment rose steadily from 1976. The implications of the
reformed structure of entry to higher education have begun to
be seen in reality, and with one particular unexpected result
that girls - who predominated in the university-bound routes
of study - have been found to be disadvantaged because they
lack the opportunity of work experience which even compulsory
military service gives to young men to add to the value of
school marks in an increasingly competitive entry process.
The new Lgr 80 curriculum will permit transfer to *gymnasieskola*
without dependence on choices made at the age of 13. And above
all the political climate has changed. Following the original
terms of reference, the first non-social democratic coalition
government, with a conservative minister of education in 1977,
instructed the enquiry to ensure that certain lines of study

should be theoretically orientated whilst others should be
vocationally orientated; at least one *gymnasieskola* line was
to give full qualification for entry to each course of higher
education. Then in 1979 the second non-social democratic
coalition, this time with a Liberal minister, partially reverted to the original directive, saying that while each line in
gymnasieskolan must have both a vocational and a study-
orientated emphasis each could give more stress to the one or
the other. Secondly, the enquiry should extend its remit to
take an overview of the goals for both compulsory and post-
compulsory schooling and consider how far and in what ways
vocational preparation should take place in both sectors of
schooling. Furthermore, the structure of and pre-requisities
for foreign language programmes in *gymnasieskolan*, the question
of the use which should be made of school marks as an entry
qualification, and the adjustment to the new Lgr 80 should also
be considered.

There is, however, another factor which bedevils planned change,
one which is common to all countries, that of changing birth
rates. There were 108,559 sixteen year olds in 1978; this
reached a peak of 123,550 in 1980, but by 1985 will decline to
108,239 and by 1993 to 96,591, rise again by 1996 and then fall
once more. Since these children are already born, the chances
of significant changes in the totals are slight. Other countries which have not expanded provision for sixteen year olds
to virtually 100% as in Sweden can, in theory, accommodate
falling rolls by increasing provision; Sweden (or the USA or
Japan) can do so only by reducing staff and facilities, or by
increasing the resources made available for the age-group, the
cost of which is formidable in a country where staffing is at
a gross level of about 1:11 for teachers, where teaching duties
at this stage are normally 24 periods per week, and where
buildings are already spacious and very well equipped.

It is therefore far from clear what will be the outcome of the
responses to the recommendations of the *Gymnasieskolan* enquiry.
What is clear, however, is that the reformed school will need
to be more flexible than it is at present, be more in accord
with the patterns of adult and working life, and make economic
use of public resources. Several current experiments contribute to its proposals. One is the idea of courses starting
on more than one occasion in the year - for example, instead
of the traditional start of a course in August or January, and
lasting for a complete term, it is possible to envisage courses
made up in modules of, perhaps, a month or six weeks or ten

weeks. Secondly, in the Kopparberg region there have been
schemes exploring more co-operation between pupils in the
theoretical and the practical lines. Thirdly, in Göteborg,
schemes have operated to interweave theory in school with
practice in a place of work. Fourthly, in Södertälje, patterns
of part-time study have been tried. Fifth, in Norrköping,
there have been schemes for a smoother transfer from the 9th
to the 10th year by, for example, seeing the final term of the
one and the first term of the other as a whole, with elements
of the preparatory vocational study brought forward and elements
of theoretical study delayed. Together with such experiments,
the results will be forthcoming of studies made of the effect-
iveness of patterns of study and work guidance, and of the co-
operation in the *SSA* Committees which bring together representatives of school and working life.

School and Work

The lack of conviction that schools can solve social problems
is one of the legacies of the seventies. The apparent end of
annual economic growth and thus relatively easy access to more
and more resources of public finance is another. Both pose
problems for schools. But both are made all the more complex
by the emergence of a phenomena which the politicians, the
economists and the educators barely envisaged until the mid
1970's - the very real prospect in a post-industrial, highly
technical and mechanised society, and especially one threatened
by the kind of industrial upheavals associated with an energy
crisis and a slump, of a society in which jobs for teenagers
simply do not exist on any large scale and the prospects of
such jobs seem remote in the foreseeable future. What, in such
a context, does an affluent and caring society do with and for
its youngsters? One answer - the simple one - is to increase
the school leaving age. But this does little more than delay
the problem, at the same time as insisting that the school
remain in essence a custodial institution to an age where its
students are legally adults.

Sweden has so far rejected the idea, even when it is at the same
time ready to provide places for more than 100% of sixteen year
olds. In part this reflects traditional Western European ideas -
that work is, in itself, a "good thing", and that schooling
tends to perpetuate a lack of responsibility in its students.
In part it also reflects an ideological perspective, that society
is necessarily divided into those who 'ought' to receive 'higher'
levels of schooling for leaders, and 'the rest' who are not

appropriate for such schooling and should follow more subordinate roles in working life. An idea was floated in the
autumn of 1980, not unrelated to the then minister of education,
the conservative ex-teacher Britt Mogård, to end compulsory
schooling at 15 and to replace the two-year *gymnasieskola*
lines with three-year courses, thus providing 11 years schooling
for most but enabling some to leave after 8 years - to do what
was not made clear.[10] In part, too, it reflects the uncertainty
of public attitudes, whether to accept that the Western
European employment prospect is really a result of structural
changes in society and is therefore likely to last a long time,
or whether it is still largely a cyclical phenomenon, well
known in the last two hundred years and merely delayed by the
circumstances and policies of the post war years.

There is no doubt that the structural changes have had a marked
effect in Sweden. The increase in mechanisation was noted
above, and it is very apparent in visiting any work place. For
example, in the late 1940's, what was then the largest match
factory in the world regularly employed 2,500 people, including
by far the majority of school leavers at (then) age 14, for a
wide range of manual and unskilled jobs; it now produces more
matches than ever and employs 250, on a wholly automated process.
The timber industry, too, which once made extensive use of male
manual labour not just to cut and transport pines in the deep
and often snow-bound forests but also in the mills to cut, trim,
plane and prepare the tree trunks, now uses little but powered
equipment. Tractors rather than horses can pull the timber to
roads and lorries transport it to spacious workhalls where
machines clasp a whole tree trunk, turn and cut it, and remove
sawdust through massive ducts - all operated by perhaps a girl
sitting in a sound-proof cabin controlling leavers, knobs and
buttons while sitting as comfortably as an airline pilot; and
as with flying, these processes can now also be controlled by
computers. Word processors in offices, computer links to
telephones, automated store-keeping, automated registering of
sales and transfer of payments: Chaplin's "Modern Times" of
the 1930's are a present reality in techniques.

At the same time, much more attention is now given to the conditions of work, and negotiations between employers and
employees have led to agreements, backed by laws, which forbid
those not legally adult to work with certain materials, or in
certain environments where the wrong use of a machine could
have disasterous consequences, or to be employed on shift work,
necessary for the machine to earn its keep. It is in these

circumstances that an increasing number of Swedes aged 16-18
have found themselves unable to obtain a job, quite irrespective
of the general employment situation in simple economic terms.
It simply is not possible to say to such youngsters that there
is work in another part of the country; even where this may be
true, the under-age cannot be told to live away from home in
lodgings or in hostels.

There is also, of course, unemployment which is clearly cyclical:
the factory which, while prepared to employ school leavers in
years when trade boomed was simply unable to do so in times when
the order books are not full; the shops which do not replace
staff when the profit margins are cut; the public services
cutting back expenditure, especially on staff, when inflation
greatly exceeds growth in productivity and the receipts of taxation. There is evidence that some employers are ready to employ
youngsters in good times: and evidence, too, that they want to
employ those who, while waiting for a job, have obtained a
practical qualification not necessarily in a specific skill but
in the habits and attitudes of work which, whether or not it
calls for some manual dexterity, above all calls for an understanding of what accuracy, puntuality, responsibility and co-
operativeness imply.

Sweden has, however, taken the significant step whereby it is
the responsibility of the school authorities to provide opportunities for those under 18 who are not in school. Since the
mid 1970's, there has been the so-called "youth guarantee", the
promise of either a job, or practical work experience, or a
place at school for all aged 16-18; and significantly, in
Spring 1980, it was decided that only exceptionally should those
under 18 be provided with "youth opportunities jobs" or with
"Labour Board Education", *arbetmarknadsutbildning* or *AMU*,
organised by the Department of Employment, in both of which the
recipient received a proper salary, largely paid for by government grants, and employment as long as it did not exceed six
months (and therefore, legally, became 'permanent').

The school authorities are now enjoined both by the National
Board of Education and the Labour Market Board to provide either
more places in the schools, or obtain practical work-experience
places, or extend their apprenticeship courses. For this, the
students receive only the normal study grant (232 kronor per
month in 1980, roughly £23) instead of 20-23 kronor an hour which
the unskilled worker might expect. One way of financing increased
provision by the school authorities is to use the state grant

which is available for teaching based on a place of work;
another is to find more practice places; a third is to extend
school-based apprenticeships. This last possibility is already
extensively used in any case: apprenticeship training in the
technical and mechanical fields has largely been conducted in
the schools for several years, and is now virtually unknown for
the future car-mechanic and such like to take an apprenticeship
with an employer who gives not only the practical experience
but also the theoretical instruction and, in conjunction with
the craft in question, sets the final tests to become a "skilled
worker" or a "master craftsman": this is now done in the
practical lines of *gymnasieskolan*. It is only in manual crafts –
hairdressing, tailoring, gunsmiths, house painters, pattern-
makers, watchmakers, opticians and so on– where the traditional
apprenticeships continue at places of work, their training programme under the general control of the Handicraft Society,
Hantverksföreningen, rather than the schools.

There is no suggestion that the world of the school should not
see meaningful employment as the end-activity of formal schooling.
Indeed, even as employment prospects for sixteen year olds have
declined, the importance of practical work experience at the 13-
16 stage has not diminished, but simply changed its emphasis:
there is still much point in the minimum of three visits in Class
8 and a week's work experience in Class 9, and in association with
the civics classes to help youngsters to understand something of
how the world of work is organised, and to challenge the stereo-
types of jobs which are only for men or for women, or are dirty
or noisy, are well or badly paid, enjoy higher or lower social
status, or are "not for the likes of us". Above all, what
employers now tend to look for is not so much traditional subject
knowledge and specific craft skills but basic skills in the use
of language and number and basic attitudes of responsibility and
co-operative life and work. All studies show that it is the less
well qualified, those who have eschewed training courses, who are
more likely to find it hard to get a job, whether at 16 or later.
Gymnasieskolan may have become a place for most 16-18's, but here
too the whole organisation stresses future employment, with its
curriculum arranged in terms of occupational categories, options
set out in terms of job prospects, and entry requirements for
higher education positively encouraging applicants who have work
experience.

Unemployment in Sweden is not as high as in the rest of Western
Europe: but while school systems absorb in one way or another

most up to age 16, the age-group 16-24 still has three times as
many unemployed as in older groups, and for every 16-24 year
old who is unemployed, there are twice as many in some kind of
"work opportunity" programme operated by the Labour Market Board.
The problems tend, therefore, to be hidden: but they are still
there. Those in small towns and sparsely populated areas which
are excessively dependent on very few major employers are particularly at risk when the mine, the saw-mill, the engineering
works closes down. The under-18s are legally, as well as
possibly socially, "immature"; girls under 18 are the more
likely to be offered lower paid jobs with longer working hours
in fields such as child care, or as home helps - and when a
place in a pre-school *dagis* costs twice as much or more compared with the cost of paying for help to be sent part-time to
the home, it is not surprising that some local authorities
prefer the cheaper alternative and welcome the availability of
16-18 year old girls. In any case, national manpower predictions
are seldom precise enough to guarantee work for the individual
in a given locality. Those most affected are clearly the less
able and the less motivated 16-17 year olds, that 10-15-20%
who did not get into the *gymnasieskola*, or if they did, were
placed in lines of study they did not really want and from which
they dropped out after a year or so. Such youngsters find
themselves in a vicious circle. They experienced low grades
throughout compulsory school, acquired a low self-image having
been told so often they were at the bottom of the heap, saw
little point in staying in school to receive two more years of
the same experience but who, because of low marks, find it hard
to get a job even if one is available, and who then run the
risk of being social misfits, justifying their rejection of
school and society in the experience of being rejected.

It is in these contexts that Sweden has attempted to respond to
the problems of relating school and work. The first in time
was the establishment, noted above, of the *SSA* committees,
Skolan, Samhället och Arbetsliv, bringing together representatives of school and working life the better to ease the transition from school to work. These began experimentally in the mid
1970's, and from 1 July 1977 have been statutory bodies in each
local authority. As an example of what they achieved, Göteborg
found 2,700 vacancies, including 500 work experience places, in
the first year. But this cannot be a "once and for all" task:
every year, and increasingly at the level of individual youngsters and individual employers, this kind of co-operation is
proving its value through personal rather than merely bureaucratic means.

Secondly, the Labour Board schemes, while no longer available
for those under 18, nevertheless provide significant opportunities for those up to 24. It has been shown, however, that
it is easier to identify a demand than to satisfy it: at one
stage in 1978 courses in welding, for instance, had a four month
waiting list, and for car mechanics as much as a year - though
courses of this kind are increasingly to be found in *gymnasieskolan* as the number of places available is expanded specifically to cater for more than just 16 year olds. Thirdly, five
projects - in Söderhamn, Skellefteå, Södertälje, Halmstad and
Karlstad, towns in different parts of the country with different
problems - have been established to study extended follow-up
procedures for the under 20's.

Fourthly, it is recognised that there is a great need for more
improved guidance services, with more personnel, and better
links between school, further study and work, and between
teachers, school administrators, labour market staff and pupils.
A study in Umeå,[11] sponsored by the National Board of Education,
showed widespread uncertainty about the role of these counsellors.
It may be that the old "careers guidance" teacher at the 13-16
stage, *yrkesvalslärare*, had an advantage over the "counsellor",
syo konsulent, in that he was a teacher, and had regular, on-
going, contact with the pupils, whereas the student has to
make a point of going to the counsellor in his office, generally
located in the "administration" part of the school. On the
other hand, the guidance teacher was less well qualified in a
formal sense and had less direct contact with the labour market,
and it is the 'counsellor' concept that is being preferred. In
both cases, however, the problem of a lack of understanding by
the traditional academic teachers and by heads and school admin-
strations, was noted; to them the subject teaching was the
purpose of the school, and further study in subjects was seen
as the goal for the most highly motivated: guidance was not
their concern.

In certain senses, the solutions to problems of relating school
and work are relatively easy. Given the co-operation of management and the shop floor, not too hard to obtain at a personal
level and supported in principle by the leaders of both the
employers' association (*SAF*) and the trade unions (*LO*), it is
not too difficult to obtain practice places and/or to devise
training schemes involving both the school and the place of
work. This is particularly so in the larger towns and with
the larger firms. A scheme of government grants also goes
some way towards meeting the problems of the smaller employer

who has to deploy staff needed for normal productive activities
to be able to afford the time needed by the young learners.
The educational responses are also relatively easily made in the
sense of providing places in *gymnasieskolan* and organising
courses in a manner more appropriate to ideas of recurrent
education, given the political and social will to do so.

Problems

There remain, however, three massive problems for the schools.
First, neither Sweden, nor any other country, has found a really
satisfactory answer to the problems of the "school-tired"
fifteen-eighteen year old. Schemes of participation in decision-
making or of individualised learning programmes may help; but
there remains a climate of opinion among teenagers themselves
and to some extent in society itself that expects school to be
"dull". It requires great maturity for youngsters to recognise
that they can be their own worst enemies in having such
attitudes.

Secondly, the plea to make school work more "relevant" is
clearly more complex than groups such as those supporting the
idea of an "alternative *Gymnasieskola*" appear to recognise.
The task is presumably to make the link between school and work
part of the educative process. But places of work are geared to
"produce" or to "serve", not to teach; their goals are necessarily different, however attractive may appear the curriculum
orientation of "polytechnic" education whether on the models of
Eastern Europe or their not wholly dissimilar "pragmatic" mani-
festations in the spirit of Dewey in the USA.

Thirdly, the ideology underlying the idea that work is itself
educative needs to adapt to changing technology. With the best
will in the world, there will be semi-literate and semi-numerate
sixteen year olds who are virtually unemployable in the more
sophisticated job processes; it is almost as if they might
need "protected work", as has been found in most developed
countries for those who come into the legal categories of
"handicapped persons".

It is at these points that questions of the purposes of schooling become dominant: in what terms is expenditure on schooling
to be justified in economic terms? The traditional answer was
the cyclical argument, that it increased production, generated
a larger GNP which made available more welfare and more schooling which in its turn further increased production. But the

western world of the 1980's is no longer convinced by this
argument. Perhaps schooling might be better measured in
qualitative terms, a quality of life. Sweden is not unaware
of this. There is a tradition of both academic study and of
vocational training in the integrated *gymnasieskola*. There is
also change towards a broader educative role which, as with the
basic school, is tending towards different concepts of school
and teaching. It is this that lies behind the idea of school
as a place where people learn to live and work together: to
know and understand different cultures through programmes of
"internationalising" education. "I can live with a bad speller;
I cannot live with a bigot".[12] Fine ideals, however, are
easier to express than to achieve.

CHAPTER 6

Higher and Adult Education

Traditional Higher Education

Traditionally, being a student meant in the first place passing
studentexamen, the formal examination at the end of a full
academic secondary school course at age 20 or 21 taken in a
dozen or more subjects. This entitled the successful candidate
to wear the white "student cap" and gave the right to register
in the so-called "open" faculties of arts and science of a university or university-level High School, *Högskola*. There was,
however, a selective entry to certain practical and vocationally
prestigious courses in, for example, medicine, dentistry, veterinary science, some fields of engineering. Until the late
1960's, the courses were of indefinite length and there were,
indeed, some "eternal" students. There was a 'normal' expectation of how long a course should take, very roughly equated with
the level of achievement being sought: a subject could be then
taken at a 1, 2 or 3 mark level, and each "mark", *betyg*, was
supposed to be a full term's work. But the student presented
himself for assessment, generally in December or May, when he
felt 'ready', and it was not uncommon to combine study with
work and to take at least half as long again, or even more, to
reach the appropriate degree level. There were, and are, no
fees, only relatively small "student dues"; and it was common
to finance personal expenses by taking a private loan, or to
interweave study with paid employment. It was far from uncommon
for graduates to repay their debts throughout the greater part
of their working lives.

A first degree, *filosofie kandidat*, or *fil-kand.*, required 6
marks, and was normally taken in two or three subjects. What
constituted a "subject" might well be much narrower than its
equivalent in an English "single subject" degree course; for
example, economic history, political theory and political history
were, and are, three 'subjects'. Those seeking posts in public

service, such as grammar school teachers, would take a particular
combination of subjects as laid down, and receive the degree of
filosofie magister, normally abbreviated *fil.mag.* Other graduates took examinations naming their speciality, for example,
agronom or *socionom.* Further study led, after two or three
years, to the *filosofie liceniat, fil.lic.*, requiring a minor
thesis; and after a minimum of two or three more years and the
submission of a major thesis, the highest degree of *filosofie
doktor, fil.dr.* (which in medieval tradition is opposed and
defended in public debate and which entitles the successful
disputant to wear a black collapsible 'opera hat' and an engraved
gold ring on the third finger of the left hand). The *lektor* in
the academic gymnasium traditionally was a *fil.dr.*; but as the
numbers attending this level of schooling began rapidly to rise
in the 1950's, it became possible for those with a *fil.lic.* also
to be appointed as *lektor*, and thus give rise to fears of lower-
ing standards.

Not only was there no fixed length of time for study. Swedish
university students never have known the kind of close residential life characteristic of the traditional British university.
They have always lived in either private rented rooms and flats,
or student flatlets in blocks built by the student union bodies
who might rent vacant accommodation to tourists in the summer.
In 1980 figures, this might cost anything from 500-1,000 kr. a
month for a furnished room. Nor was there much direct guidance
on precisely what was required in the course of study, or in
the humanities at least any closely structured programme of
instruction. There might, for example, be lectures on periods
of English Literature at stated times, and the audience might
include freshmen and post-graduates: but the lecturer would
not necessarily know how many of each or have any real personal
contact with any of them. The student would read, independently,
knowing little more than he would be required to have detailed
knowledge of so many thousand pages of literature from a given
list of books. But perhaps it did not matter so much in the
early fifties, when only about 3% of an age group went to university: the student 'read his subject'.

In the fifties and especially the sixties, student numbers
rapidly increased, as Table 13 shows. More and more students
completed a full secondary school course, more and more entered
university after *studentexamen*, more and more older students
returned after a period of absence (undergraduate credits gained
at the 1,2,3 mark level never lost their value), more and more

TABLE 13:   University Student Enrolment 1940/41 - 1977/78

Year	New Enrolments	Total
1940/41	2,000	11,000
1950/51	3,800	17,000
1960/61	8,000	37,000
1970/71	26,000	125,000
1973/74	20,000	108,000
1977/78	34,100*	150,000

* Expanded concept of higher education in 1977

candidates sought opportunities to study in the smaller towns some distance from the main university centres of medieval Lund or Uppsala, nineteenth century Stockholm or Göteborg: or the foundations in the 1960s of Umeå and Linköping; more and more public money was being spent on higher education. Obviously more staff were appointed, and lecturers ran seminars; but the professorial staff became even more remote, the burdens of the heavy loans became more widespread, and the drop-out rate remained at about 50%. Some, of course, dropped out of the university and enrolled instead in teacher colleges and the like: a practice which makes it very hard to follow the published statistics. Furthermore, some of the drop-outs returned later. In these senses, "short cycle" and "recurrent" higher education was known in Sweden long ago, and was highly respectable.

In these circumstances, it was perhaps inevitable that changes would be proposed. The first moves in this direction in the 1960's came from a working party of the University Chancellor's Office known (by the initial letters of its Swedish title) as UKAS, which proposed fairly fixed groupings of subjects to give the studies greater coherence; a points system of 40 points for a 40-week to replace the old 1,2,3 mark system; some provision for part-time students; and the beginnings of the idea that most, if not all, courses should have some occupational end

in view. These ideas were bitterly criticised in academic
circles, and were in fact modified by a parliamentary decision
in 1969 known irreverently as "PUKAS"; but courses were nevertheless grouped into nineteen "lines" and students in the so-
called "open" faculties where no *numerus clausus* operated were
to be expected to complete a notional one year (two term) course
in no more than three terms if they were to be entitled to re-
register. A measure of decentralisation was also begun, with
what were known as university *filial* being opened in smaller
towns, colleges affiliated to a parent university and offering
20-point or 40-point courses in the popular subjects and the
ones which did not require specialised facilities. It was at
this time that a revised system of state-backed study loans,
with repayments linked to a cost of living index, was introduced,
the 1980 pattern of which is summarised in Appendix V.

These plans, however, related only to university work as traditionally conceived. There was a growing issue of what framework of higher studies might best meet the needs of some of that
70% of an age-group which, as the sixties were drawing to a close,
could be expected to complete at least two years of the post-
compulsory schools. The validity of the traditional distinction
between university and non-university level work also began
seriously to be questioned, especially as an increasing number
of training programmes called for a greater theoretical component
as well as for practical skills, as was the assumption that
entry to university level work necessarily required *studentexamen*.
Furthermore, means of implementing ideas of "democratisation" in
education, as in other spheres of life, were being sought in the
1960's. Clearly the students of 1968 were not happy, and there
were riots in Sweden that year as there were in France, Germany,
the USA and elsewhere. It was in this climate that Sweden set
up, in 1968, its major committee of enquiry into the capacity,
location and organisation of basic higher education, known as
U68.[1] It envisaged a much wider conception than traditional
university education, but it explicitly excluded research and
the question of the levels of scholastic competence required
for entry: these were the subjects of two other committees of
enquiry.[2]

U68 and 1977 Reforms

The U68 committee worked in a manner similar to other major
educational official commissions. A small central committee of
four officials (the Under-Secretary of State for Education;
Chancellor of the Universities; the retired Director General

of the NBE) worked with three "reference groups" representing
the political parties, the education system, and the labour
market organisations of both employers and employees. Some
enquiries were commissioned, and on four separate occasions
50,000 copies of "debate pamphlets" were published: _on structure
and function in higher education; on aims of higher education;
on relationships between studies and subsequent occupation;   and
on developments at the school level. As in other fields it was
an attempt to generate an informed debate, an attempt to achieve
that feeling of consensus which is a characteristic goal of
Swedish social democracy. That the final decision would be a
political decision in parliament was not in dispute: but if
that decision were to be effective, it would be desirable to
have not only a political decision, but also the understanding
and support of the public at large and especially of the participants involved.

In this case, however, the approach was not wholly successful.
Opposition from traditional academics to increasing public
control was not surprising. But the proposals also reflected
changing political attitudes.[3] The Social Democrat Minister of
Education in the 1960's, Ragnar Edenman, wholly supported the
idea of 'open faculties'. He resigned in 1967, to be replaced
by Olav Palme, later to be Prime Minister. A new Ministry of
Higher Education was also created at this time, which led to
the appointment of Lennart Sandgren as Under Secretary and
Chairman of U68. He had different views on control of quantitative growth, and until 1973 at least there was intra-party
dispute on the matter of *numerus clausus*.

U68 defined higher education as "essentially ... education ...
based as a rule on the general qualification requirements adopted
in 1972":[4] in effect, the successful completion of any line in
gymnasieskolan with specific requirements in Swedish and English
for those from the two-year lines; alternatively, special
admission requirements for adults who had either taken courses
at the Folk High Schools after leaving compulsory school, or
were over 24 years old and had been gainfully employed for five
years (which could include care of one's own children). It
also started "from the premiss that higher education is to prepare students for subsequent occupational activities".[5] There
were seven basic proposals, and after much debate these were in
essence adopted in the Higher Education Act of 1977, but with
amendments to the administrative structure, the academic autonomy
of the individual institutions, and the extent of selectivity.

These proposals were:

a) All educational programmes should be organised in five
    occupational sectors - technology; administration and
    economics; medicine and care services; teaching; cultural
    work and information services. These sectors would replace
    the traditional university faculties for basic higher educa-
    tion, and would be the basis on which grants of public
    money were allocated.

b) Each sector would have a number of "lines", and each "line"
    would be made up of a number of "courses" of a stated points
    value. Each term of full-time study would count as 20
    points, each year 40 points. In all, about 100 "lines"
    were proposed, (Appendix VIII lists the lines available in
    1980/81); and each course would be graded either Pass/Fail/
    Credit (*spets*), or simply Pass/Fail. No first degree titles
    would be used - simply a statement of subjects studied for
    so many points.

c) Programmes could be "general", "local" or "individual". "It
    is not necessary that every individual course should have a
    clear occupational relevance ... The important thing is
    that the combination of courses making up the programme
    should constitute a good preparation for future occupational
    activities".[6] General programmes fitted into a national
    pattern; local and individual ones met local and individual
    needs.

d) Entry to all courses should be selective, and "positive
    steps" were to be taken to promote the idea of recurrent
    education, by better guidance, better grants for adults,
    decentralised locations of study, and by giving credit for
    work experience in the system by which applications were
    graded. (This selective idea was not, initially, adopted
    for those kinds of programmes which had traditionally been
    offered in the "open" faculties, but was in fact introduced
    in 1979).

e) Total intakes numbers would be decided annually, for each
    sector and each line.

f) The country would be divided into six regions, in each of
    which there would be one of the existing university areas -
    Uppsala, Stockholm, Lund-Malmö, Göteborg, Umeå, and

Linköping - together with institutions in a number of other
towns. In each region, programmes within each of the five
occupational sectors would be offered. These regions were
then sub-divided into nineteen areas. (This was also
amended later).

g) All higher education would be administered centrally by a
new Office of Universities and Colleges, *Universitets-och
Högskoleämbetet,* or *UHÄ*. In each area it was proposed to
have a Higher Education Board with the "public interest"
in the majority. (This was also amended).

That this total reorganisation would meet opposition was
apparent almost from the start of the U68 commission's work, in
the sixteen notes of reservation to its main report in 1973,
and in the subsequent public reviews. As a generalisation, in
favour included the National Board of Education, teachers and
employee groups; those in opposition came from traditional
university opinion, student opinion and the bourgeois political
opposition of the day. At root, the U68 ideas challenged the
highest level of academic tradition. To question the functions
and structures of universities was to challenge the authority
of *universitas,* those deeply held views of the nature of knowledge, of access to it and the process by which it was dissemi-
nated. Students, too, felt that the direction of their studies
was being steered by labour market forces, and that as individuals they were thus being 'manipulated' yet again, as they had
been at school.

The parliamentary committee charged with the preparation of the
bill to implement the proposals had already by 1974 amended the
original proposals by giving more power to academic opinion at
the institutional level; by having the higher education boards
only at the regional level; by stressing the research function
which, while not part of the U68 remit, appeared to be given
too little consideration in its plans; and by delaying the
process of decentralisation to more *filial.* It took, however,
two more years of debate before final decisions could be made
on the relationships between central government, regional
boards and institutions; on selectivity and equality of opportunity; and on how to effect the integration of studies into
appropriate occupationally orientated programmes without des-
troying academic coherence. By this time, the political
climate had changed and the first non-Social Democrat bourgeois
coalition for forty-four years had formed a precarious government, one of whose actions was to pass the 1977 Higher

Education Act.

The extent of the change in basic higher education as envisaged by U68 is reflected in the issue of administrative control. Traditionalists wanted to maintain a distinction between the university and other post-secondary school courses; and when university entry meant perhaps only a small proportion of an age-group, it was relatively easy to justify in terms of academic freedom the absence of public control over the numbers permitted to enter and over course content and structure. But U68 was considering a 'mass' entry age group, together with a wide range of more overtly vocational studies, often of relatively short duration, the development of a much wider concept of basic higher education.[7] The debate really centered on the control of what was a major public provision for perhaps 30% of an age-group, far more than the proportion which in the 1930's had entered even the lower selective grammar schools. Obviously "the public interest" must be involved: but to what extent and what level?

The outcome of these discussions led to the present structure shown in Fig. 10. <u>Parliament</u> determines the framework for higher education and votes the necessary monies. The <u>Ministry of Education</u> prepares the material for parliament in the name of the government and administers its policy decisions, with the Ministry of Agriculture accepting this responsibility regarding the Federal Agricultural University. The <u>Office of Universities and Colleges</u>, <u>UHÄ</u>, executes the policy as it affects state institutions and the <u>National Board of Education</u>, <u>SÖ</u>, does so for municipal institutions, mainly for health care and training, which had been part of the upper secondary school system. Together they co-ordinate plans, determine annually the number of places available in each line of study, and decide the total annual allocations of finance. <u>UHÄ</u> has five planning sections; one for each of the five study sectors. In each of the <u>six regions</u> - Stockholm (incorporating the counties of Stockholm and Gotland); Uppsala (the counties of Uppsala, Södermanland, Örebro, Västmanland, Kopparberg and Gävleborg); Linköping (the counties of Östergötland and Jonkoping); Lund-Malmö (the counties of Kronoberg, Kalmar, Blekinge, Kristianstad, Malmöhus and Halland); Göteborg (the counties of Göteborg - and Bohus, Älvsborg, Skaraborg and Värmland); and Umeå (the counties of Västerbotten, Jämtland, Västernorrland and Norbotten) - there is a <u>regional board</u> appointed by the Crown, with two-thirds of its members from the "public interest". These boards plan and co-ordinate provision within the region and are responsible for

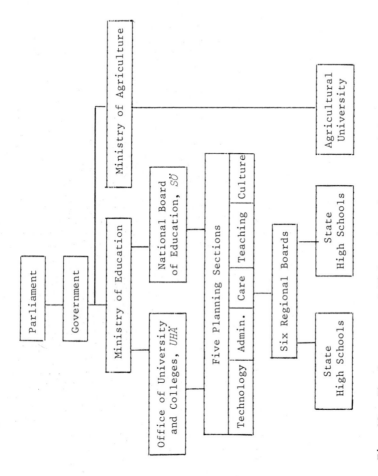

Fig. 10. The Structure of Higher Educational Provision

allocating available finances to local and individual courses, and for encouraging association between basic level studies and research in the region. Locally, there are the separate units of Higher Education, either state or municipal, together with two private institutions, both in Stockholm, the Commercial High School, *Handelshögskolan*, and the Institute for Social Pedagogy, *Socialpedagogiska Institutet*. The Agricultural University is spread all over the country, its centre being in the Ultuna area of Uppsala.

The organisation of the 32 state Universities and Colleges, eleven of which have regular research functions, is shown in Fig.11. Each will have a Board, *Styrelse*, where a third of the members represent the public interest and two-thirds comes from the staff and students. The board co-ordinates the work of the University or College, the links between basic courses and research, provides the premises, sets up lines of study and determines the budgetary submission annually to *UHÄ*. Each unit will have a *Rektor*, appointed in the first instance for six years by the Crown on the recommendation of the local board or following election by the staff. There may also be an Admissions Board on which the public interest would be represented. The content of courses is determined by a "Line of Study Board", *Linjenämnd*, which can be separate for each University or College or may be common for the whole region, and has equal numbers of representatives from the world of work, academic staff and students. Research studies are the responsibility of Faculty Boards, sometimes sub-divided into sections. These are chaired by the Dean, and include academic staff members elected by those staff who have doctorates, together with representative non-academic staff and students. In every University or College where there are academic appointments for which a doctorate is a pre-requisite, there are appointment boards with members appointed by academic and non-academic staff, students, and experts relevant to the post in question.

The teaching and research is carried out in Institutions: and it is for the University or College Board to decide which institutions to set up. These are also headed by Boards, chaired by a *prefekt* with membership drawn from the staff and students. These boards decide how an institution's resources are to be allocated and how teaching and assessment is organised.

The Municipal Colleges have a similar pattern of organisation. They are immediately responsible to the County Council, *Landsting*, the local authority board, *kommunstyrelse*, with the County

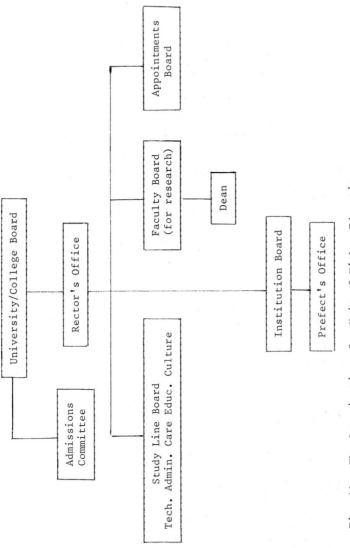

Fig. 11. The Organisation of a Unit of Higher Education

Education Board of the Local Authority School Board acting on
their behalf. Unlike the boards for state higher education,
these county and local authority school boards are political
bodies, and neither employees nor students have any place on
them. They have, however, the same responsibilities as do the
state higher education boards; there are Lines of Study Boards
for the county and local authority Higher Education; and
admission to their courses is carried out by admission committees.

The planning process in higher education follows a sequence
normally running over at least two years. *UHÄ* sets out general
guidelines in July; in the coming months, regional boards
advise the local planning groups, and individual institutions
and study boards respond through the local *UHÄ*. Meanwhile,
faculty boards have also sent direct to *UHÄ* their research proposals, though university and college boards have an opportunity
to comment on them. Regional boards make their observations to
UHÄ by the end of April in the following year. By the beginning
of September, *UHÄ* makes its proposals to government for implementation twelve months hence. During the autumn, government
deliberates its policy and in January presents to parliament its
budget proposition, together with proposals for the disposition
of the monies being sought. By June, parliament will have made
its decisions, and a formal letter, *regleringsbrev*, summarises
the regulations for the coming financial year. At the same time
as parliament is deciding the state budget, the counties and
local authorities are determining theirs. By the beginning of
February, each region should be able to say what resources will
probably be available for local and individual courses of study;
and between the end of March and the middle of May each High
School Board draws up its own budget, assuming that parliament
will not make any major changes in the government's proposition.
It is intended that the process should be a continuing dialogue,
with all concerned aware of both current and longer term perspectives.

It is perhaps also worth noting that in Swedish procedures in a
public collective body, a member of a formal committee or board
cannot simply absent himself. Except for sickness and similar
reasons, there is a duty either to be present in person or to be
represented by a recognised substitute. Furthermore, every
member must vote either for or against a proposal, and those
voting against the majority are obliged to record their reasons
for taking a different view.

Selection

U68 proposed that all higher education should be selective. The
parliamentary preparatory committee in 1974 prevaricated: the
liberal party wanted to retain the traditional faculties, at
least for those who had obtained a grade average of 2.3 in the
final result from the 3-year and 4-year *gymnasieskola*, and the
committee referred the whole matter to the commission considering
"competence" to enter higher education. Understandably, the
student body wanted to retain such open access. At the same
time, it was becoming clear that there was a growing tendency
for students not to proceed directly from school to higher
education, and from the early seventies, there had been experiments making it possible for students aged 25 or more with five
years of gainful employment to be admitted on the basis of
scores on a scholastic aptitude test rather than school results.
Indeed, in 1974, for the first time, a majority of new entrants
to universities were in fact aged 25 or more, and ever since
it has been increasingly recognised that higher education is no
longer simply that which follows on from a full period of
schooling to age 18/19, albeit with a break for military service
for the men.

The increasing numbers of students completing a two-year
gymnasieskolan course, the recognition that at least some of
these might be eligible for higher education, and the large
numbers of the adult population who needed extended educational
facilities if they were not to be permanently disadvantaged on
grounds of age by a choice made perhaps at age 13/16, made it
even more necessary to consider the extent and the manner in
which limited resources were to be made available. Availability,
however, is not simply a question of academic competence judged
by scholastic success in an academic secondary school course.
It is also a question of motivation on the part of the student,
of social need, of the nature of student support systems, of
the location of the proposed course of study. Equality is a
goal accepted by all major political parties in Sweden: the
problem is how to obtain it with equity and justice. But
equal opportunity to study what?

Basic to the *UKAS/PUKAS* ideas of the sixties, to the ideas of
U68 and to those of the 1977 Act is the notion that higher
educational courses should have in mind some occupational outcome. This poses formidable social and political questions:
how right is it to use manpower planning models as the basis for
planning higher education?[8] U68 and the 1977 Act assumed that

manpower needs should be used to help determine the size of a
given intake of students. It is clear, however, that it is
possible for manpower planning not only to be misused but also
to be dysfunctional. Two examples suffice. The first was
recognised by the Swedish submission to the OECD studies of
teacher supply,[9] where it was noted that if all estimates of
manpower need were added together, there are more demands than
there are people to meet them: each planning sector tends to
operate on its own, and it is unrealistic to expect a totally
effective global forecast over all sectors of occupational life.
The second example is the change which takes place in occupational needs in a free society, not by planning, nor by expectation, nor even a planned change when technological and political
events intervene. There was little evidence in the mid-1970's
to suggest that the 1980's would begin with an economic crisis
in the western world which drew parallels with the slump of the
1930's. The energy crisis, the north-south dichotomy in economic
terms between the developed and the Third World, and the change
in political climates have also all altered the bases of planning.
Furthermore, the directive nature of such a basis for planning
numbers in higher education does seem to be in conflict with
the notions of an open democratic society which loomed so large
in Swedish school reforms of the 1950s and 1960s, and of the
notions of self-realisation which have been emphasised in the
study and work orientation, *syo*, activities in the schools.

Politically, the Liberals in the post 1976 government were able
to insist in the 1977 Act that the 2.3 grade average in *gymnasieskolan* would indeed suffice for entry to the so-called "open"
faculties. By 1979, however, harsh economic reality had required
the next coalition government to rescind this decision, and
since then, the U68 idea of total selectivity has prevailed.
How does it work?

First, applicants may consult the seven booklets, each of 40-50
pages, issued by *UHÄ* describing how higher education is organised,
how to apply, and what courses are available in the five occupational sectors into which the courses are organised. There is
a new intake every term, August and January, but some courses
are available only once a year. The application procedure is
centralised in an office of *UHÄ* and is wholly computerised.
The applicant puts up to twelve choices of course and location
in rank order, and after a deadline date cannot change this.
For selection purposes, each applicant applies under one or more
of four quotas:

1a - for those with a final leaving certificate from the three
      or four year *gymnasieskola*, the grade average of all
      subjects is calculated (with certain remissions - for
      example, the mark in gymnastics can be excluded if it is
      below the overall average). The maximum is 5 points.

1b - as for 1a, but with points added for extra experience.
      Work experience must include at least 9 months in one
      employment and at least 15 months in all; and originally
      an extra 1.0 point could be earned by voluntary work cover-
      ing at least two years with, for example, sports organisa-
      tions or trade unions, making it possible to earn a
      maximum of 2.5 extra points; this was reduced to 2.0 in
      1980, and with the elimination of the voluntary work
      merits in 1981, to a maximum of 1.7.

2a - for those with a leaving certificate from the two-year
      gymnasieskola, maximum 5 points, as in 1a.

2b - as for 2a, but with added points for experience as under
      1b.

3a - for those with formal education from Folk High Schools,
      with a maximum of 4 points as judged by the Folk High
      School marking system (4,3,2,1).

3b - as for 3a, but with added points for experience as under
      1b and 2b.

4 - for those who are aged 25 or more with four year's
      experience (no longer five years), and who take a scholas-
      tic aptitude test, the scores on which are then scaled
      to give a maximum of 2 points.

      quota 4a: for those who can apply only under this quota,
                 and for whom half the places available under
                 quota 4 are reserved.

           4b: for the remainder of those offered places under
                quota 4, and shared between all quota 4
                applicants.

The number of places offered is in proportion to the number of
applicants under each quota. Applications are submitted by mid-
June for the August entry or the end of October for January
entry. At the end of July (or mid-December), the first computer

selection takes place. Applicants are sent a form to be returned, either accepting the offer made, in which case all
other choices are withdrawn, or rejecting any offer and asking
to be considered for remaining choices in the second round of
selection in mid-August, (or early January), after which the
same "acceptance/rejection/try again" process is repeated a
third time for the August applicants, with the selection being
made at the end of the month. At each "draw", a candidate not
selected is told the "reserve number" his merits have earned,
from which an estimate can be made of the chances of success in
the later "draws". After the final selection, it is possible
that a place is not in fact taken up when the term begins, and
each university or college has a duty then to seek those applicants next in rank order to see if they want the place available.
In the event of two or more applicants having the same points
total for one vacancy, the choice is finally made by drawing
lots. When terms begin, there may well be notices in student
common rooms trying to arrange an exchange with somebody who
has obtained a place in another town and would prefer a change;
on a limited scale, this is possible.

To prevent an excessive emphasis being placed on points gained
for work experience, it was originally decided that 20% of the
places in quotas 1 and 2 would be determined by school marks
alone. Research on experiences since 1977, however,[10] has led
to this being raised to 30% as from 1981, together with the
reduction to 1.7 of the points value for work experience. It
was apparent that while it was desirable to ensure that applicants who came from backgrounds other than directly from school
should have real opportunites to enter higher education, those
who did come direct from school, and especially the girls for
whom work experience and "society merits" were less commonly
available (the young men, at least, could do their compulsory
military service, which counted as work experience), were
becoming increasingly disadvantaged.

The current pattern of entry requirements and course structures
certainly opened the way to higher education for new groups of
students (see Table 14). The largest percentage of those from
the two-year *gymnasieskolan* lines tend to obtain places in the
administrative and teaching sectors. Table 15 shows the
importance of work experience. There is, however, considerable
variation between different lines of study within a sector, as
is shown by Table 16. It is also clear that the more selective
a course of study, the more likely it is for the successful

TABLE 14: Newly Enrolled Students 1977/78

| | Basis for Eligibility | | | | |
	3-Year Upper Secondary	2-Year Upper Secondary	25/4's	Others	Total
Study programmes	63% / 11,660	10% / 1,780	5% / 1,020	22% / 4,160	100% / 18,620
Single courses	49% / 15,860	12% / 3,760	17% / 5,630	22% / 7,095	100% / 32,345
Total	53% / 26,380	11% / 5,385	13% / 6,530	22% / 11,065	100% / 49,360

Source: (Kim, 1979)

TABLE 15: Entrants to Line of Study, Autumn Term 1979

	Technology	Admin.	Care	Teaching	Culture	Local	Total
Total Entrants	4,256	5,455	816	1,696	534	512	13,269
Group 1A	845	789	122	231	100	175	2,262
B	3,088	3,027	486	491	321	247	7,860
2A	53	228	15	122	11	29	458
B	105	761	31	232	20	86	1,235
3	18	144	18	91	13	20	304
4	147	506	144	229	69	55	1,150
% age Group 1	92.4	70.0	74.5	60.3	66.4	62.9	76.3
2	3.7	18.1	5.6	20.9	5.8	22.5	12.8
3	0.4	2.6	2.2	5.4	2.4	3.9	2.3
4	3.5	9.3	17.7	13.5	12.9	10.7	8.7

Source: *UHÄ, Siffror från CA HT-79* (Numbers from Central Admissions, Autumn Term 1979), 1979-10-01

TABLE 16:   Examples of Applications to Different Lines of Study,
            1979

Course/Location	Group 1 %	Group 2 %	Group 3 %	Group 4 %
Marine technology, Stockholm	94.7	3.9	–	1.4
Economics, Stockholm	83.8	13.1	0.5	2.4
Law, Stockholm	84.5	5.7	1.0	8.7
Psychology, Stockholm	50.0	17.1	3.8	29.1
Social Science, Östersund	38.5	45.2	6.7	9.6
Medicine, Uppsala	70.2	5.7	1.6	22.5
Teacher 7-10's, Jönkoping	37.4	47.0	7.8	7.8
Guidance Teacher, Stockholm	33.0	22.2	5.4	39.4
Cultural Services, Lund	76.5	9.4	4.2	9.4

Source: *UHÄ, Siffror från CA HT-79* (See Table 17), p.7.

applicant to have work experience. In Autumn 1978, for example,
in the socio-medical and teacher-training fields, about half of
those accepted had more than four years' work experience, compared with only one in ten of those with no experience. Furthermore, between 1977 and 1979, between 20% and 30% of all entrants
were successful because of the points they added for work with
clubs and societies, and this was twice as common for men as
for women. For the more selective courses, the combination of
both high academic marks and work experience had clearly become
necessary by 1980: in the first stage of the selection process
in the summer of 1980, two-thirds of the fifty teacher education
lines required the maximum grade average of 5.0 from the three-
year *gymnasieskola* and virtually all of them required over 5.0
if the applicant was applying on school marks plus work
experience. Of all the 130 lines available, the lowest grade
average for those direct from the three-year *gymnasieskola* at
this stage was 3.9, and that only in the Public Administration
lines in Uppsala and Stockholm: every other was taking an
average of 4 or better for quote group 1A.

Effects on Schools and Higher Education

It was these kinds of development which led to changes in 1981,

and discussion of even more radical amendments: a less centralised procedure; or consideration of the Danish system where
the number of places in different quotas is determined in advance
as a deliberate act of social policy to favour this or that
category. For school leavers, application to higher education
had by 1980 become a complex and saddening game. An example
might be of a student who was thinking of becoming a teacher in
Geography and Biology. The Autumn 1979 figures are set out in
Table 17.

TABLE 17:   Application for Geography/Biology Teacher Training,
            1979

	Uppsala	Stockholm	Göteborg	Lund	Total
No. Places	8	3	10	2	23
No. Applicants	92	91	86	68	236
No. 1st Choice rankings	3	7	7	8	25
Acceptances	9	3	10	2	24
Grades					
Group 1A/Acceptances	3.7)/2	4.0/1	4.5)/2	4.6/1	3.7/ 6
1B	)/6	4.3/2	)/7	-/-	3.7/15
2A	4.0 /1	-	-	4.7/1	4.0/ 2
3	-	-	5.1/1	-	5.1/ 1
% age applicants Group 1	93	100	92	86	
Group 2	7	-	-	14	
Group 3	-	-	8	-	

Source: derived from *UHÄ, Siffror från CA HT-79*

Obviously, there can be none of the certainty which once characterised the attitudes of most pupils at the end of a full
secondary education. The potential applicant might well ponder:
"do I apply to the famous university city of Lund, or the big
city life of Stockholm or Göteborg? Do I leave to seek a job -
any job - to raise my average by a point or two and try later?
(About 40% of those rejected in 1977 had found places they wished
within two years: but what happened to the 60% who did not?)
And what if my grade average turns out to be below the 3.7 or
better required for the Geography/Biology teacher line? Is it

better to get a place in the general, non-specifically vocational
Biology line? (there was in fact little chance in the Autumn
1979 intake: the lowest grade average for that was 4.3, even
though there is something of a glut of graduate biologists at
present). Or look to a wholly different possibility – for
example, Public Administration? There were 220 places available
for that in Autumn 1979 in Uppsala, Stockholm, Linköping,
Göteborg, Karlstad, Lund or Växjö – and the average grade required
was 2.5, and over 3 in only three of the places".

It is perhaps not surprising that there has been a slight tendency
for average school marks to rise by a decimal point or so as
competition has become more severe, especially from the 3-year
and 4-year lines; something of a "drift" in this direction in
teacher behaviour. Further, if a job is available, it is more
likely to be taken by somebody with good school grades who is
seeking more points from work experience. An unintended consequence of *numerus clausus* in an "integrated" and "mass" system
of higher education which at the same time deliberately seeks to
improve opportunities for adults and can justify this in terms
not only of social equality but also in terms of social need in
a changing employment situation, is that the less well qualified
teenager, and the one who comes from a background where the
"deferred gratification" of a period of higher education is not
a prevalent social value, is likely to find himself – and
especially herself – joining the ranks of the unemployed on
leaving school. The opening of access to higher education, even
a system of higher education which embraces fields of study previously excluded from the walls of academe, to students such as
those in the 2-year lines of upper secondary school has so far
attracted only 10-12% of applicants from these lines (see
Table 14 above).

Schools, however, cannot solve employment problems nor, beyond
a certain point, alter conventional social values or social and
economic priorities. They now face, in effect, a custodial role
for significant numbers of 16-19's. The 35-40% of an age-group
now in the 3 and 4-year academic lines cannot all hope for higher
education, even if two-thirds of them might get there eventually
after work experience; a handful of the 15% on special courses
might go on to the new vocational technical institutions of
higher education, known as *YTH*. And a handful of the 40% or so
in the 2-year lines might continue their studies eventually,
again after work experience: perhaps 2-3% might be able to do
so immediately on leaving school, judged by intake patterns
1977 to 1980. For the teachers of the 2-year lines, this is

perhaps less disturbing: those with vocational backgrounds are less likely to have had experience of higher education, however defined. The teachers of the 3 and 4-year lines, however, were themselves almost certainly products of the universities: it is a new experience indeed for them not to envisage higher studies to be the normal future for most of their students.

How far the administrative changes in 1981 will solve some of the problems and tensions which have arisen remains to be seen. They are, however, unlikely to lead to reopening places for those who, prior to total selectivity, could find a place with a 2.3 grade average in the "open" faculties. Indeed, it may well be that the 30% rule will lead to even more emphasis on school marks, especially in those programmes where there is already stiff competition for places, such as class teaching of younger children (now just as selective as medicine, dentistry and veterinary science). Until the proposals of the Upper Secondary School Enquiry are debated and agreed, there is no question of changing the principles of the present admission rules. The best – or worst – that can be expected until 1986 is changes in the details of admissions every year or so, in response to preceived problems and trends.

The changes in structures, organisation and admission procedures on higher education itself have had effects quite different from those on the schools. The most obvious among the student body is the age balance, indicated in Tables 18 and 19 (for an annual intake, these figures may be roughly doubled to take account of the January intake). Over a longer time span, the proportion of all students aged over 24 has risen from 4% in 1970 to 60% in 1978. To a greater extent than before, institutions of higher education are very much "adult" centres. It may be noted, however, that the extent to which this is true varies in the different sectors. While in total about 30% of the intake is over 24, it is only 14% in the technological field but 54% in the care services and 56% in teaching.

A second change is the phenomenon of students reading "single courses" rather than full undergraduate programmes (see Table 14 above) – and strikingly, 49% of these are taken by applicants from the 3-year upper secondary school, the traditional source of all university students. Of all students in higher education, the proportion of those not intending to read for a full degree rose from 32% in 1970 to 72% in 1978. It is easier, too, to take single courses by part-time study, and the proportion of part-timers (whether on full or single programmes) rose from 12%

TABLE 18:   Age Distribution, Autumn Term Intake 1979

	Men	Women	Total	%
Age range under 20	2,338	2,116	4,454	31.9
20-24	3,630	1,562	5,192	37.2
25-29	1,327	729	2,056	14.7
30-34	581	565	1,146	8.2
35-39	209	406	611	4.7
40-44	82	209	291	2.1
45+	61	91	152	1.1
Total	8,224	5,678	13,942	

TABLE 19:   Age Distribution by Field of Study, Autumn Term Intake 1979

	Technology	Admin.	Care	Teaching	Culture
Age range under 20	1,918	1,822	141	252	169
20-24	1,880	2,170	263	490	193
25-29	424	832	211	428	72
30-34	135	500	158	270	34
35-39	63	291	80	165	31
40-44	17	137	28	75	22
45+	7	76	4	32	22
Total	4,454	5,828	885	1,712	543

Source: UHÄ, *Siffror från CA HT-79* (Numbers from Central Admissions, Autumn Term 1979, 1979-10-01, pp 5-6

Note: These totals should be consistent between both tables, and the additions correct; there are minor errors in the original text, but these do not affect the general picture.

in 1970 to 32% in 1978.

A third change, not unrelated to the "single course" pattern,
is the tendency for teaching in these as well as the normal
courses in the full lines of study to be offered in classes
which remain together for only a few weeks, perhaps a full 20-
week term at most. The catalogue for Stockholm University,
for example, for 1980/81 lists 328 20-point(20 week) single
courses; 116 10-point courses; and 129 5-point courses - all
in addition to the normal lines of study. Fourthly, as was
seen above (Tables 17 and 18), while the scholastic background
of the students still emphasises the 3 and 4-year upper secondary
lines, this differs between the different lines in higher
education.

The impact of these factors - older people (and therefore more
likely to be married and to have their own social lives less
dependent and less near the university itself), many reading
short single courses, and most coming from backgrounds which
include experience of a working world foreign to the traditions
of academe - is likely to alter the traditional image of the
community of scholars engaging in an on-going dialogue in pursuit
of truth. As many of the critics of the U68 proposal, such as
Professor Segerstedt in Uppsala, made clear, there is a danger
of a divorce of research and undergraduate teaching. There is
no longer the normal expectation that all staff will be engaged
in research. Post graduate study, access to which is selective
from those with 80 undergraduate points in appropriate fields,
offers taught courses and a thesis requirement for the doctorate.
Much research is institutionally or individually inspired; much
more, however, is financed by government through research
councils, and there is here some fear of constraints on academic
freedom. Time will tell what the effects will be, not only on
the institutions themselves but also on the expectations of
higher education which youngsters will receive from the experience
of their mentors. Consider, for example, the difference to the
student who moved from living in a flat in Göteborg and attending
classes in a complex of buildings which is more like than a
school that a university campus, to living in one of the student
union blocks of flatlets in Lund, within walking distance of the
centre of the town, and being able to feel part of the intellectual as well as the social life of an ancient university
city; and contrast both of those experiences with that of the
student who attends an institution in one of the small and new
centres of higher education.

As far as the "undergraduate" is concerned, the new institutions of higher education are in general probably more organised and structured than were the universities of their parents' day and perhaps, too, more like a "super secondary school". Each course has a built-in assessment procedure, a *tenta*, taken on completion of the course; and there is thus likely to be a major test every five or ten weeks. It will be marked either pass/fail or merit/pass/fail, and access to post-graduate study is likely to be easier for those with "merit", *spets*, on the record sheet. The prospect of failure is also daunting: one course starts almost immediately after another ends, and if the failure has to be redeemed, the study for it has to be done along with study for the new course. There are, too, more seminar-size classes than there used to be.

Strict control of entry numbers, however, has not removed the drop-out phenomenon. Three examples, all from different universities, may make the point. A mathematics class in one university started in August 1978 with some two dozen students; by Christmas, there were 12 left: nobody seemed to take any overview of the total programme - the students simply moved from one class to another with more or less understanding of what they were doing. In another case, it would seem as if the lecturers were still operating the "fail them the first time round to get a better performance from those who really want to stick the course" approach which was not unknown a generation ago: of the 300 entrants admitted under selective *numerus clausus* rules to read Law in Autum 1978, only 3 had passed all the required *tenta* by January 1981 - yet the principle of manpower planning would imply that something like 300 law graduates would be needed by summer 1981. A third case, however, showed 100% success: a selective architecture programme where students regularly attended different classes, but where they belonged to kinds of "tutor groups" familiar in an English context but relatively rare in Sweden, the function of which seemed to be to make the total course coherent; there were no failures and no drop-outs in two years.

It is, however, too early to measure the effects of changes on levels of scholarship. University teachers have been much engaged in devising the new courses. They have also been much engaged in devising new decision-making procedures. The risk that the "public interest" would impinge on academic course content seems not to have been well founded. By 1980 at least, the boards of study proposed for the various lines suggest that traditional academic views continue to prevail and that the

ideas of breaking the hold which separate academic disciplines
and fields of study have traditionally maintained have been
thwarted. A report by *UHÄ* of a study of eight such boards in
1980 was entitled "Vision and Reality": there was little discussion of policy in the boards, and planning was delegated in
effect to the separate institutions and subjects, whereas the
original intention had been that these boards should have a
vision of a total student programme. By associating representatives from the world of work within which the particular line
of study was located, it had been hoped that the programmes would
have greater vocational relevance. The report recognised that
new ideas took time to establish themselves, but regretted the
apparent unwillingness of the new bodies to take responsible
policy decisions. There was a need, it said, for the members
of these boards, who are appointed for three-year periods, themselves to have courses of training to further their knowledge
both of the pedagogy and the management of the area they were
responsible for. It was also argued that the boards should
have responsibility for several related lines in a geographical
region, and have greater direct control over the allocation of
funds so that they could "buy" appropriate courses at different
institutions. Such is the painting of the brave new world of
higher education.

As with the school reforms, however, it is likely that while
decision-making will bring about structural changes, institutional decision-making processes will change much more slowly.
There will still be lectures and seminars, reading lists and
assignments. While the tight rein of regular tests will make
demands on students, some of those students will still find
time to talk or dance all night and still get "merit", while
others will struggle to succeed whether they study hard or not,
and others again will develop perceptions of themselves and the
world which take them away from the standards and values of
academe. University staff, too, will find various satisfactions
and regrets: too much or too little undergraduate teaching;
too much or too little concern for research and publication;
too much or too little academic freedom in their relations with
those governmental bodies which fund research or seem to ignore
the results of research. It is unlikely that academe can ever
again enjoy the relative peace and isolation of years ago: "mass"
higher education, largely financed by public monies, prevents
that.

But Sweden is a long way from "universal" higher education; and
a long way, too, from narrowly technical training courses dominat-

ing higher studies. In theory, courses of study are of equal value wherever they are followed; in practice, it is unlikely that this is in fact the case; the prestige of certain institutions remains unimpaired: Karolinska in Stockholm for medicine, philosophy in Uppsala, history in Lund. Standards of scholarship in first year courses may be lower than was once the case - though the evidence for this is equivocal, especially where the grade-point averages for entry are so high.[12] The standard of scholarship at the research level continues to enjoy a high international reputation.[13] Response to reforms of higher education as it is emerging tends to depend on whether the bottle is seen as half empty or half full.

Adult Education

While numbers in higher education exploded in the 1960s, so too did numbers in various forms of adult education. The commonly quoted figure[14] of about a third of the adult population studying something or other in its spare time is perhaps not wholly accurate. A sample survey by the Central Statistics Bureau, *SCB*, in 1976[15] showed that while there were over two million enrolments in courses run by the major adult education voluntary agencies, in fact this covered only some 650,000 different adults. Nevertheless, the enrolment figures do suggest that the great variety of forms of adult studies in Sweden attract by world standards a very large proportion of all adults. They flock to courses which vary from study at the level of school and university courses, through a whole range of vocational courses to the purely leisure-orientated studies which may combine the social pleasures of weekly meetings with conversational Italian or Spanish prior to a charter holiday to the sunny south.

Popular education has long enjoyed public support in Sweden, and in its organised forms enjoys considerable state and local authority subsidy in a society which believes that it should make it possible for older people, many of whom have received little formal education in their youth, to raise their levels of general knowledge to that of today's youth; to receive advanced training and retraining to meet the needs of a changing labour market; continually to have the opportunity to improve the quality of the political, social and cultural life of the country; and to do these things in ways which allow all to participate, regardless of working hours, family status or place of residence.[16] Since 1976, employers are required to pay a payroll tax in 1979 of 0.25% of an employees' annual wage

bill to make it easier for employees who have families to support
to take study leave as well as to finance courses in priority
subjects such as Swedish, English, Mathematics and Civics and
to make such courses available at places of work. Furthermore,
all permanent employees enjoy the unconditional right to leave
of absence for study during working hours, and to receive
grants for loss of income. Adult education takes 12% of the
National Board of Education's expenditure.[17]

Popular Movements

There are essentially three stands in the historical development
of this network of facilities over the past hundred years. The
oldest derives from the popular movements of the nineteenth
century, especially the churches, the labour movement and the
temperance movement. Its best known form is the Folk High
School, *Folkhögskola*, which came from Denmark to Sweden in 1868
and sought to give young rural adults better opportunities for
general education. Of the 110 Folk High Schools open in 1980,
29 were founded before 1900, a further 22 before 1918. More
recently, 31 were founded 1945-60 and 10 since 1960. The Folk
High School Decree[18] set as their task "to give the students
insight into their responsibilities as individuals and as
citizens. They should be organised so that the students'
abilities to work co-operatively are strengthened, their abilities for independent thought and critical judgement are developed
and their maturity and interest in study is encouraged". Each
school is then free to design its own curriculum, and most will
offer either short courses of 1-8 weeks, and winter courses of
30-34 weeks which last for two, and sometimes three, years.
Most of the winter courses are forms of continuing education at
school level, but some schools have specialities in, for
example, aesthetic studies in music and theatre, or media
studies or third world problems.

A study in 1973 of those on winter courses[19] showed that 61% of
students were women; the average of men was 22.9 and of the
women 20.7; (the normal minimum age is 18, but there is one
Folk High School taking students aged 16+); 40% had no more
than 9 years schooling; 22% had interrupted study between
school and attendance at the Folk High School; 67% had come
from the world of work; 9% had some kind of physical or psychological handicap (there are some schools especially designed
for the handicapped, for example those at Hjo and at Furuboda,
near Kristianstad, symptomatic of the contemporary concern for
those in special need). A quarter of those in "church" Folk High

schools themselves belonged to some church, compared with only
7% of those in other schools; similarly, a quarter of those in
schools run by the labour movements were members of a political
organisation, compared with only 8% in other schools. In all,
17% were teetotal, and 3% were members of teetotal movements
(18% in schools run by the teetotal movements and 25% in schools
run by churches). 32% of the students were politically of the
centre-right, 25% social democrats and 24% communist orientated;
the rest "did not know" or did not answer. 37% of the students
had learnt about the courses through friends who had experienced
the Folk High School world, compared with only 6% through
advertisements. 57% were resident, and a quarter of all felt
that their school had to a large or to some extent a characteristic ideology (this was felt by 45% in the schools run by the
labour movements and 36% in the church run schools). About
13,000 students a year enrol for the winter courses. Tuition
is free, but students pay for board and lodging, frequently
recovering the cost through grants and/or study loans (see
Appendix V for details).

As school and post-compulsory facilities increased in the 1970's,
there was some idea that the Folk High Schools might become less
significant in providing adult education. But as Fig. 12 shows,

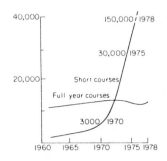

Fig. 12.   Folk High School Students

Source: Marklund S & Boucher L, The Curriculum for 13-16
           Year Olds in Sweden: A Review of Changes,
           1950-1980, Compare, 10,2,1980, p.164.

this has been far from true, especially for the short courses,
which now enrol 150,000 a year compared with only 3,000 in 1970.
Large numbers of these have been sponsored by the voluntary
educational agencies in co-operation with the Folk High Schools,
and have been encouraged since 1973 by the law entitling
employees to leave of absence and, since 1975, making it possible
for all adults, including housewives, to claim a discretionary
grant for study of a minimum of half a month full-time or full
month part-time in any six-month period. Furthermore, the proposals of the Folk High School Enquiry, which reported in 1976,
led to an increase in culturally and vocationally orientated
courses according to student demand, as long as they do not
compete with courses already available through other sources;
for courses of two weeks duration; and at least one course per
year of 15 weeks. It was clear, too, that half of the Folk
High School students came from the lowest of Sweden's three
social groups, and an increasing number were from the growing
immigrant population.

The mass enrolments in courses provided by the voluntary popular
educational movements, however, are for a peculiarly Scandinavian
phenomen, the study circle. These began in 1902, through the
IOGT, and the first study society, the Workers' Educational
Association, *Arbetarnas Bildningsförbund* or *ABF*, was founded in
1912. Since the mid-1970's, following various amalgamations,
there have been ten recognised voluntary agencies, nine of which
are linked with one or more of the popular movements. The ten
recognised "study associations" are in (Swedish) alphabetical
order:

Workers' Educational Association, *Arbetarnas Bildningsförbund*,
ABF
People's University, *Folkuniversitet*, *FU*
Free Church Study Association, *Frikyrkliga Studieförbund*, *FS*
YMCA/YWCA Study Association, *KFUK-KFUM Studieförbund*
Teetotal Movement's Educational Activity, *Nykterhetsrörelsens
Bildningsverksambet*, *NBV*
Study Promotion, *Studiefrämjandet*, *Sfr*
Citizens' School Study Association, *Studieförbundet Medborgar-
skolan*, *Mbsk*
Adult School Study Association, *Studieförbundet Vuxenskolan*, *SV*
Swedish Church Study Association, *Sveriges Kyrkliga Studieför-
bund*, *SKS*
Administrative Staff Study Educational Activity, *Tjänstemännens
Bildningsverksambet*, *TBV*

These, together with the Swedish Folk High School Teachers'
Union, *Svenska Folkhögskolans Lärarförbund, SFHL*, and the Swedish
General Library Society, *Sveriges Allmänna Biblioteksförening,
SAB*, form the National Adult Education Association, *Folkbildningsförbundet*, which has an office in each of the 23 counties.
In many of the local authorities, the adult educational associations form "co-ordinating committees", but these have no formal
connection with the county or National Association. The current
regulations require that the educational activities are carried
out in a manner which permits "an objective and many sided view
of the subjects of study". To earn a state grant, which in 1980
covered some 45% of the costs, a circle must have between five
and twenty members, and be held for at least twenty hours over
at least a four-week period, and with no class lasting more than
three consecutive hours.

The growth in study circle activity since 1960 has been striking.
The number of circles rose from some 150,000 to 289,000 in 1980;
the number of enrolments, 800,000 in 1960, doubled by 1967, and
reached 2,700,000 by 1980; the number of study hours, 1,800,000
in 1960, doubled by 1967, doubled again by 1974, and reached
eight million by 1980. Every autumn, the letter boxes in all
households receive a regular flow of advertising material from
one or other of the main associations or its affiliations.
Courses in civics and economics, literature, arts and crafts,
and languages each enrol well over half a million: indeed, the
Folk University in the Stockholm area advertised in 1980 some
750 different language programmes. University level courses,
especially those in non-vocational subjects such as religion,
philosophy and psychology, account for more than 1% of the
circles. In recent years, the largest single group of circles
has been in the area of priority subjects: Swedish for immigrants, for example; or Swedish, English, mathematics or civics
for those with only an elementary school background. In
general, however, it remains true that despite "outreach" programmes to small places of work and special subsidies for courses
in rural areas and for handicapped persons, the majority of
those enrolling in study circles are already among the better
educated. The economies in public expenditure in the early
1980's, which are forcing cuts in current provision of grants,
will no doubt result in increased costs for participants. As
problems of financing all kinds of education become increasingly
severe, as may be expected in the 1980's, it will be interesting
to see what effect changes in grant regulations for the more
leisure-orientated adult education work will have on enrolments.
It is quite possible that "those that hath" will continue to

seek more.

Retraining

But it is precisely to benefit the less well educated or the less secure that more modern developments have occured in Swedish adult education. The first in time was the introduction in 1960 of retraining programmes, notably those run by the National Labour Market Board, *Arbetsmarknadsstyrelsen* or *AMS*, but increasingly including courses offered by employers and by trade unions. Currently, over 100,000 persons a year may be involved, over and above those provided within the framework of *gymnasieskolan*. Grants, which in total cost a tenth of national educational costs, are available for those who are, or run the risk of becoming, unemployed; who are difficult to place in employment; who are over age 20; who are registered as unemployed and for whom permanent employment would not be possible without retraining. There are also special courses in trades where manpower has been in markedly short supply. The National Board of Education, in fifty special centres, has in recent years provided about half the courses available, and some 85% of those trained have obtained jobs within three months, 85% of them in occupations within the branch of employment to which the training course was directed. Since the main object of this work is to maintain employment, the courses tend to be specific to certain trades, and tend to be organised on a modular basis so that there can be continuous admissions, with various degrees of specialisation. It is obvious that such a pattern fits easily into the ideas noted above (Chapter 5) for the reorganisation of *gymnasieskolan* into monthly blocks of study. Because, however, some of the applicants lack basic educational skills, eight week pre-training programmes are also available.

Other forms of occupational training are offered by employers and trade unions. Employees in the public services have regular training programmes, and for those in the Customs Service, the Post Office and the Labour Market Board there are complete vocational training courses. Private employers, and their association, *Sveriges Arbetsgivares Förening* or *SAF*, arrange similar programmes. The two major employee organisations, the Confederation of Trade Unions, *Landsorganisation* or *LO*, and the Central Organisation of Salaried Employees, *Tjänstemännens Centralorganisation* or *TCO*, also have extensive programmes, one or two weeks or occasionally six month courses, subsidised by government grants.

Schooling for Adults

A further kind of adult education is the adult school, *Vuxenskolan*, in which the local authorities run systematic school-level studies. This began formally in 1968, but its origins were in the 1950's when the voluntary study associations began offering study circles in separate subjects which by special dispensation could lead to university entry, alongside the existing courses leading to *studentexamen*. These were very hard roads indeed. Students paid full fees, and there was often as little as a quarter of the teaching which a student at school could expect. The enquiries into reform of the traditional academic *gymnasium* in the 1960's suggested that the local authorities might run schools for such adults; a few "evening *gymnasia*" in the larger towns led in a few years to "adult *gymnasia*" practically everywhere. By 1970, numbers following courses at the 13-16 stage had trebled from 11,000 to 37,500; there were 44,500 in academic post-16 courses, 5,000 in the *Fackskola* courses and 79,000 in *Yrkesskola*, trade school, courses. By 1973/74 the total volume of all local authority adult education was 30% of all study circle activity, and its costs per pupil, half met by the state, nearly half by the local authority and about 7% by fees, were about the same as ordinary study circles and clearly less than the Folk High School work. It was, too, recruiting as well as other forms of adult education from those who had only an elementary school background. The municipal adult school was beginning to offer to adults much the same schooling as was available to youth, though with greater emphasis on concentrated study of individual subjects, on a modular structure which straddled the line and course structures of the ordinary schools, and which required only about half the contact time of the ordinary school.

Except for a small decline in recruitment in the early seventies, numbers in the local authority adult schools grew year by year. In 1975, there were over 150,000, 23% at the 13-16 age level, and 32% at the 16-19 academic level. By 1978, the total was 210,000, with over 40% at the upper secondary academic level and some 30% at each of the 13-16 and the vocational 16-19 level. By the early 1980's there were more students in the adult secondary schools than there were in the 16-19 school itself. In this context, two forms of adult school provision are worth special mention. The first is the two state schools for adults, at Norrköping and at Härnosand. These are for students who do not have access to adult education in their own

areas and who cannot attend regular courses. They recruit
nationally from students aged over 16, and offer school courses
either wholly by correspondence or by five week contact courses
per term at the school followed by correspondence material from
either *Hermods* or *Brevskolan*, who are responsible for marking
the assignments. Subjects are studied one at a time in concentrated programmes, the schools carry out all guidance work,
and the courses are expected to take no more than six months
longer than the normal school programmes. The other special
provision is in some twenty or more local authority areas
where there are full-time or part-time schools for gypsies.

Basic Schooling

But as in so much educational work, new target groups begin to
be identified. In 1970, at the instigation of the Confederation of Labour and the WEA, a committee to experiment different
forms of teaching, *FÖVUX*, was set up. Reporting in 1973, it
noted that nearly 70% of adults aged 20-65 had no more than
elementary schooling; about 20% had 9-year schooling; less
than 10% had post-compulsory schooling and only 3% had university degrees or their equivalents. It proposed a massive
expansion of provision for adults, a twelve year programme
before the demand for 9-year schooling for all had been met.
The committee had discovered that about half their sample of
under-educated adults wanted to take courses, 40% in English,
30% in mathematics, 20% in Swedish and 10% in civics; and
64% preferred to study in their spare time with a small grant,
while 30% would prefer to share both work and study. An experimental recruiting drive showed that shift workers were the most
difficult group for whom to provide courses, and for them, and
for other similarly disadvantaged groups, the study circle was
the method recommended. It was the view of *FÖRVUX* that the
local authority adult school provision could well be reduced
because it provided to such a large extent for those already
well schooled and with normal working times.

The most recent target is the illiterate adult who needs basic
education, below the level of the 13 year old at which the local
authority adult schools normally begin. In 1974/75, some
1,100 persons, 300 of them Swedish and the rest immigrants,
were being taught functional reading and writing skills, defined
as those below the average level of 13 year olds: and it was
estimated then that there were probably at least 40,000
immigrants, plus 100,000 Swedes, whose literary skills were at
that level.[20] Since 1977 provision for such people has legally

become a responsibility of the local authorities, and in 1978, some 2,700 were enrolled. Analysis of this group makes clear some of the immediate problems. 40% lived in the county of Stockholm: most were Swedes, Turks, Syrians, Kurds and Greeks; two-thirds of them, and nearly all the Turks and Greeks, were women; only 11% had taken leave of absence from work in order to study; 18% needed individual rather than group instruction. As the Head of an adult school in Stockholm commented,[20] officials from social welfare offices or places of employment ring up to plead for their hopeless cases, but the school can barely cope. There is a need for teachers, premises and materials, all to be available more or less on demand. Pupils can feel frustrated when they are unable to adjust either to work or to study; but at the same time, they need support over longer periods than the grant regulation permits, for example for classes in the summer to bridge the gap between school terms or for longer than the two years for which grants are available.

It is always easier to identify, quantify and legislate for new problems than it is to solve them. In traditional adult education it was early recognised that the idea of recurrent education, *återkommande utbildning*, could not be achieved overnight. Changes in attitudes are necessary among participants as well as providers. The relative failure to reach the mass of the less well educated and the dangers of adult education providing for those already relatively well equipped are well known. So too are the problems of co-ordinating efforts between central and local authorities, between formal and informal providing agencies, between educational and social services, between employee and employer organisations. Very much indeed is done: more remains to be achieved.

CHAPTER 7

Teachers

There is no country in the world which, in quantitative terms, staffs its schools as well as Sweden. The annual teacher census[1] for Spring 1980 showed there were 140,600 teachers in employment, 130,514 of whom were actually in post. Even allowing for the 11% who work part-time, this gives a gross pupil: teacher ratio of around 11:1.

Table 20 lists, in summary form, the distribution of these teachers.

In all, some 61% of all teachers are women; some 10% serve as Special Education teachers, over half of whom have a qualification in this area; over half of all teachers are aged under 40; and 18% (23,620) are not technically qualified - 15% in *Grundskolan*, 18% in *gymnasieskolan*, and 42% in other types of school.

Why Sweden should staff its schools so well is an interesting historical and sociological question which appears never to have been researched. The simple explanation is that Sweden has traditionally had a respect for scholarship. This is certainly true: the village teacher, much as the *adjunkt* and *Lektor* in the town, was one of the intellectual elite, along with the parson, the doctor and the lawyer. In a society where occupational titles were until recently the formal mode of address, to be a teacher (and preferably, of course, an academically qualified teacher) was socially significant.[2]

Another explanation is that the teacher unions are relatively united and have great power. This is also true. There are three main teacher unions, themselves amalgamations of smaller groups. Tow of them, the class teacher union, *Sveriges Lärarförbund*, *SL*, and the union of vocational teachers, *Svenska Facklärarförbund*, *SFL*, are members of the white-collar composite

TABLE 20:   Teacher Deployment

Category	Approx %	% Women	Swedish Title
Class Teacher 7-10's	20+	99	*Lågstadielärare*
Class Teacher 10-13's	20+	64	*Mellanstadielärare*
Subject Teacher 13-16-19	25	45	*Ämneslärare/Adjunkt**
Single Subject 16-19	2	14	*Lektor**
Director of Studies	2	24	*Studierektor*
Head	2	9	*Rektor*
Practical Subjects (Gymnastics, Music, Art)	10	50	*Övningslärare*
Vocational Subjects	7	?	*Yrkeslärare*
Part-time Teachers	10	?	*Timlärare*

Adjunkt and *Lektor*: these were the normal academic posts in the grammar schools. The *Adjunkt* studies two or three subjects to stated levels in stated combinations, the *Lektor* (now employed only at *gymnasieskolan* or in higher education) takes a higher degree, *licenciat* or *doktor*.

union, *Tjänstemännens Centralorganisation, TCO:* the third, the union for the academic subject teachers, *Lärararnas Riksförbund, LR,* is a member of the prestigious union of occupations which require university qualifications, *Sveriges Akademikers Central-organisation, SACO.* Of course there are differences of interest between these teacher unions, especially between LR and SL, and these are reflected in negotiations of salaries and conditions of service. Nevertheless, separately and collectively, they are very powerful pressure groups, and even more so now that employee participation in decision making, acting through the unions, is part of the law. This union power, however, is relatively recent, and cannot explain the public support for teachers in earlier times.

A third explanation might be found in a study of personal and
political contacts, especially in the early days of Liberal and
Social Democratic reforms. Parliaments of those days tended to
include a large number of teachers; many of the wives of leading politicians were teachers; and in a small and relatively
homogeneous country with limited access to higher studies, there
was a great chance that persons of influence in different walks
of life would be known personally to each other: before 1920
less than 3,000 pupils a year passed *Realexamen* at age 17, less
than 2,000 a year passed *Studentexamen* at age 20.

The educational explosion between 1950 and 1970, caused partly
by rises in the birth rate, partly by the school reforms extending compulsory schooling to 16, and partly by rising aspirations
and the increased retention rate after 16, made great demands
on teacher supply, which could only come from age-groups smaller
in size and with fewer opportunities for higher education than
that it was called on to serve. Inevitably, too, there was an
explosion of training provision, at both the initial and in-
service levels.

Initial Training

For initial training, output increased from barely 4,000 a year
in 1959 to 10,000 a year in the early seventies. In all, from
1959/60 to 1973/74, 107,000 teachers were qualified, including
11,600 ex-elementary teachers who had taken subject teacher
qualifications at university, either by full-time attendance or
by correspondence study. Significantly, however, only about
two-thirds of those qualified during this period were actually
serving as teachers in 1973, a fact which does not match well
with the ideas of manpower planning which have formed a major
base for the re-organisation of higher education. The explana-
tions for it, however, are no doubt simple enough: some will
decide not to teach; some are unable to teach in the area in
which they live; some find their qualifications do not match
local vacancies; some - and especially teachers of music, art
or craft - can find work, either part-time or full-time, outside
the schools; and some women simply do not continue at work
when they are married and have families: the training of women
class teachers, as of nurses, has traditionally been "wasteful"
in this sense.

In general, teacher shortages in the 1980's are limited to specific parts of the country, especially the sparsely populated
north; to certain areas of the curriculum such as languages,

including Swedish, for immigrants; to certain age groups such
as pre-school and adult provision; to specific vocational
courses where there is a need for theoretical as well as practical knowledge, and to the problem of providing courses to
qualify those 18% who are unqualified. A major reduction in
output took place in 1975, with an entry for subject teachers
48% lower than in 1971, for class teachers at *Mellanstadiet*
73% lower, and for class teachers at *Lågstadiet* all of 93%
lower. Gross calculations for the 1980's foresee the possibilities of even more cuts, especially because of the fall in
birth-rates in the 1970's. By 1985, the 7-10 stage will
certainly have 14% fewer pupils than in 1980; the 10-13's will
decline by 4% and the 13-16's by 8%; and these trends will of
course follow through the rest of the educational system in
succeeding years. The budget proposals presented in January
1981 pointed out that it was cheaper to give short courses to
the "unqualified" than to follow normal teacher education programmes: Table 21 shows the relationship between teacher
training and teacher deployment.

TABLE 21: Teacher Training and Teacher Deployment

Percentage Category of Teacher	Examined	Take Post	Full-Time Equivalent	Proportions employed after 3-5 years
7-10	91	89	77.1	62.4
10-13	88	85	77.1	57.4
Gymnastics	98	85	71.2	59.3
Home Language	86	90	78.3	60.6
Music	90	65	66.1	38.7
Crafts	100	77	66.9	66.9
Special Ed.	100	99.5	76.3	75.9
Art	90	46	71.6	29.6

Source: quoted in *Lärartidningen/Svensk Skoltidning*, 2/1981,
p.19

Calculations of "shortage" and "need", however, are inevitably
related to questions of what constitutes "qualified" and what

constitutes "teaching service". In these respects, Sweden
categorises its teachers in terms of the course followed. A
"qualified teacher" is thus one who has taken a specific course
for a specific teacher post. Class teachers are normally
"qualified" to teach either 7-10 year olds or 10-13 year olds
(though an elective taken in the course of training for each
age-range does permit teaching that subject at the next older
age-range): and subject teachers are "qualified" only in the
teaching of the subjects in question, either at the 13-16 stage
or, if the subject is studied in sufficient depth, at the 16-19
stage. Teachers of the practical subjects of Music, Gymnastics,
Art, Textile Crafts or Wood and Metal Crafts can be qualified
for all age ranges. In all, there are 102 different categories
of teacher - 21 in *Grundskolan* and 81 in *Gymnasieskolan* (see
Appendix IX).

Underlying the present categories of teacher, however, is an
age-old division, closely linked to the parallel system of
elementary and (selective) secondary schools which the reforms
in Sweden since 1950 have swept away: the division between
class teachers - traditionally non-graduate, following a shorter
length of training, requiring lower entry qualifications, and
leading towards the teaching of younger pupils in non-selective
schools; and subject teachers - traditionally either graduates
in "academic" subjects or taking specialist courses in practical
and vocational subjects, requiring for the academic subject
study at least the traditional university entry qualifications,
and leading towards teaching older pupils in selective schools.
As noted in Chapter 2, class teachers went either to an Elementary Teacher Training College, *Folkskoleseminariet*, to take a
four-year course based on the lower secondary leaving examination,
Realexamen, or a two-year course based on the upper secondary
leaving examination, *studentexamen*; or to an Infant Teachers
Training College, *Småskoleseminariet*, for a three-year course
following *Realexamen*, or a two-year course following *studentexamen*. Subject teachers took a university degree, followed
(since 1865) by a 'practice year', *provår*. This dualism - or
three or four-part system if one separates the practical and
vocational subjects - still remains despite repeated recommendations that the new integrated and unified school system requires
a new kind of teacher.

The first suggestion for change came in the report of the 1946
School Commission. The new school sought to end the division
between "better" and "worse" children, elementary school children and grammar school children, class teachers and subject

teachers. The purpose of the teacher was to educate the whole
child, its intellect, temperament and emotions, not simply to
teach more or less complicated pieces of knowledge. It was
this which led to the idea noted in Chapter 2 of Teacher High
Schools, *Lärarhögskolor*. These were first proposed in 1952,[4]
to be established in the then four university towns and in
perhaps other places due to have a university. All pedagogical
teacher education should be concentrated in these High Schools,
which would be of university standing. Thus the old teacher
colleges, *folkskoleseminarierna*, began to disappear: Stockholm
became a Teacher High School in 1956; Malmö in 1960, Göteborg
in 1962, Uppsala in 1964; Umeå in 1967 and Linköping in 1968,
to train both class and subject teachers (the class teacher
lines at Uppsala closed in 1975).

At the same time, some training colleges for class teachers
remained; in Falun (now closed), Gävle, Härnösand, Jönkoping,
Kalmar, Karlstad, Kristianstad (now closed), Luleå and Växjö.
Art teachers train at the Art School, *Konstfackskolan;* Craft
teachers at the Craft Training College, *Slöjdseminariet*,
Linköping; gymnastics teachers at one of two Gymnastics and
Sports High schools, *Gymnastik-och idrottshögskolor*, in
Stockholm and in Örebro; music teachers at the Royal College
of Music, *Musikhögskolan*, Stockholm, or at the conservatories
in Göteborg and Malmö; home economics teachers at colleges in
Göteborg, Stockholm, Umeå or Uppsala; pre-school teachers at
colleges in Borås, Falun, Gävle, Göteborg, Halmstad, Härnosand,
Jönköping, Kristianstad, Luleå, Malmö, Norrköping, Solna,
Stockholm, Södertälje, Umeå, Uppsala, Västerås, Örebro. Teachers
of vocational subjects were trained at Institutes of Vocational
Pedagogy at Göteborg, Malmö, Linköping, Solna and Umeå, under
the auspices of the National Board of Education, but since 1972
these have been incorporated in the relevant Teacher High School;
the Boards of Agriculture and of Forestry have their own courses.
With the reorganisation of higher education after 1977, all
these colleges are being incorporated into the Universities and
Colleges of Higher Education in the six regions described in
Chapter 6.

The reform of teacher education which fully takes account of the
reform of the school system, however, has yet to take place.
There was in 1957/58 a plan whereby teachers for the 10-13 stage
might specialise so that they could also teach at the 13-16
stage, but this was quietly filed away and lost. The Teacher
High Schools, and the remaining teacher colleges, did begin in
the 1960's to move away from the school-like atmosphere of the

old colleges, where students followed a 35-period a week programme of classes, even on a Saturday afternoon, and were
treated in a manner similar to the old *Gymnasium*:   work has
become more individualised and research based.

But the Teacher High School courses for class teachers do not
yet give any real sense of equality and identity with the
university, and the year of pedagogical study offered to graduates is likely to be as divorced from the previous academic
studies as is the PGCE course in England.   A new Expert Committee was set up in 1960, *Lararutbildningssakkunniga*, *LUS*, which
produced sixteen reports before concluding its work in 1965,[5]
leading to a governmental proposition in 1967[6] institutionalising
the distinct categories of *lågstadiet* (7-10) and *mellanstadiet*
(10-13) class teachers alongside the subject teachers.   It was
recognised that teachers must be able to teach "over the stage
boundaries":   hence, assuming a full academic secondary schooling prior to entry, the course would be $2\frac{1}{2}$ years for the 7-10's,
3 years for the 10-13's, and would include a system of electives,
the courses chosen qualifying the teacher to offer these subjects at the higher stage. 7-10 teachers elected for further
study of one of Swedish, Mathematics, English or Social Studies,
together with one of Drawing, Music or Gymnastics.   The 10-13
teachers elected for further study of one of religious studies,
Swedish, Mathematics, Chemistry or Civics, together with one of
History, English, Physics, Biology, or Geography, and one of
Music or Gymnastics (though these latter two did not give competence to teach 13-16's).

It also became clear that in fact, only in the smallest local
authority areas was a class limited to one teacher only;   at
the 10-13 stage, less than 4% of all classes were taught
exclusively by one teacher, and 20% had more than five teachers.
Furthermore, as Table 22 shows, it was clear in classes 4-6,
that teachers avoided where possible teaching one or other of
the practical subjects, Music, Drawing or Gymnastics.   It was
studies such as these which led to the decisions on the electives
to offer.

As Table 23 shows, however, the proposals still emphasised the
traditional differences in training between the class teachers
and the subject teachers, the former having much more pedagogy,
methodology and practice and much less subject study than the
latter.

TABLE 22:   Attitudes to Teaching

Percentages	Music		Drawing		Gymnastics	
	Men	Women	Men	Women	Men	Women
Taught subject and wanted to	29	34	49	63	54	39
Taught subject but would prefer not to	34	38	27	22	27	38
Did not teach subject	37	28	24	15	19	23

Source: SOU 1965:31

TABLE 23:   1967 Teacher Education Syllabus Proposals

Percentages	Subject Study	Pedagogy	Methodology	Practice
Class Teachers: 7-10	42.9	11.9	12.6	32.6
10-13	53.7	11.0	10.0	26.3
13-16	71.0	9.0	3.0	17.0
16-19 *Adjunkt*	77.0	7.0	2.5	13.5
Lektor	83.2	5.1	1.8	9.9

LUS, when approved in principle, was followed by *LUR*, the proposals of the working group in the National Board for implementing the reform. This published, just in time for the 1968
student revolts in Europe and the USA, two massive volumes,[7]
the 512 sides of the "Red Book" for class teacher courses and
the 324 sides of the "Green Book" for subject teacher courses -
so-called after the colour of their covers. Behaviourism

and the scientific method loomed large: psychology would
explain pupil behaviour, and by analysis of causes it would be
possible to change the factors which influenced behaviour. By
1971, revised (and very much smaller volumes) were introduced,[8]
in which teacher education was to be more individualised, "an
active task carried out by each student, and planned in co-
operation with his teachers and supported by their teaching and
guidance"; and the 1975 version included a chapter on "joint
Decision-Making and Responsibility", which bore little relationship to the structured programmes being offered.[9]

Figure 13 summarises the structure of courses offered in the
Teacher High School in Göteborg in 1979, revised to take account
of the reorganisation.

Term	_Lågstadiet_ Line (7-10's)	_Mellanstadiet_ Line (10-13's)	Subject Teachers Line (13-16's)
1	20 weeks	20 weeks	20 weeks*
2	18 weeks + 2 weeks practice	19 weeks + 1 week's practice	20 weeks*
3	16 weeks + 4 weeks practice	18 weeks + 2 weeks practice	20 weeks*
4	20 weeks practice	17 weeks + 3 weeks practice	20 weeks*
5	16 weeks + 4 weeks practice	20 weeks practice	20 weeks*
6		16 weeks + 4 weeks practice	20 weeks*
7			12 weeks + 8 weeks practice (2 + 3 + 3)
8			20 weeks practice (9 + 11)

*   120 weeks divided 40-40-20-20; 40-60-20; 60-60;
      80-20-20 according to subject combinations

Fig. 13: Class and Subject Teacher Lines, Göteborg Teacher High
         School 1979

The content and points value of the courses was:

	7-10's	10-13's	13-16's
Subject Study			120
Teaching Practice:			
Observation	10	10	5
Block Teaching	20	20	19
Introductory Course)	5	4	1
Child Development)	11	11	6
Pedagogy)			
School Today)	22	29	
Man and Society)	9	10	
Influences on Teaching)	15	16	9
Electives	8	10	

For Class Teachers:

a) Methodology for Basic Skills in 'School Today'; for science
    in 'Man and Society'; for practical subjects in 'Influences
    on Teaching'.

b) Electives 7-10's: one of: Drawing, Music, PE.

c) Electives 10-13's: one of: Religious Studies, History,
    Biology, Chemistry, Physics.

For Subject Teachers: Lines for

a) History/Social Sciences - two or three of Swedish, Religious
    Studies, History, Social Studies, Civics, Geography, Math-
    ematics, Psychology, Economics.

b) Languages - two or three of Swedish, English, German, French,
    with subsidiary in History, Geography or Social Studies.

c) Mathematics/Natural Sciences - two or three of Mathematics,
    Physics, Chemistry, Biology, General Science.

Between 1968 and 1973, a further committee, known as *LUK*, looked
at the education and status of teachers of practical and vocational subjects, and soon found itself involved in the same
issues as *LUS* had been: *LUK* wanted gymnastics, drama, home

economics, textiles and similar subjects to be included in
higher education and combined with traditional academic disciplines.

These ideas were approved in that music or gymnastics could
henceforth be combined with another subject, though drawing
remained a single subject and relatively little has yet developed regarding the more overtly vocational subjects. It wanted,
too, greater emphasis placed on in-service studies, and on work
experience outside schools for all subject teachers. One particular proposal was readily implemented by government, the
replacement from Autumn 1974 of paid teaching service during
the practical teaching term by unpaid "teaching practice", much
to the dismay of student teachers who would now cover their
costs within the normal student grant and loan system.

Teaching practice takes place in the ordinary schools - special
'practising schools' disappeared in the 1960's. The local
school board and the school itself will decide whether or not
to accept students and has the right to reject a candidate who
simply does not fit in. But the Teacher High School selects
established teachers with whom it will place students and pays
(about 1,000 Kr per student per term) that teacher to be a
tutor, who then accepts the responsibility of attending seminars
on 'supervision' at the High School and of giving daily
guidance. Assessment of practical teaching, on a 3 point scale
with some 35% getting the top mark, is the responsibility of
the method *lektor* from the High School who makes two or three
visits per term to the school. This mark is a major element
in obtaining an appointment (see below), and can be reassessed
during one's teaching service.

The 1968 reforms were evaluated in two qualitative studies in
the early 1970's, through the Teacher High Schools of Stockholm
and Linköping for both class teacher lines (KUL-K) and subject
teacher lines (KUL-Å). Significantly, they found that the
official emphases on internationalism, democracy and personality development made little impact during the courses, and
that students had little opportunity to influence the content
of their courses.

By the mid 1970's, it was clear that not only was there a need
drastically to reduce the quantitative scale of teacher education, it was also necessary to tackle once again the content
of programmes and the range of competence of the teachers it
qualified. A new Teacher Education Committee known as *LUT*

was set up in 1974, and reported in 1979.[10] It started from
the belief that in the future teachers will have more responsibility for the total personal development of pupils; that
their role will become more one of support and stimulus, and
not restricted to imparting knowledge; that greater emphasis
will be placed on the pupil acting independently in searching
for knowledge, analysing, making decisions, exerting influence
and effecting changes; and that there will be a more open
school, with greater co-operation between different levels of
school, between pupils and staff within the school, and wider
contact between school and the rest of society at home and in
other countries. Such attitudes pre-suppose a teacher with a
wide range of competence and one whose education is itself con-
ducive to personal development.

The proposals were for a teacher competent to teach throughout
the compulsory school, and for a separate qualification for
those teaching at the post-compulsory level. *LUS* studies had
shown (Table 21 above) that a pure class teacher system was
rare in any case; studies for *LUT*[11] pointed out that most
pupils now start *grundskolan* with the experience of daily contact with several adults in pre-school, leave *mellanstadiet* in
class 6 seeing 4-5 teachers every week, in class 7 meet on
average 12-13 teachers a week and throughout *högstadiet* see on
average 22 different teachers and a range of between 16 and 32.
Clearly to see many teachers at once makes demands on adolescent
pupils, especially at a period in their lives when guidance and
stability is of prime importance; it also makes demands on
högstadiet teachers, each of whom normally meets some 200 pupils
a week and up to 400-500 if teaching a practical subject. The
same study also showed that whatever the subject teachers might
say about the desirability of a competence to teach at both the
13-16 and the 16-19 level, in fact only 3-4% of teachers in
gymnasieskolan in the general subjects also teach at *högstadiet;*
only 1-2% of teachers at *högstadiet* teach either 10-13's or
16-19's, except for teachers of gymnastics, music or craft where
40-50% of them also teach younger pupils; and barely 3% of
mellanstadiet teachers teach at *högstadiet*, indeed, barely 10%
of those who qualified under the 1968 regulations and were thus
qualified to do so in one subject have at any time made use of
that qualification. Within *högstadiet*, it was not teacher
shortage but a desire to give better guidance that encouraged
45% of teachers to work outside the formal framework of their
appointments, and 35% to work outside the formal framework of
their subject competence.

In these terms, the proposal for a 'teacher for the compulsory
school' is a realistic proposition, and would thus break the
age-old assumption that there is a necessary division in the
teaching force within the compulsory age range. Furthermore,
as noted in Chapter 6, the limited number of places in all
teacher education courses since 1977 has made it possible to
ensure a high academic standard and work experience from practically all candidates. Figure 14 shows the main essentials
of the course proposed by *LUT*.

For the teacher at the post-compulsory level, including *gymnasieskolan* and adult education, *LUT* proposed a 4½ year course,
3½ years of subject study, with a concurrent general course of
practical pedagogics, preceded by a term of the elements of
pedagogics, methodology and teaching experience and followed by
a term of final teaching practice. It also recognised that many
persons with appropriate academic knowledge might wish to move
into teaching at this level after experience elsewhere, and
might then take a separate practical pedagogical course. Proposals are also made to ensure that teachers of the practical
and the vocational subjects also have a full year of pedagogical
studies and the equivalent of 3½ years of subject study.

Finally, *LUT* proposed that newly qualified teachers should have
an induction period for a term, with support from "companion
teachers" for a half day a week, and a programme of induction
drawn up by the school management, the companion teacher and
the newly qualified teacher. In its proposals for in-service
training, *LUT* distinguished between school-determined courses,
provided by the five days every year which form part of the
current annual conditions of service; individually-determined
courses, for which ten working days per year were proposed,
days which could be accumulated over several years; and socially-
determined courses, required by society at large and to be
followed at the direction of central government on an *ad hoc*
basis.

The extent to which *LUT* will be implemented will depend as much
on the economy of the 1980's as on the intrinsic merits of the
proposals or the reactions to them by both the public and the
profession. Government presented a proposition to Parliament
in Spring 1981. Predictably, perhaps, the right-wing press was
critical of *LUT*, seeing its ideas as an example of what was
regarded as a decline in the concern for knowledge. So, too,
was the subject teachers' association *LR*, which hoped to retain
the possibility of competence to teach 16-19's and felt that the

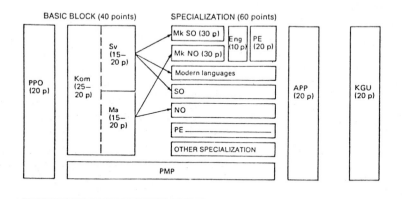

PPO:	general course of practical pedagogics
Kom:	communications block
Sv and Ma:	alternative advanced courses (i.e. special options) in Swedish and mathematics
Eng and RE:	English and practical aesthetical subjects (music, physical education and drawing/pictorial studies); obligatory for teachers intending to serve mainly in lower grades
MkSO and MkNO:	environmental education as per social science and natural science variants respectively (ecology being common to both variants), focussing primarily on the teaching of lower grades
Modern languages, SO and NO:	alternative specialities comprising English and German/French, natural sciences or social sciences, and focussing mainly on higher grades. The languages alternative also entails linguistic practice for each language (5 points).
PE:	alternative specialities comprising one of the following practical aesthetical subjects: wood-work and metal work, textile work, domestic science, music, physical education or drawing/pictorial studies, aimed principally at strengthening the position of these subjects in lover grades
OTHER SPECIALIZATION:	alternative specialities for teachers intending, for example, to serve as home language teachers
PMP:	elements of pedagogics, methodology and practical training in basic block and specialized studies
APP:	concluding practical and pedagogical training
KGU:	supplementary basic education which teachers wishing to do so may devote to subject studies and/or advanced/wider practical pedagogical education within 2–8 years after the commencement of service.

Fig. 14.   Proposed Teacher Education Courses for *Grundskolan*, 1979.

Source: *Teachers for a School in Transition*: a summary of new points and proposals by the 1974 Swedish Commission on Teacher Education, 1979, p.17.

time allowed for subject study in the *grundskolan* course, at
least 20 points less than at present, was too little. The class
teachers in *SL*, too, while supporting the "total view", were
critical of the refusal to link the plans with a proposal for a
common appointment in *grundskolan* rather than to the separate
stages as at present. *LUT* itself was divided on this point:
six members of the committee wanted two kinds of post, which
would effectively lead to a profession divided between class and
subject teachers, and five of the "experts" on the committee
also reserved their positions on this issue. *SL* itself was
divided: 103 of the local branches were in favour of specialisation based on the age-level of pupils, and 66 were against.
It would be easy to solve the problem of the extent of subject
study, simply by incorporating the proposed half term of in-
service study after qualification into the initial course: but
the cost of a four-year course for all is a major obstacle.

The question of a formal distinction between the teacher for
the compulsory school and for the post-compulsory sector, however, is the more fundamental issue of principle. As with
earlier attempts to reform initial training the better to
relate to a changed school system, it is not unlikely that the
reality wil defeat the rhetoric, that there will be at least
as much tradition in the prestige of subject specialisation
over class teaching, the prestige of the traditional academic
disciplines over the practical and vocational subjects.

In-Service Courses

In-service courses in Sweden are referred to either as "further
education", *vidareutbildning*, or "continued education",
fortbildning. The former is always individually determined,
because it implies studies which, once complete, will give a
specific formal competence, *behörighet*, and thus qualify for a
specific salary. One example of this was the practice, common
in the 1960's, whereby elementary teachers took university
courses to qualify themselves to teach specific subjects at the
13-16 stage. Since 1977, the growth of single subject courses
in higher education noted in the previous chapter is in part
explained by subject teachers who have taken leave of absence
for a term or a year to refresh or add to their earlier studies.
It is also possible to do this by part-time study, and this is
now made easier by the increasing tendency for certain popular
subjects to be offered in small towns under the auspices of
the regional higher education board.

Another such "conversion course", in Stockholm and Umeå in the late 1970's, was for infant teachers, *småskollärarinnor*, who after completing a ten-week practical experience, took a one term course to train as pre-school teachers. There are also one year courses to convert junior teachers, *lågstadielärare*, to be middle years teachers, *mellanstadielärare*; and one term courses for *mellanstadielärare* to be *lågstadielärare*. A final example, and in recent years taken by far the largest number of teachers, is the training of teachers for special education. This is offered in Stockholm, Göteborg, Malmö, Uppsala and Umeå, and since the mid-1970's has been qualifying about 1,000 teachers a year in one year full-time courses. About two-thirds of the places are for the General Course, *Gren 1*, the structure of which is shown in Fig. 15, and which qualifies for teaching remedial classes in the ordinary school or in a special school, teaching children who have difficulties with reading and writing, who are physically handicapped or partially sighted, or who, for a variety of causes, might be taken individually or in a small group for "clinic" teaching in the ordinary school for limited periods in a week. Only about one in four of applicants for the course, who must be establi-shed teachers with at least three years' experience, are able to obtain a place.

Subject Area	Contact Hours
Pedagogy:	
Goals and organisation of special education	30
Education psychology	120
Education sociology	10
Medical orientation	40
Child and Youth Psychiatry	30-230
Methodology:	
General	20
Special Methods	90
Teaching Aids	20-130
Practical Experience	220
Subject Study: One of:	
a) Swedish, Phonetics, English or Mathematics	72
b) Social Studies, English or Mathematics	
c) History, Geography, Civics and Careers	
d) Mathematics, Physics, Chemistry	
e) Physics, Chemistry, Biology	
Special Study	5-6 weeks

Fig. 15: General One-Year Course in Special Education

The thrust for courses of this kind was especially stimulated by
the debate in the early 1970's on the inner workings of the
school and the subsequent *SIA* report, together with the related
ideas of teams of teachers at all stages of schooling working
together to meet the needs of the pupils, one of whose members
should have special skills in diagnosis, giving special instruction, and being able to work with colleagues. The special
studies followed in the course are to enable the candidates to
extend their skills in particular areas, such as difficulties
in one or more of the basic skills, or dealing with emotional
problems, social maladjustment, speech difficulties, hearing
problems, the use of creative work in teaching the handicapped.
By 1978, it was estimated that 22% of pupils in *Grundskolan*
were receiving remedial teaching of one kind or another at any
one time, and that 35-40% would receive such teaching during
the course of a school year[12]; but as noted above, about half of
their teachers are technically unqualified.

A second line for Special Education, *Gren 2*, with some 200
places available each year, is for work in special schools for
the blind, the deaf, the maladjusted and the aphasic. Most
applicants are qualified teachers with established appointments
and a minimum of three years experience, but for the maladjusted,
candidates should be qualified in social work, physical therapy,
occupational therapy or in teaching a vocational subject. Here,
too, the course has four elements, pedagogy, methodology,
practice and subject study. A third line, *Gren 3*, trains pre-
school teachers for special schools or hospitals and, for
occupational therapists, leisure time teachers and vocational
teachers as well, for work in training centres.

By far the largest amount of in-service work, however, is by
short part-time courses of continued education, *fortbildning*.
A very thorough four year survey between 1970-74 by the National
Board of Education, known as *SMIOF*[13], suggested five kinds of
course - to enrich initial training, recognising that such
training could never be complete; to meet local needs, especially
in relation to the decentralising of decision making envisaged
by *SIA* and changes in the grant system away from totally specified uses; to meet those needs which the central or regional
authorities indentify; the better to implement on-going curriculum changes; and to meet the needs of individual teachers.

The issues with which *SMIOF* dealt were fundamental: what kinds
of courses should be available; what resources should be made
available in terms of money, personnel and time; which bodies

should control the availability of those resources; and who
should determine how they are to be used. The National Board
necessarily has overall control and might require certain themes
to be taken up. There are regional needs, bringing together
four or five counties on the lines of the regional higher
education boards and which have, since 1977, been a framework
within which Teacher High Schools have been able to develop
programmes sometimes originating in their own staffs and sometimes in response to public requests. There are county needs.
There are needs from individual school units. While the precise
recommendations of *SMIOF* were overtaken by other studies such
as that on the relationships between schools, the state and the
local authorities,[14] the functions of the county school boards,[15]
and the *LUT* teacher education enquiry,[16] the effective co-
ordinator is the County Board. To take one example: in 1978/79
the county of Skaraborg, with a population of 267,342, employed
a full-time in-service leader, *fortbildningledare*; nine consultants for *Grundskolan* covering the different age-ranges and
subjects; nine other consultants for special topics - for those
with hearing problems, sight problems, physical handicap, other
handicapped, religion, traffic, and questions the misuse of
alcohol, drugs, and tobacco; nine native-speaking language
assistants - three for English, two for German, two for French
and one for Spanish; and in co-operation with the four other
counties making up "region 4" with a total population of
1,915,706, seven consultants for *gymnasieskolan*.

The most immediate form of in-service training is through the
five "study days" which form part of the teachers' year of duty
and which are fitted into the school year in such a way that
the pupils have a long week-end holiday. In 1974/75, for example,
Skaraborg published the following programme:-

Day 1:   A County programme for class teachers and music teachers
         at *högstadiet* on Rhythm and Creativity, known as *ROS*
         or a regional programme for teachers in the two-year
         technical line of *gymnasieskolan*;
         or a regional programme for minority subjects in
         gymnasieskolan: Philosophy, Latin, Psychology, Russian,
         certain technical subjects, aesthetic subjects; or
         for librarians, shcool psychologists, school curators,
         school nurses.

Day 2:   A regional programme for all teachers on "The role of
         the school in a changing world".

Day 4:   A county programme for teachers of aesthetic subjects
            and for special education.

Days 3   Freely chosen by the schools, but with the county
and   5:   offering:

            a)   information on *SIA* (then about to be published)

            b)   sex education (supported by the County Council and
                  with the help of staff from the Maternity Hospital,
                  to consider contraception)

            c)   local environmental plans

            d)   pupil-parent-society relationships (assisted by
                  staff of a county child guidance clinic)

            e)   English for teachers in *Mellanstadiet*

            f)   courses for those who want to become local AVA
                  leaders (following a national programme on the
                  use of AVA).

Inevitably, new issues emerge, and new ways are devised to deal
with them. In the early seventies, there were national projects,
incorporating some of the study days as well as additional days
over a number of years so that all teachers could be involved,
on topics such as individualised teaching in Swedish for class
teachers (known as *SIS* project); Modern Mathematics (the *DELTA*
project); teaching English in Class 3 (the *JET* project); study
and work guidance for all levels of school from class 1 upwards
(the *SYO* project); and on learning to live together (the *SU*
project). Much time was also given to studies of *SIA*, the proposals for improving the daily work of schools. In 1976/77,
three national projects began, each of which would run for five
years and involve all teachers, deliberately seeking to change
attitudes; one was on sex stereotyping; another on equality
and internationalisation of teaching (the *JIE* project), an
attempt to develop broader horizons in fugure generations; and
the third on co-operation between school and the society of
which it is a part. Leaders of study groups are trained in
voluntary vacation-time courses and subsequently lead the work
of study days. The courses themselves are quite often the product of action research projects at the Teacher High Schools.

There are also three larger thrusts for the 1980s, involving
longer courses which can only be covered by the employment of
supply teachers. The first is for four-week courses in special
education, part of the movement to provide for the individual
special needs of about a quarter of the school population, as
well as to respond to a widespread public concern to ensure
that the handicapped of any kind receive every assistance. The
second and third projects also relate closely to the ideas of
SIA, to train the senior staff of schools the better to promote
staff development and the activities of the school unit, so
that its work is more meaningful for the pupils, increases
internal democracy and openness and creates a better balance
between the activities of the school which aim to develop pupil
performance and good personal relationships.[17]

The first part of this "Plan for the training of school leaders",
known as *PLUS*,[18] started in 1976 and will run for several years.
The training period consists of 85 days of study spread over
two years. There are 2-4 course days on each of four occasions,
January and February, October and November in the first year and
on three occasions, February, March and November in the second
year; two periods of about ten days each in June and September
of the first year for what is known as "social practice" -
working in local industry and commerce on one occasion and with
other local authority agencies such as the social workers,
child care personnel and youth workers on the other; and the
equivalent of about 40 days of "home study" in between the
course periods and the practice. All education officers, heads
and deputy heads are required to take this course, which is
the responsibility of the National Board and is run regionally
by teams drawn from the association of local authorities, the
county school boards, the school leaders' professional associations and academic personnel.

As Ekholm notes,[19] the scheme owed much to US theories[20] and to
Swedish studies.[21] Each school should be organised in such a
way that its activities correspond to its curriculum. Evidence
suggested that the most effective model for promoting change
was to present "concrete descriptions of reality". A series of
"observational reports" of what is happening in a school are
discussed with others in the school so that discrepancies between
what is seen by different people become the basis for fruitful
discussion and decision making. It has already become clear
that to change the forms of work and the relationships in
schools between different individuals takes a long time, five
to seven years: the two-year training course is only a begin-

ning; and training must not stop with the leaders.

Thus the second project has also begun, the training of personnel teams, *personallagsutbildning*, PLAG. This takes ten
days of term-time, divided into five, three and two days over
a year, the first two periods being residential and the third
period local within a *Rektor's* district, and should involve all
teachers in the 1980's. Each team should have 10-15 people,
and should include senior and junior teaching staff and other
adults who work within the school. The course begins with
techniques to show how groups behave and leads on through a
dialogue between all concerned to identify needs and together
to make a plan to meet those needs and then to evaluate the
decisions arrived at. As with the school leaders, participants
are intended to learn how to make a development plan, negotiate
its implementation, observe the consequences and use this as a
basis for revision.

If this plan is successful, it will go a long way to meeting
the comment of the 1960's that the problem of school reform is,
to a much greater extent than was then recognised, a problem
of teachers.[22] A formal evaluation is the subject of a project
led by Ekholm at the University of Linköping. Two issues are
already clear: first, it is an expensive activity; secondly,
management processes involve much time being spent is discussion.

The booklet for Skaraborg in-service courses and conferences
for 1978/79[23] also illustrates a number of other interests.
One was for traffic education to change the attitude of children towards traffic rules, ensure continuity in traffic
education and work towards better understanding between various
groups involved in traffic education. A second was how best
to meet the mismatch between the availability of lines of study
in *gymnasieskolan* and the fluctuation in student demand. A
third was a wide range of practical teaching problems at
gymnasieskolan level - to achieve a more student-centered mode
of work, especially in year 1; to improve self-confidence and
communicative competence in the use of English; to improve
command of Swedish by using teaching groups of different sizes
for different aspects of work in three parallel classes; to
share experiences between third-year natural science line
students on the use of computers in civics as well as Mathematics and the sciences (the *DIS* projects); individualised
study in economics subjects; short courses for unemployed
youth; ways in which theoretical studies in the school could be

better linked with special projects for the 420 youths aged 16-20 who, in March 1978, despite the short vocational courses already available, had not sought a place in the schools and were nevertheless unemployed. A fifth was to seek to increase the in-service opportunities for teachers in *gymnasieskolan*. A sixth was to provide opportunities for teachers to acquire better understanding of the world of work outside the school. A seventh was to enable teachers of vocational subjects in *gymnasieskolan* to have between one and four weeks practical experience of work in industry and commerce.

In an attempt to plan what courses to offer, where, and on what scale, teachers are asked to notify their interests before the end of September so that the in-service co-ordinating committee for the county can make its plans. The range of activities outlined above makes it possible to envisage that each teacher will have some in-service training in excess of the required five annual study days at least once every four years. The kinds of course suggest the range and pace of change in teaching. Proposals in the 1981 budget for greater control on the amount of money available from central funds for in-service work, on determining the goals for the courses available, and on the criteria by which local authorities may decide which teachers may go on which course also suggest a change of emphasis in less affluent days. It is hardly surprising then, that teachers feel concerned about their conditions of service.

Conditions of Service

Practically everything of significance in the conditions of service for the Swedish teacher is subject to agreements, *avtal*, negotiated by the unions with the state.

As noted above, what constitutes a qualification for the different categories of teacher is defined in terms of the length, level and content of the course followed. When applications are invited, normally advertised in both the national and the professional press, and in the official gazette *Post- och Inrikes Tidning*, the applicant sends in his "papers" which consist of copies of formal qualifications, together with certificates of service and of attendance at courses, all on standard forms and all duly signed and witnessed. These are then assessed on stated criteria known as *Meritvärdering* which follow a process specified for each category of teacher and listed in 100 pages of the Handbook UFB 2.

There are three stages: the first is the possession of the
basic qualifications; the second is level of achievement in
that qualification, followed by further qualifications; the
third is for experience. Grades in examinations are given a
numerical equivalent, averaged to two decimal places; service
as a teacher counts two merits per year, in other work as 1
merit per year, with a maximum of 30 merit points. Representatives of the unions have a right to examine the papers of
applicants to ensure that the merits have been correctly
assessed and that the rank order of applicants is correct.
The person with the highest number of merit points must then
be offered the post. If the point totals are equal, "local
considerations" can be taken into account, for example,
experience of a particular kind, perhaps as a consultant, a
temporary spell as a deputy head, work with one's union, or
even matters such as age or sex in particular circumstances.
There is no formal system of references, though it is not
wholly unknown for informal comment to be sought or offered
or for a local school board to interview those whose merits
entitle them to be considered.

Teachers have worked for many years to remove bias as far as
possible in making appointments, and the elementary teachers
had experience enough of bias in the days when appointments
were made by the local parish. Now, when normal teaching
appointments are made by the County (albeit on the recommendation of the local school board) and senior appointments by
the National Board of even "the Crown", there is almost total
resistance to ideas of increasing decentralising decision making
by making appointments the responsibility of the local authority.
As Appendix IV shows, however, a move in this direction is
part of the decentralising trend in administration.

As noted in Chapter 3, appointments are of three kinds:
established, known as *ordinarie*; non-established, known as
extra ordinarie or *e.o.*; or "temporary", known as *extra*,
either full-time or by the hour as *timlärare*. There are, of
course, also supply posts, *vikariat*. It is an agreement that
some 85% of all normal full-time posts should, if possible, be
offered as "established", and the holder of such a post has
virtually complete security of tenure. Leave of absence from
the post can be taken virtually indefinitely, enabling the
holder not only to take up a non-established post elsewhere
but to return later to the established post. There are,
however, suggestions in 1981 that the distinction between

ordinarie and *extra ordinarie* appointments be abolished in
order to achieve greater flexibility of staffing.

Teaching hours (of 40 minutes) are also laid down: normally 29
four class teachers and teachers of skill subjects, 24 for
subject teachers and 21 for the *lektor*. Certain posts also
earn remission of teaching duties; heads; deputies; equipment
teachers, *tillsynslärare*; guidance teachers, *yrksvalslärare*;
and those with union responsibilities. The scales of remission
are laid down in the negotiated agreements.

Salary structures are closely related to qualification and
teaching duties. Under the current scheme for public employees
governed by state regulations, there are 26 salary scales, L1
to L26, with ten increments in each scale. The scales overlap
to a very high degree, the top of L1 being higher than the
bottom of L11 and the bottom of L26 being lower than the top of
L22. There are additions for those who live in the far north,
known as "cold place additions", *kallortstillägg*, divided into
four categories (the lowest allowance at the bottom of L1 was,
in June 1980, 57 kronor a month; the highest at the top of L26
was then 1,280 kronor a month).

The salary scales as at 1st December 1980 are set out in Fig. 16.

There are allowances for being the equipment teacher, *tillsynslärare*, or Head of Department, *huvudlärare*, of around
500 kr. a month, with additional sums depending on the number
of "points" earned, related to numbers of pupils at different
age-levels.

A teacher who teaches classes regularly in addition to a normal
duty is paid by the hour for doing so, at a rate of between
50-150 kr. an hour depending of the level of qualification and
the level taught. A supply teacher without qualification in
the lowest class is paid around 250 kr. a day, qualified as a
subject teacher between 300 and 400 kr. a day depending on
experience.

Teachers who take leave of absence may have certain salary
deductions; about 3% for those who take on 'official' duties
(e.g. to serve on a committee) where no salary is paid
(A-avdrag); about 10% for voluntary courses of study for up
to 240 days in ten consecutive years if the employer approves
of the course *(B-Avdrag)*; or without pay *(C-Avdrag)* for purely
personal absence .

Category		Salary Class	Scale (Kronor per month
Class Teacher 7-10			
On appointment:	3 terms	L1	5,332
	then	L4	5,706- 6,414
after 4 years		L6	6,683- 7,808
Class Teacher 10-13			
On appointment:	1 term	L3	5,584
	2 terms	L5	5,816
	then	L7	6,109- 7,432
after 7 years		L8	7,767- 8,143
Subject Teacher			
On appointment:	1 term	L5	5,816
	2 terms	L7	6,109
	then	L10	6,629- 8,221
after 8 years		L12	8,917- 9,128
Adjunkt			
On appointment before training		L5	5,816
after training			
for 112 days		L8	6,263
for 310 days		L10	6,629
then		L12	7,018- 8,706
after 12 years in same salary class and after 7 increments		L13	8,929- 9,349
Special Education Teacher			
In *Grundskola* classes 1-3		L7	6,109- 7,999
classes 4-9		L10	6,629- 8,619
In Special Schools			
classes 1-3		L9	6,444- 8,374
classes 4-9		L12	7,018- 9,128
Methodology *Lektor*, Teacher High			
School classes 1-6		L14	7,481- 9,651
for subject teaching		L16	8,073-10,293
with higher degree		L20	9,530-11,910
Deputy Head, *Grundskolan*		L18	8,750-11,160
Head		L20	9,530-11,910
Head as School Chief (*Skolchef*)		L22	10,406-13,006
Director of Education		L23	10,883-13,603
(on size of area)		L24	11,390-14,240
		L25	12,095-15,115
		L26	12,953-16,193

(Assume £1 = 10 Kronor)

Fig. 16: Teacher Salary Scales: Kronor per month, December 1980

The normal retirement age is 65, though teachers of classes 1-3 may leave at 63, and there is provision for early retirement after at least twenty years service and no sooner than five years before normal retirement age. The normal pension for teachers with a full thirty years of service is 65% of final salary, but teachers, who contribute some 3% to their own pension scheme, are also entitled in addition to the basic old age pension. Surviving husbands and wives receive 40% of the spouse's pension on death. The pensions are subject to automatic increase on a scheme related to, but not absolutely fixed by, a cost of living index. In recent years, schemes have been introduced whereby teachers reaching age 60 may work part-time.

By international standards, teachers in Sweden are well paid, enjoy public status and work in good, well built and well equipped surroundings. Their unions, annual membership of which costs about 10% of a month's gross salary, are careful to resist what are seen as erosions of standards and to work for improvements and safeguards.

But there remains not inconsiderable teacher dissatisfaction. In 1971 it was noted "That a third of the teachers in *Grundskolan* regard their working conditions as unsatisfactory, and a half of the *högstadiet* teachers would like to change their jobs (70% in the large towns) is clearly a very serious matter".[24] This was the period when the class teachers' association *SL* conducted their enquiry into working conditions in school;[25] when the subject teachers' association *LR* published regularly in their weekly journal[26] evidence of the pressures felt by their members as a result of the inadequacies of the schools themselves: classrooms which were too small, no place to prepare lessons and mark exercises, insufficient materials; the period when an enquiry was launched into teachers working conditions, *Utredningen om lärarnas arbetsförhållanden, ULA,* which showed how the introduction of *grundskolan* had increased teachers' duties;[27] the period when the National Board of Education set up its major study, chaired by the then Director General on Co-operation in the School, *Samverkan i Skolan, SISK.* At that time, solutions tended to be seen in methods of teaching such as group work; in co-operative committees of pupils, parents, teachers and other adults; in reducing class size; in negotiating recognition of "conference time" as a legitimate part of the working week; in curriculum reform.

It was hoped that improvements would follow the *SIA* report in 1974, the subsequent parliamentary decision to implement its

ideas, the moves towards decentralisation and joint decision-
making by the MBL law. The data on the extent of leave of
absence in 1977, the extent and nature of teacher stress documented between 1976 and 1980, and the increasing evidence of
violence in schools showed that the problems had not been solved.

Some 12% of staff are normally on leave of absence,[28] a third
for study, 20% for child birth, 5% for sickness and all of 40%
for "other reasons". Of these, 7% or 10,086 in 1980 were in full-
time employment; the remainder were absent from part-time posts.
A study of these "other reasons" was carried out by the National
Board with the full co-operation of the three main teacher unions,
LR, SFL and *SL*. It covered all stages and kinds of teaching in
grundskolan, and of gymnastics teachers in *gymnasieskolan*, and
it questioned both those who were absent and those who were not,
and those employed both full-time and part-time. It was clear
that class teachers, especially of the youngest age-groups,
were the most content (96% for 7-10's, 89% for 10-13's), compared
with barely 75% for teachers of academic subjects). There was
some suggestion, too, that there was a more positive attitude
among teachers of the large urban areas than in the sparsely
populated areas; and among *mellanstadielärare* it was those who
were absent for study who were the least satisfeid: it may be
that there are many who realise that they have chosen the wrong
job and want to find a way to leave it.

This is also suggested by the studies of stress.[29] In 1977, *SL*
made a case-study of 500 teachers in a "typical" town of 35,000,
Enköping. Figure 17 summarises the findings.

Teachers – %	7-10's	10-13's	13-16's	16-19's
Had seriously thought of changing jobs	33	49	49	54
Would not enter teaching again	26	29	48	37
"Went sick" because unable to cope	6	9	10	2
Stress as reason for dissatisfaction	80	80	77	62

Source: Quoted in *Lärartidningen/Svensk Skoltidning*, 14/1977,
         p.8.

Fig. 17: Stress Study, Enköping, 1976

97% found job satisfaction through good contact with pupils;
84% through good and helpful colleagues; 82% from freedom to
plan their own work and to have a good head teacher; and only
17% were attracted by the salary and 10% by the prestige of the
job.

A more recent and thorough study by the Stress Research Labora-
tory at the internationally famous Karolinska Hospital in
Stockholm,[30] which includes a Scandinavian dimension, suggests
that one in four of teachers are under stress, especially those
who teach older pupils and who see many pupils in their weekly
work. The influence of the social situation in the school is
clearly demonstrated. One source of stress derives from poor
relations between the pupils themselves as well as between pupils
and teachers, and this is more obvious among older pupils.
Another source is organisational: poor relations with the
school leadership leads to poor co-operation, poor influence,
and thus feeling of harassment. But while in statistical terms
the *högstadielärare* is more likely to be under stress than his
colleagues working with younger children or more selective older
ones, how the sum of stress factors is made up is an individual
matter, with variations within each teacher category likely to
be larger than the variations between the categories. How far
purely physical factors affect the situation has yet to be
analysed: it is suggested, however, that while poor facilities
make a job more tiresome, they are less likely than the social
factors to be of dominant influence. It is clear, too, that
catchment areas with one-family houses rather than apartment
blocks, well settled rather than with changing and increasing
populations, and with schools which have space in which to work
and materials ready to hand are least likely to have teachers
under stress. A particularly interesting finding was that
school leaders, and particularly the women among them, were more
content: it was suggested that they were more experienced, and
the women were more likely to emphasise the social and psychological aspects of their work.

The consequences of such feelings and attitudes for the work of
schools is obvious; and is made worse by the feeling that the
society does not really care. The Head teacher study in
Göteborg in 1977 quoted in Chapter 4 above (note 22) was followed
later by a quarter page advert in *Göteborgs Posten*[31] signed by
535 teachers asking parents to support their pressure for better
premises, resources for teaching materials, better staffing, less
bureaucracy.

In an era of growing violence,[32] a teacher in Göteborg was
killed in December 1979, knifed by a drunken 15-year old boy at
the end of term party. Ministerial condemnation was unequivocal:
The Minister of Education made it clear that adults must be
active in their educative roles, that parents often betray their
children by failing to give guidance and exercise legitimate
control. The Minister for Social Services stressed the need for
adults to stamp out boot-legging, especially to youngsters. The
Minister of Justice emphasised the right of teachers to all the
protection of the law - necessary indeed when a few months later
a school in Lindingö, near Stockholm, was closed in order to
protect staff after a teacher had been assulted by a pupil.

Of course it is wrong to imagine that schools are full of
aggressive pupils and highly dissatisfied teachers. Equally,
however, it is not merely selfishness of those who enjoy conditions which their fellow teachers in other countries might
envy, in salary, social status and general working conditions,
to seek to maintain their position relative to the improvements
which undoubtedly characterise Swedish society in the last
thirty years. Teaching, however, is a more complex activity
than it was when the 1940 School Commission wrote of "The School
is the Service of Society" if only because society itself is
more complex. As with the pre-school, the compulsory school,
the post-compulsory school, higher education and adult education, teaching retains many of its traditional features,
especially to instruct and to help develop acceptable social
values. At the same time, the context within which this
teaching takes place has changed and is changing. It is not
surprising that problems result.

CHAPTER 8

After 30 Years of School Reform

Readers of *Göteborgs Posten* found in their first issue for 1980,[1] under a headline "Are we not the best in the world?), a column which drew on press clippings from foreign comments on Sweden collected by the Foreign Office, "interesting and while not always cheering, nevertheless amusing reading". The most acrimonious in 1979 came from the French weekly magazine, *Paris Match*, its 800,000 copies readily seen at hairdressers and dentists' waiting rooms. To quote: "Violence reigns on the streets and in the underground, pensioners dare not go outdoors, youth live in a constant narcotic dream, computers can expose all about our private lives, the police watch everybody but seldom interfere, all crime is excused on social grounds (except for tax avoidance), non-socialist politicians follow socialist policies, the students cannot spell, Olav Palme has led a campaign for ignorance in the name of equality, the state brings up the children, the school is ambitious only for sex education – and equality between the sexes has gone so far that the Swedish man is suppressed about as much as a woman in South Morocco".

The Swedish ambassador in Paris commented that "social pornography of this kind has happened before and will happen again; the article can do harm, though hopefully as little as a load of manure passing down a village street ... But we have to recognise that our characteristic puffed-up perfectionism and somewhat mean and nit-picking accuracy can make us absurd. It does us no harm occasionally to get our knuckles rapped and be snubbed".

The sheer extent and rapidity of educational change in Sweden since 1950, and the processes by which it has been implemented, has understandably made the country the focus of considerable attention. The OECD examiners in 1969[2] noted the "general recognition which Sweden is accorded as a "lead country" in educational policy ... Educational concepts accepted in Sweden, such as

192

extended postponement and flexibility in school career choices, equalization of social participation in higher education, insistence upon a rapid expansion of numbers and a simultaneous increase in quality in an already highly developed school system, and the introduction of scientific investigations into educational policy issues, are only representative of this position".

There is little doubt that the changes were very thoroughly prepared: discussion papers, field research, report, public debate, legislation where appropriate, follow-up studies, revised schemes. There is little doubt, either, that the process has generated an enormous literature. Indeed, it is hard to believe that there is anybody who has read literally all of it; suffice to know one area in real depth, and hopefully have an overview of the total.

Nor has the process yet come to an end. There is still considerable room for development at the pre-school level, and to decide whether it really is most appropriate for this sector to remain the responsibility of the social services rather than the educational services: the OECD examiners in their 1979 review thought not.[3] The report on a revision on *gymnasieskolan* in June 1981 will certainly lead to much discussion and heart-searching, as will the report of the Child Care Committee. Government motions in Parliament in Spring 1981 include proposals for teacher education deriving from the LUT report of 1979; the organisation of study and vocational guidance at all levels of schooling; new time-tables for the existing *gymnasieskolan;* the administration of the public school system, especially the relationships between central government, the counties and the local authorities (see Appendix IV); grant aid for private schools - an area which, in quantitative terms, is minute but the existence of which demonstrates that Swedish education is not totally in the hands of the state;[4] and for staff development and school research.

There will also be summaries of the *remiss* on a number of earlier reports, which will form the basis for parliamentary discussion at a later date: on teaching aids, following an enquiry on the marketing of educational equipment; on home and school, following an enquiry on how to strengthen contacts between home and school: on women as school leaders, following a special report on that subject; on a proposal for pupil and student participation on ways to improve the working environment of schools and institutions of higher education, prepared respectively by the National Board of Education and the Office of Universities and Colleagues. The Ministry of Education in 1981 is also involved

in a study of the working conditions for school leaders, to form
the basis of a budget proposal in 1982.

The context of future change, however, is very different from
that of the previous decades of reform. The optimism of the
1960s has given way to the doubts of the 1970s and the uncertainties of the eighties. In Husén's phrase,[5] euphoria gave
way to disenchantment about the contribution of educational
reform to social change. Clearly there was a shift in attitudes
early in the seventies, not infrequently expressed in society
at large by critics of the burden of taxation: the feeling of
being excessively controlled by "them" in big business, management, government – especially central government; and the constantly increasing prices, especially following rises in the
cost of oil. So much of Sweden's prosperity is based on high
per capita energy consumption; in a country where there is no
possibility of further development of water power, no source of
coal or natural gas, and no prospect of off-shore oil deposits,
sources of energy could only be from imported and increasingly
expensive oil or the development of nuclear power, which could
make use of some large uranium deposits.

The occasion for the fall from office of the Social Democrat
party at the election of 1976 was essentially the issue of nuclear
power, a major issue in the pre-election television debate between
the Social Democrat Prime Minister Olav Palme, arguing that without such power industrial activity and employment would decline,
and Thorbjörn Fälldin, leader of the Center Party, who was so
patently concerned for the human and environmental risks of
nuclear development and the disposal of nuclear waste. Palme
never projected the warmth and avuncular appeal of his predecessor
Tage Erlander: for many in the middle of the political road, he
was too clever by half, the architect of a prosperity living off
borrowed foreign capital on borrowed time. Fälldin the "simple
farmer" from central Sweden, touched a spark of conscience in
those who felt that perhaps the unending pursuit of growth was
not worth the human, let alone the economic, cost even though
the alternative political strategies were not wholly clear,
especially when the right wing Moderate party, whose co-operation
was necessary for a non-socialist parliamentary coalition strong
enough to form a government, was in favour of nuclear power.

Palme lost in 1976. Fälldin's Center-Liberal-Moderate government fell on the nuclear issue following a national referendum
in 1978 which supported the continued development of some nuclear
power stations. A caretaker Liberal-led government survived

until the 1979 election, when another political cliff-hanger
resulted in a return to power by Fälldin leading a one-seat
coalition majority over the Social Democrat and Communist group.
The self-confidence of a generation had been shaken by the energy
crisis, world-wide recession, unemployment, inflation and economy
cuts.

Educational economies began in 1980, when the National Board's
estimates for 1981-82 were, in response to governmental guidelines, 2% lower in real terms than for the current year, and
included a change which, in view of the prospect of falling rolls
in the 1980's, would have significant consequences - to use the
local authority as a whole, rather than the school unit, as the
baseline for calculating the number of teachers needed. This
was followed late in the year by an attempt to cut current
expenditure by a further 2% as the first part of a five-year plan
to reduce public expenditure, and while the proposal was defeated,[6] it was revived in the normal budget proposition in January
1981. Increasing the average class size in *Mellanstadiet* from
21.8 to 23 saves 1,000 teaching posts; limiting the range of
lines in *gymnasieskolan* saves a further 1,500 teaching posts;
reducing the normal length of further training for special
education teachers from two terms to one; reducing grants for
teaching materials; abolishing "heads of department" posts in
schools;[7] limiting funds for school research; cutting costs in
higher education by 3% per year for a five-year period; limiting
support for purely leisure-orientated adult education courses;
limiting administrative costs - these and other measures heralded
an era of retrenchment, particularly in staffing costs, which had
not been known for over forty years.[8]

One suggested saving was to limit initial teaching education and
use resources instead to give teacher training courses to the
unqualified teachers in posts; another was to abolish the concept of "established" posts for teachers; a third was to encourage local authorities to draw on a "savings bank" of useful ideas
which, while not perhaps new, might be revived - to use the
energies of children for useful social training in helping to
keep clean or to help run libraries; co-ordinate transport for
school and pre-school children; give the local authority more
control over in-service training so that leave of absence might
be less easy to obtain and more emphasis could be given to courses
desired by the authority; co-ordinate the timing of all school
meals; increase the length of life of school equipment; cheaper
means of copying; spelling out the consequences of vandalism;
less money for educational visits; and using non-teachers in

appropriate circumstances - something deeply challenging to the
teacher unions who had spent a hundred years fighting for "professional standards" defined in traditional terms.

Parallel with the savings have emerged ideas whereby special
resources might be made available to meet areas of need, an idea
which presupposes some agreement about how 'need' is measured
and who should allocate the resources. Here questions are raised
about the relationships between central and local government,
between different sectors of the educational system, between
"public" (political) and professional influence in the process
of decision making; and above all between different views on
the purposes of education, especially in the light of the experience of recent educational change.

Reflections on Reform

It is in this context that Sweden looks back somewhat ruefully at
thirty years of non-stop reform. So much was expected; so much
desired in terms of equality, of knowledge levels, of social
behaviour. The search for equality has been in many respects a
chimera. In social class terms, it is still the children from
the homes of manual workers[9] who achieve lower grades at school,
who are less likely to elect to take the academically more prestigious choices at *högstadiet* or *gymnasieskola*, who are less
likely to proceed to higher education. Their chances of "success"
in these terms have increased, as has been shown by studies of
cohorts born respectively in 1934, 1948 and 1953;[10] for example,
the proportions of the 'manual worker' group in higher education
increased from 6 to 13 and 20% between 1950/1960 to 1970. It
has, however, rightly been noted that "when formal mechanisms
of selection are abolished in order to improve accessibility to
higher levels of education for children from working-class homes;
this freedom of access is exploited more extensively by groups
who are already well-represented in the selective system.[11]

The disadvantaged, then, still tend to leave school having followed less demanding courses, with lower grades and with more limited horizons than those already favoured. The bookish ways of
working in schools still tend to favour the privileged. For all
the fine words about developing independence and co-operativeness,
classrooms remain dominated by teachers who talk and who give
instructions to passive and dependent pupils.

In terms of knowledge, too, there is criticism. No doubt average
levels of attainment have increased: indeed, it would be very

disturbing if this were not the case now that so many stay at
school well beyond the statutory learning age of 16. It is
also true that Sweden scores highly on those measures of scholastic attainment examined in the International Studies of
Educational Achievement,[12] and the variations of attainments
between schools in Sweden is less than in the other countries
studied,[13] thus making one's place of residence much less significant that it once was. Nevertheless, there is widespread
criticism that the average and below average levels in the
basic skills, especially in reading, are lower than would be
preferred; that the scope for extending the interests and
attainments of individuals could well receive greater emphasis
without cost to the disadvantaged; that first year university
students straight from school lack some of the grounding in
formal disciplines which their parent's generation displayed.

Above all, in a system designed to teach people to live and
work together in harmony and with responsibility, social behaviour in and out of school leaves much to be desired. As was
noted above, especially in Chapter 4, the school curriculum
stresses the need to support and strengthen democratic principles
of tolerance, co-operation, a respect for truth and right, a
respect for the sanctity of human life and the right to personal
integrity. The reports of truancy, nonchalance, lack of care,
lack of interest, vandalism, apathy and violence, however, are
too widespread and too well documented to be ignored.

Indications of dissatisfaction[14] were clear enough. In the
first six months of 1977, for example, a dozen paperbacks with
titles critical of current schooling were published. As Husén
categorised them[15] there were first the conservative critics
who argued that more open access to secondary schooling had
lowered standards; that the removal of formal school marks and
examinations and the emphasis on social development led to a
decline in intellectual rigour; that gifted children were
sacrificed on the altar of dogmatic egalitarianism; that the
equality-orientated school over-emphasised its custodial function.
Strands of these arguments are clearly to be seen in the differences between Lgr 69 and Lgr 80 for *Grundskolan*.

Secondly, there were the humanistic critics who rejected "life-
adjustment" programmes as anti-democratic, "need reduction"
programmes as a fragmentation of knowledge, positivist philosophy
as lacking guidelines. Here too, Lgr 80 stresses the central
place in schooling of a study of values.

Thirdly, the New-Marxist voices were also heard. The young are
clearly alienated in a society which manipulates them to serve
its own capitalist, consumer orientated profit dominated
interests. Drawing on arguments from French and U.S. critics
such as Bourdieu, Bowles and Gintis and Carnoy,[16] they conclude
that "the technocratic-meritocratic ideology of equal educational
opportunity serves as a kind of opium for the people ... it was
thought that schooling liberated people ... but though education
... seems to assist people in escaping from traditional hierarchies ... It creates new hierarchies ... it is a process that
causes alienation".[17] Dialogue pedagogy is no answer; a
revolution is needed.

It was not necessary, however, to be a Marxist to be a revolu-
tionary. The fourth kind of critic sought salvation in the
ideas of the de-schoolers - Illich, Reimer, and the Norwegian,
Christie.[18] The best known activity of this kind in Sweden was
Experiment Gymnasiet, EG, in Göteborg, referred to in Chapter 6
in the context of the "Alternative Gymnasium Enquiry" of the
late 1970's, *DAG.* One study[19] suggested that *EG* became chaotic
because the freedom it offered lacked direction: it was wide
open for gutter-press journalistic reporting, parents became
uneasy, political opposition grew, the school lacked pedagogical
guidance, and therefore it failed. But as with Christie's book,
and the evidence from similar experimental schools in Oslo and
Copenhagen, it did make many ask awkward questions about schools:
why we have them and what we would do if they did not exist.

It is relatively easy to point to the failures of the reforms in
terms of egalitarianism, levels of scholastic achievement, social
responsibility. It may well be true that the school in a capitalist society is a tool of that society - no less than the
school in a communist society is a tool of communist ideology.
It is apparently true in all developed societies, whether
capitalist or communist, that school is relatively meaningless
for many people. Certainly no country has yet discovered how
best to cater for its adolescents in a neo-industrial society
which simply cannot employ many teenagers and dare not let them
run wild in the streets. The negative attitude to schools among
15-16 year olds in so many developed countries was documented
in one of the IEA studies.[20]

It is unfair, too, to allow the critics to have all the argument.
Much has indeed been achieved. The search for greater equality
has without doubt been successful in many respects. Opportunities for those who live in rural and relatively remote areas

have improved out of all recognition. So, too, have the opportunities for those who suffer from social, physical or intellectual handicaps. Great care and concern has been lavished on
provision for the immigrant population, and the insistence on
offering tuition in the language of the home in areas where
perhaps thirty different languages are spoken in a school and
where the children range from non-readers to near school-leavers
with considerable fluency is a remarkably liberal approach to a
problem which bedevils many countries. Adults, too, have widespread opportunities to obtain the same schooling as is available
to the young. It is not the fault of the educational authorities
that educational provision has not been able to overcome social
prejudices against immigrants. The expression *djävla utlänningar*,
damned foreigners, may well be heard, albeit *sotto voce:* about
those immigrants who take our homes, our jobs, our girls and our
social services for granted. Nor can the authorities be blamed
for the failure of disadvantaged groups to avail themselves of
the educational opportunities that are there for the asking.

Perhaps the young do not know as much as one might like them to
know. Nevertheless, there is abundant evidence in the IEA
studies to conclude with Husén[21] that "... the comprehensive
system, by its openness, lack of selective examinations during
the primary and lower secondary stages, and its high retention
rate, is a more effective strategy for taking care of all the
talent of a nation during mandatory schooling. By casting the
net as widely as possible the prospects of 'catching' an optimum
number of fish are increased". Husén also recognised,[22] however,
that there is a cost-benefit problem to answer. Perhaps more
and fatter fish could be raised more quickly if greater efforts
were put into nourishing the weakest of the shoal at an earlier
stage, rather than seeking to catch more, including the tiddlers,
at a later stage. Suppose it were possible to raise the reading
and writing "age" of the bottom 15% of 16 year olds by one
chronological year, from $12\frac{1}{2}$ to $13\frac{1}{2}$: and the cost of doing so
was to employ x% more teachers or spend y% more on materials, at
the expense of some other desirable end-product, would society
find that cost? Or do we simply accept that for the less able
there is a need for a kind of 'protected place' in the adult
world, just as there are 'protected jobs' for certain categories
of handicapped persons?

It is also true that while all the goals of social and educational equality have not been achieved, one might expect future
generations to seek more for their children on the basis of the
argument that scholastic attainment and aspirations are related

to social background. The vast numbers who take adult classes
for school level courses may well seek to ensure that their
children do not have to follow such a strenuous route. Furthermore, while pupil behaviour is not all that the public would
wish, Sweden is quite sophisticated enough not to blame that on
the schools alone. It is highly significant that for all the
criticism in Sweden in recent years, there is no serious
suggestion that the school reforms should be unscrambled. There
is no desire to return to the separate schools of a generation
ago, to select out those who, for whatever reason, find satisfaction with traditional academic or vocational schooling and
leave the rest in some "sin-bin". To give them so-called
practical-vocational courses is no answer: employers in a technical society do not know what to do with the semi-literate and
the semi-numerate. Sweden has certainly learnt that much from
its experience of school reform.

It has learnt, too, that not one of the three main theories put
forward for achieving educational equality[23] is enough on its
own. Changes in the structure, content and organisation of
schooling are necessary but not sufficient. A "cultural" input
is also of value, with its emphasis on early childhood and
early stimulation and compensation. So, too, are "structural"
changes in the whole social system, which bear upon changing
patterns of social relationships and the value of different
"paths" within education systems.

Sweden has seen that, given a general public consensus, it is
relatively easy to change the structure of schools. It is very
hard indeed to change the processes by which they operate.
Partly this is because effective goals, seeking to change
attitudes, need methods of teaching which are different from
those traditionally accepted for the pursuit of intellectual
goals. People do not learn for themselves or become responsible
for their own actions by being told what to do. It is hard
enough to change teacher behaviour; it is doubly hard when at
the same time it is necessary to change the expectations which
the pupils bring to the school - whether this is quietly to be
the 'ideal school pupil' who does what he is told, or is to sit
back and challenge the teacher to "entertain" a captive audience.
Partly, however, it is the slow realisation of what Sadler noted
so long ago, that school questions are part of larger social
questions; that schools - their staff and pupils - need to work
in much closer collaboration with the local, national, even
international society if their aims are to be achieved.

One aspect of this greater integration of school and society
will no doubt have to be greater decentralisation of decision-
making within the national framework. As the OECD examiners in
1979 noted,[24] schools have become very uniform and teachers too
afraid to individualise, to treat different children differently.
Merely to decentralise from the National Board to the County and
Local School Boards is not enough: it is argued that changes
have to come within the individual school, in the responsibilities of and relations between individual teacher, pupils and
parents.

The implications of these trends would seem to be that the
education system in Sweden and all concerned with it - teachers,
parents, pupils, politicians, the general public - are vaguely
coming to terms with role change in at least three respects.
First, for the compulsory school, the custodial role looms
larger. Furthermore, most pupils cannot find work at 16 even
if they want it. To some extent, therefore, even the post-
compulsory school becomes custodial. In these circumstances,
school is a major institution of social policy, one which has
two tasks which might well be in conflict. It has to teach
intellectual skills. It also has to foster social values. In
neither of these can it hope to achieve its aims without the
wholehearted co-operation of other educative institutions in
society, notably parents but also other cultural institutions
such as public libraries, leisure time organisations, the media.
Schooling is part of education, not the whole of it.

This bears on the second role change. School has a wider social
role, which brings it much more directly in contact with working life, both in the provision of general courses of study
and of more specific technical and vocational instruction. In
both contexts, it implies contact with groups of people outside
the walls of the traditional school, and implies a readiness to
organise its working day, week and year in such a manner that
fits the needs of other groups. Hence the importance of accepting the *SIA* ideas of an integrated school day; the importance
of accepting that recurrent education begins at 16 plus; and
the importance of the various moves towards decentralisation of
decision making, which are clearly part of a trend throughout
the seventies, common in principle to all political parties:
this is not simply a feature of the change of political power
in 1976.

Such changes also imply a change in the professional role of
teachers. At the level of participators in the decision making

process, it is already apparent that there is uncertainty. On
the one hand, teachers welcome involvement in curriculum
decisions; on the other, once they become part of the decision
making body they are also part of "management" and hence involved
in decisions affecting their conditions of service which may
well be different from those being agreed elsewhere. An article
in the class teachers' journal commemmorating the centenary of
the foundation of the original association in 1880 of the General
Soceity of Elementary Schoolteachers, *Sveriges Allmänna
Folskollärareföreningen, SAF*, quoted a statement in 1881: "that
the school teacher should in law be guaranteed the right to take
part in the deliberations of the school board, but make decisions
only if he is a member of the board".[25]

Secondly, it involves teachers as partners rather than as deter-
minators in the teaching-learning process. It was easier when
the teacher alone decided what to do and how to do it. Now
teachers have to discuss content and method with non-teachers,
perhaps find themselves involved in activities not traditionally
associated with their role, and be obliged to work with non-
teachers such as pre-school staff or those trained to lead
leisure time activities, or perhaps even the general public.
Thirdly, it involves ideas derived from the notion of "working
units" of 60-70 pupils with a "team" of staff.

Such approaches encourage ideas implied in the reformed school
of an environment wherein people learn to live and work together.
It also implies a more learner-centered rather than teacher-
centered pedagogy and a more general and less subject-centered
teacher qualification.

It is unlikely, of course, that the inner workings of Swedish
schools will change totally within a generation. For one
thing, well over half the serving teachers still have at least
twenty years to serve before retirement: and in any case, the
newly qualified teachers for the rest of this century will be
products of the existing schools. People do not change as
rapidly as systems. Schools of the future will doubtless continue to have many of the traditional characteristics of schools
as old as western civilisation. They will have one teacher
working with a class of about twenty-five; and the total curriculum will be the same "collection" of subjects that has been
offered for generations. To expect anything else would be to
expect a total rejection of traditional theories of knowledge,
the structure of the disciplines which the western world has
inherited from ancient Judea, Greece and Rome, and has been

interpreted by the medieval schoolmen, the philosophers of the
renaissance, and of the enlightenment. Locke and Descartes,
Rousseau and Hegel, Dewey and Marx or Lenin are all part of a
common intellectual heritage. At the same time, these traditions
are being challenged, and will continue to be challenged as
schools adjust to the characteristics of a new and, as yet, only
partially recognisable post-industrial society.

Sweden's generation of school reform might look, in retrospect,
as if it were a carefully planned scheme to implement a current
ideology. But there never was any 'grandiose plan'. Rather
there was, and is, a general commitment to what might be called
social liberalism, a desire for individual self realisation
within a framework of the common good. In such a context, there
is likely always to be "unity in diversity", traditional features
interacting with changing ideas.

Postscript

It is a unique situation to write about a foreign country which
is, at the same time, partly one's home and where one's wife
teaches 10-13 year olds and one's daughters have been through
the reformed educational system yearly since 1962. The insights
that this family connection have provided are, it is to be
hoped, balanced by academic and professional judgements. Clearly
it is wrong simply to look at the "official" view of Swedish
education. Equally clearly it is wrong simply to listen to
Sweden's own critics. Both impressions give a one-sided view.
It is wrong, too, to imagine that because Sweden has a centrally
administered system with centrally determined curricula and
organisational frameworks that all schools are alike. They are
not. And they differ not simply between town and country, ✷
industrial and rural area, inner city and lush suburbia, old
and new, but also within these categories. There are, of course,
similarities, just as there are in the schools of any country;
but the individual Swedish school can have its "climate", its
"style", just as uniquely as schools elsewhere.

There is also a danger of "lifting" ideas and structures from
one country in the belief that they will naturally transplant.
That is highly unlikely to be successful. Nevertheless, there
are characteristics about education in Sweden which are worthy
of consideration. The most obvious is the evident public concern for matters educational. This is apparent not only in
the regular major news items in all the press, not just the
"heavies", but also on radio and television where at peak viewing

or listening times there is likely to be a serious educational discussion for half an hour or more. It is no doubt this which has in part made it politically possible to engage so whole-heartedly in educational reform in recent years. It also relates to the very obvious desire to see school as part of society, for schools to be able to negotiate with employers and trade unions the circumstances which permit wide-scale work experience to be an integral part of the curriculum, to be ready to apply to schools and their staffs the same kind of concern for good working conditions as apply in other work-places, not just in salaries and hours but in the physical environment of class-rooms and rest rooms.

The network of opportunities is also striking. No group is ignored; no approach is rejected. The idea of recurrent educa-tion is a reality in Sweden, and has none of the slight stigma of "second best" for those who avail themselves of the second, or third, or fourth, chance. There is no stigma, either, about the idea of part-time study, or indeed of the value of study *per se*. There appears to be a not unreasonable balance between those who value "practical experience" and those who value "theory": a well educated person knows why and how, how as well as why.

Part of this seems to derive from a broad and balanced curricu-lum. For an Englishman, it was invaluable to have one's pre-judices rudely shattered: to discover that for example, unlike foreign language study in England, the Swedish upper secondary student does not devote a large part of his English studies to the study of English literature, which is then examined through essays written in Swedish; or to see at close quarters the value of ensuring that every child continues to study his mother tongue, some Mathematics, some Science, at least one foreign language, something of the social environment, and something of the creative arts right through school to age 19. It simply is not possible to give up, say, Physics, or indeed all science, at the stage when Archimedes climbed out of his bath; or any-thing to do with craft and design. Perhaps that goes some way to explain the evident style as well as the technology which is part of contemporary Sweden.

It may be that the very best schooling in England is very good indeed. The very worst can be very bad. In Sweden, the range is narrower. But faced with the choice of average school matched with average school, there is little to regret and much to be grateful for in the Swedish experience. There is no 11+

to face; no 16+; at 19+, at least one knows one's grade
average at the end of the term, but waiting to know the results
of applications to college plays havoc with the month of August.
The children profit from the broader curriculum; they go as a
matter of course to a co-educational school; there are no
petty arguments about school uniform. On the other side of the
coin, it is probably true that more could be demanded of them,
and some could progress faster; but no doubt the same might
well be said of schools anywhere.

What is undoubtedly true is that those in school and higher
education from 1962 have suffered at one time or other from the
disruptions of re-organisation. From 1962 to 1971, *Grundskolan*
was being introduced, year by year through class 1 to class 9;
the *gymnasieskolan* in 1971 was "integrated" only on paper; and
higher education had yet to be reorganised. For those who
started in 1966, *Grundskolan* was settling down, and by 1975,
Gymnasieskolan was likely to be in a brand new building with
excellent facilities; but by 1979, the school leaver faced
the wholly selective higher education system with its five
occupationally orientated lines of study. Only a fool would
wish the experience of reorganisation on his own family.

A dispassionate evaluation of the system as it enters the
1980s, however, suggests that Sweden has asked and is asking
significant questions even if it has not yet found all the
right answers. In finding those answers, it is highly unlikely
to discard the virtues of traditional schooling merely to
satisfy what could be no more than transitory change. It is
likely, however, to continue to search for a school which can
continually adjust to meet the changing needs of both individuals and of society.

Notes and References

Except when given in these notes, full bibligraphic details for books and articles are to be found in the Bibliography, where texts in Swedish and in English are listed separately.

CHAPTER 1

1. *Kommun:* as explained in Ch. 3, the literal translation "Municipality" does not adequately describe this unit of local government. The term "local authority" is preferred throughout this text.

2. Sweden is the fourth largest country in Europe. Of its 173,630 square miles, 50% is forest, 10% farmland and 9% lakes. Its forests are $1\frac{1}{2}$% of the world total, and yield 3% of the world's sawn timber and 8% of its pulp.

3. *Göteborgs Posten:* election debate reports, August 1979, and article *Partierna överens om utbildingen: skolan ingen valfråga* (Parties agree on education: the school no election issue), 26th September 1979. The left wing communist group *VPK* was the only party not to agree that there had been an excess of confidence in the importance of school to recreate society.

4. Landqvist, J (1946) p.48. (in Swedish)

5. Ibid., p. 20. (in Swedish)

6. Isling, Åke (1973) p.12. (in Swedish) See also Boucher, L (1974) in Cook TG (Ed.) pp.67-84.

7. Isling (1973) op. cit., pp. 29-30. (in Swedish)

8. Quoted in SOU 1963:42. (in Swedish)

9. Paulston, RG (1968).

10. Jägerskiold, S (1959). (in Swedish)

11. SCB (1960) Tables 192-205; also SCB (1974). (in Swedish)

12. Hedin, A (1883). (in Swedish)

13. Wennäs, O (1966). (in Swedish)

14. Berg, F (1883). (in Swedish)

15. Quoted in Isling (1973) op. cit., p.46. (in Swedish)

16. Danielsson, A (1981). (in Swedish)

17. Egidius, H (1978a) pp.75-76. (in Swedish)

18. Bergstrand, N-O G (1972). (in Swedish)

19. Moberg, V (1949); (1952); (1956); (1959). (in Swedish)

20. Erlander, T (1973). (in Swedish)

21. Egidius (1978a) op. cit., p.79.

206

22. These kinds of schools are rapidly disappearing. By 1978/
    79 they accommodated about 1 in 5 of all classes and 1 in
    20 of all pupils aged 7-16. (Statistisk Årsbok 1979,
    SCB, Table 372). They are now found mainly in the sparsely
    populated north. In the 1950's, they were common in all
    rural areas.
23. SOU 1944:20.

CHAPTER 2

1. Marklund, S and Boucher, L (1980), *Compare*, 10,2,161-178.
2. Marklund, S (1966), *Educational Research*, 9,3,16-21.
3. Richardson, G (1978) (in Swedish: final summary chapter
    in English, pp.312-324).
4. Marklund, S (1979).
5. Quoted from SOU 1944:20 p.45 and SOU 1946:31 p.21. (in
    Swedish)
6. Paulston (1968) op.cit., pp.88-102.
7. Richardson (1978) op.cit., p.177, quoting SOU 1945:60
    pp.25ff. (in Swedish)
8. SOU 1948:27 p.8. (in Swedish)
9. *Riksdagen, Proposition* 1950:70. (in Swedish)
10. *Särskilda Utskoltets Utlåtlande* (Special Committee's
    Report) SAU 1950:1 pp.117-118. (in Swedish)
11. *Skolöverstyrelsen* (1959). (in Swedish)
12. Ibid., p.237.
13. *Riksdagen*, SU 1956:102, p.21 (Special Committee Report on
    interpretation of the Unity School Act, 1950). (in
    Swedish)
14. *Riksdagen, Proposition 1957:106*, pp.19-21. (in Swedish)
15. SOU 1961:30.
16. Bjerstedt, Å (1968).
17. Boalt, G and Husén, T (1964) (in Swedish: an English
    translation was published, Husén, T and Boalt, G (1968).
18. Svensson, N-E (1962).
19. Dahllöf, U (1971a).
20. SOU 1959:35, Orring, J; SOU 1960:13, Härnqvist, K;
    SOU 1960:15, Dahllöf, U; Bromsjö, B (1961); Johansson, E
    (1961); SOU 1963:5, Härnqvist, K and Grahm, Å. (all in
    Swedish)
    See also Husén, T, Dahllöf, U and Bromsjö, B (1965)
    Educational Research, 7,3,165-185.
21. OECD (1967); OECD (1971).
22. Marklund, S (1970). (in Swedish)
23. The School Law, *Skollag*, SFS 1962:319 and its associated
    Decrees, *Förordningar*, SFS 1962:439.

24. *Lärartidningen Svensk Skoltidning* 20/1971, p.17.
25. SOU 1963:42; SOU 1963:50. (in Swedish)
26. SOU 1966:3. (in Swedish)
27. SOU 1952:33. (in Swedish)
28. SOU 1965:29. (in Swedish)
29. SOU 1973:42. (in Swedish)
30. SOU 1978:86. (in Swedish)
31. SOU 1973:2. (in Swedish)
32. SOU 1972:26/27. (in Swedish)
33. Marklund and Boucher (1980), *Compare*, op.cit.

CHAPTER 3

1. An issue of this kind occurred in August 1980 when the
   Department, through which the NBE draft for the text of the
   new *Grundskolan* curriculum Lgr 80 had to pass to the Minister and Cabinet, substantially altered certain passages.
   Both texts were published in *Dagens Nyheter*. Constitutionally, both the Department and the NBE were acting
   correctly. In the final version of Lgr 80, 98% of the text
   originated in the NBE.
2. See Appendix IV for the proposals in Spring 1981 for decentralising the responsibilities at present held by the
   NBE, the county boards and the local authorities.
3. Marklund (1979) op.cit., pp.53-54.
4. SOU 1974:53; Proposition 1975/76:39. (in Swedish; on
   SIA)
5. *Lärartidningen Svensk Skoltidning* 27/1980 p.35. (in
   Swedish)
6. Marklund (1979) op.cit., p.14.
7. Ibid.

CHAPTER 4

1. *Dagens Nyheter*, 2nd April 1978. (in Swedish)
2. OECD (1979).
3. Rosengren, B (1976), *Current Sweden*; see also Rosengren,
   B (1974) *Current Sweden*.
4. *Lärartidningen Svensk Skoltidning* 42/1973. (in Swedish)
5. Ibid.
6. Stukat, K-G (1976).
7. *Statistika Centralbyrån*, 28th August 1980. (in Swedish)
8. *Dagens Nyheter* 29th August 1980. (in Swedish)
9. *Lärartidningen Svensk Skoltidning* 3-4/1970 p.40, quoting a
   report by Sven Bring, Pedagogical Institute, University of
   Stockholm. (in Swedish)

10. *Lärartidningen Svensk Skoltidning* 6/1979 pp.16-23. (in Swedish)

11. School Law SFS 1962:319.

12. Lgr 69 p.11; Lgr 80 p.17. The Swedish text uses the verb *fostra*, literally "to nourish, to foster, to bring up". It is here translated as "to educate".

13. Lgr 69 p.11, pp.14-15; Lgr 80 p.13, pp.16-19.

14. National Board of Education (1975), 17th November.

15. In "A" school units (i.e. with one age-group in its own class) in 1979, over half the classes for 7-10's had less than 20 pupils and about half the classes for 10-13's and 13-16's had less than 25 pupils. See SCB 1980:6, Table 5, p.26.

16. Traditionally, the subjects of the official curriculum, *Läroplan*, have been listed in a hierarchical order. At the top came the basic skills and languages (*läroämnen*); followed by the experiential subjects (*övningsämnen*). Lgr 80 alters this for the first time, the subjects being listed in (Swedish) alphabetical order. Lgr 80 also changes the name of Drawing (*Techning*) to Images (*Bild*); and of Gymnastics (*Gymnastik*) to Sport (*Idrott*).

17. In 1978/9, the average school unit for 7-10's had under 200 pupils; for 10-13's under 300 pupils; and for 13-16's under 600 pupils. Only 0.5% of all school units had more than 1,000 pupils.

18. Sellergren, U (1970) *Lgr 69 i praktiken: den obekväma friheten* (Lgr 69 in practice: the uncomfortable freedom) *Lärartidningen Svensk Skoltidning* 42/1970 pp.8-10. (in Swedish)

19. *Lärartidningen Svensk Skoltidning*, 29/1980, *Malmölärarnas enkät om skolförhållanderna* (Malmö teachers enquiry on conditions in schools).

20. See Marklund and Boucher (1980), *Compare*, op.cit.

21. See *Lärartidningen Svensk Skoltidning* 35/1980, articles by Gunilla Svingby and Tomas Englund *Regeringen har inte följt riksdagens direktiv för de nya kursplan* (The Government has not followed Parliament's directives for the new curriculum); and a reply by Ulf P Lundgrem from Utbildningsdepartmentet, *Centrala begrepp har lyfts fram i de hya kursplanerna* (Central concepts have been high-lighted in the new syllabuses). See also *LT* 34/1980 for an interview with Sixten Marklund on Lgr 80. (all in Swedish). Marklund has been a leading member of the NBE in preparing the original revisions of Lgr 69, *Skolöve-styrelsen* (1978b), and discussed in Marklund and Boucher (1980) *Compare*, op.cit. Appendix VI gives an example of

the way in which curriculum aims, objectives, content and method are set out in Lgr 80.

22. *Göteborgs Posten* 29th December 1977, *Rapport från Skolsalen* (Report from the Schoolroom). (in Swedish)

CHAPTER 5

1. Urban Dahllöf, speaking at the annual education fair, *Utbildningsmässan*, in Göteborg, January 1981.
2. King, EJ, Moor, CH and Munday, JA (1974) and (1975).
3. See Table 1, p.40.
4. *Lärartidningen Svensk Skoltidning* 19/1980. (in Swedish)
5. Reported in *Lärartidningen Svensk Skoltidning* 40/1975, p.7. (in Swedish)
6. Figures calculated from SFL *Årsbok* 1979/80.
7. SOU 1977:9. (in Swedish)
8. DAG (1979). (in Swedish)
9. Sundén, CG (1973), *Göteborg School Administration.*
10. *Lärartidningen Svensk Skoltidning* 8/1961 p.6 *Mogårds spökskrivare träder fram* (Mogård's ghost writer appears), discussing a paper by Lars du Rietz, political adviser to the Ministry of Education, entitled *Förläng Gymnasieskolan* (Lengthen the upper secondary school). (in Swedish)
11. Åsemar, C (1978); also Åsemar, C (1977). (in Swedish)
12. Fred Wilhelms, ASCD Conference, Chicago, March 1970.

CHAPTER 6

1. SOU 1973:2. (in Swedish)
2. SOU 1977:52-55 (on research); and *Kompetensutredningen, KU* leading to the Law of 1972:84 on entry to higher education. (in Swedish)
3. Premfors, RIT (1980), *Comparative Education Review,* 24.3, 302-322.
4. U68 Summary *Utbildningsdepartment* (1973) p.8.
5. Ibid., p.9.
6. Ibid., p.32.
7. In effect, it was the distinction between "elite" entry (under 15% of an age group) and "mass" entry (15-50%). See Trow (1972) *International Review of Education,* 18,1,61-84 and Trow (1974) *in* OECD (1974). See also Bergendal, G (1977).
8. See Anderson, CA (1974) *Comparative Education,* 10.3,167-180.
9. OECD (1968).
10. UHÄ (1979b), Kim, L. (in Swedish)

11. For example in *Svenska Dagbladet* 28th December 1977, p.4.
     Interviewed on his retirement, Prof. Segerstedt envisaged
     a one year "post upper secondary college" as a way of
     improving quality after what he regarded as the decline
     of recent years. (in Swedish)

12. *Göteborgs Posten* 19th April 1979. The leading article
     Vad kan dagens nya akademiker? (What do today's new
     academics know?) recognised the debate, but also recogni-
     sed the changing demands in courses. For example, there
     might be less on parliamentary government but more on
     "political sociology" in courses on Government; more
     theory and special education in teacher training; a
     broader life orientation instead of biblical studies in
     theology. (in Swedish)

13. *Lärartidningen Svensk Skoltidning* 11/1980 p.15,
     Lärartjänstutredning (enquiry into academic appointments
     inhigher education) which proposed to link teaching with
     research in all posts in the State sector, and to create
     some three-year contract research assistant posts. (in
     Swedish)

14. For example, Swedish Institute, *Fact Sheet on Sweden*
     (1978) *Adult Education in Sweden,* Swedish Institute.

15. Reported in Times Education Supplement 17th December 1976,
     quoting a study by SCB on 1973-74 enrolments.

16. Swedish Institute *Fact Sheet* (1978) op.cit.

17. *Skolöverstyrelsen* (1980) *Petita: Skolväsendet* 1980/81.
     Adult education took 7% of the total NBE expenditure in
     1970/71, 11% in 1975/76, 12% in 1979/80. (in Swedish)

18. *Folkhögskoleförordning,* SFS 1958:478, para 1.

19. SOU 1976:16. The study was made in November 1973. (in
     Swedish)

20. *Skolvärlden* 17/1975 p.6. (in Swedish)

21. *Lärartidningen Svensk Skoltidning* 19/1978 p.12.

CHAPTER 7

1. The SCB publishes annual summaries of staffing.

2. Occupational titles are still used in formal circumstances.
    They are also found in telephone catalogues to differen-
    tiate between people of the same name.

3. SOU 1948:27. (in Swedish)

4. SOU 1952:33. (in Swedish)

5. The five main reports were SOU 1964:44; SOU 1965:25;
    SOU 1965:29; SOU 1965:30 and SOU 1965:31. (all in
    Swedish)

6. *Riksdagen*, Proposition 1967:4. (in Swedish)
7. *Skolöverstyrelsen* (1968a) (1968b). (in Swedish)
8. *Skolöverstyrelsen* (1971a) (1971b). (in Swedish). Revised versions were also issued in 1974 and 1975.
9. Egidius, H (1978a), op.cit. (in Swedish)
10. SOU 1978:86. (in Swedish)
11. *Utbildningsdepartmet* (1977). (in Swedish)
12. Times Educational Supplement 24th November 1978, "Remedial help is well integrated".
13. SMIOF: *Skolöverstyrelsens artbetsgrupp för utredning av mål, innehåll och organisation för fortbildning* (The NBE working party on the goals, content, and organisation of in-service short courses).
14. *Skolan, Staten och Kommunerna, SSK* (1978) (in Swedish: the School, the State, and the Local Authorities).
15. *Länskolnämndsutredningen* (The County School Board Enquiry) and *Skoladministrativ Kommitten, SAK* (1980) (The School Administration Committee).
16. *Utbildningdepartmentet* (1977), op.cit.
17. Ekholm, Mats (1980) in Hoyle, E and Megarry, J *The World Yearkbook of Education*.
18. The guidelines for the schemes are set out by the NBE in PLUS-75:1 and its supplements PLUS-75:11. The legal bases for the work are found in ASÖ 1976/77 nr 46 and circulars SAV nr XV:8 1976 and SAV Und:2 1977.
19. Ekholm (1980) op.cit.
20. For example, Miles, MB (Ed.) (1974) *Innovation in Education*, New York, Teachers College Press; Gross, N, Giacquinta, J and Bernstein, M (1971) *Implementing Organisational Innovation*, New York, Harper & Row; Rogers, EM and Shoemaker, FF (1971) *Communication of Innovation:* a cross cultural approach, London, MacMillan; Smith, LM and Keith PM (1971) *Anatomy of Educational Innovation*, New York, John Wiley; Havelock, RG (1973) *The Change Agent's Guide to Innovation in Education*, New York, Educational Technology Publications.
21. Ekholm, Mats (1976); Carlberg, T (1978); Lander, R (1978) (Carlberg and Lander in Swedish).
22. Marklund, S and Söderberg, P (1967).
23. *Skaraborgs Länsskolnämnd* (1978). (in Swedish)
24. *Lärartidning Svensk Skoltidning* 19/1971 p.5, *Lärarnas syn på arbetssituationen i skolan: måluppfyllnaded i grundskolan klart otillräcklig* (Teachers view of working conditions in school: clearly impossible to achieve goals in the basic school). (in Swedish). See also Ch. 2 above, pp.32ff.

25. *Sveriges Lärarförbund* (1971);   see also a summary in
    Lärartidningen Svensk Skoltidning 19-20/1971.   (both in
    Swedish)
26. *Skolvärlden* 14/1970 p.25;   15/1970 pp.3-4, p.12;   16/1970
    pp. 3-4, 6-7;   19/1970 p.4.
27. Set up in 1964, it reported in 1971: see *Skolvärlden*
    22/1971 pp.3-4, 6-8, p.18;   also *Lärartidningen Svensk
    Skoltidning* 36/1971, pp.10-25;   20/1973 pp.30-31.   (in
    Swedish)
28. A study by SCB, reported in *The Times Educational Supplement*
    15th April 1977, "More Teachers Go Absent";   and in
    Lärartidningen Svensk Skoltidning 25/1977 *Var åttonde
    lärare är tjänstledig, Var Fjärde kvinnlig lärare har
    deltid* (Every eighth teacher on leave of absence, every
    fourth woman teacher on part-time);   and 16/1978 p.6
    Vad ligger bakom ökande tjänstledighet? (What lies behind
    the increased leave of absence?);   and pp.28-30, *Bristande
    tjänstunderlag främsta orsaken för vissa lärargruppen*
    (Lack of staff posts the main reason for certain teaching
    groups).   (in Swedish)
29. *Times Educational Supplement* 28th October 1977, Vast
    majority of teachers complain of stress;   and 12th May
    1978, Teachers under more stress than other professionals.
30. *Lärartidningen Svensk Skoltidning* 18/1980 pp.11-18,
    Nordstress (Stress in the North).   (in Swedish)
31. *Göteborgs Posten* 2nd April 1979, *Föräldrar! Skolsituation
    för Göteborgs arbetarbarn* (Parents! The School situation
    for the children of Göteborg's workers).   (in Swedish)
32. *Lärartidningen Svensk Skoltidning* 2/1980 pp.5-8, *Skolvåldets
    ursprung* (The origin of violence in school);   28/1980
    Är det verklingen våldet som är problemet? (Is it really
    violence which is the problem?).   (in Swedish)

CHAPTER 8

1. *Göteborgs Posten* 2nd January 1980 p.3, *Är vi världsbäst?*
    (Are we the best in the world?)   (in Swedish)
2. OECD (1969) p.7.
3. OECD (1979) op.cit.
4. It is legally possible to run a private school in Sweden
    under the decree *Privatskolförordningen* SFS 1967:270 as
    amended.   The National Board of Education supervises the
    staffing, curriculum and facilities.   A state grant,
    normally 60% of approved expenditure, is available for
    teaching staff salaries.   (SFS 1964:137, para 15).   There

are a few boarding schools catering for children of persons
serving overseas and for a small number of children whose
parents seek a particular (perhaps religious) atmosphere.
There are also a few day schools with special approaches,
such as the Rudolf Steiner schools. The number of pupils
in private schools is under 1% of the total school population. An enquiry into private schools was set up in
autumn 1979, its terms of reference including the need for
such schools, criteria for state grants, and the recruitment
to such schools.

5. Husén, T (1979)

6. The election of 1979 resulted in a majority of one for the
non-socialist parties. In the vote on cuts in December
1980, a conservative member was unexpectedly absent, and
votes were tied. Under a procedure agreed in the early
1970s, lots were drawn, and the government motion was lost.

7. *SIA* had proposed oversight tasks for directors of studies
and Parliament decided in 1976 that the existing allowances
for heads of departments should be abolished and the duties
reallocated. This changed a nationally negotiated agreement and was rejected by the teacher unions. In 1981, it
was proposed that each local school board could provide
for these leadership roles by local negotiations for
remission of teaching duties rather than to continue paying head of department allowances.

8. The conservative Minister of Education in 1980 pointed out
that while Sweden has one teacher for every 16 pupils at
the 10-13 stage, USA has one for 20, Japan one for 25 and
West Germany one for 23. From age 13 upwards, Sweden has
one for 10, USA one for 19, Japan one for 18 and West
Germany one for 15. But the social democrat chairman of
the Education Committee in Parliament in the 1970s was
also known for pointing out that Sweden holds a world
record in teacher-pupil ratios, and that teachers who
grumbled should acknowledge this fact. (Quoted in
Lärartidningen Svensk Skoltidning 6/1980 p.8).

9. Social class classification in Sweden is normally in three
categories: Social Class 1 (5%) for senior civil servants,
professional people and senior managerial executives;
Social Class 11 (35%) for lower grade non-manual workers,
small businessmen and foremen; and Social Class 111 (60%)
for manual workers and farm labourers.

10. SOU 1958:11, Härnqvist; SOU 1971:61, Bengtsson, J and
Gesser, B; also Reuterberg, SE (1968). (all in Swedish)

11. Härnqvist, K and Bengtsson, J (1976) *in* Scase R (Ed.)
pp.205-222.

12. For example, Husén, T (Ed.) (1967); and Husén, T. et. al. (1973: in Swedish).
13. Marklund, S (1980) *in* Hoyle, E and Megarry, J *The World Year Book of Education* pp.115-130.
14. For example, *Dagens Nyheter* 9th September 1977, *Missmod i Skoldebatt* (Dissatisfaction in the School Debate). Titles summarised included Emmanuelsson, Ingemar (1977); Ekholm, Mats (1977); Erasmie, Thord (1977); Husén, T (1977); and Sjöberg, Chris (1977). (all in Swedish)
15. Husén, T (1979) op.cit.
16. Bourdieu, P (1964) *Les Méritiers: Les Étudiants et la Culture*, Paris, *Editions de Minuit*; Bowles, S and Gintis, H (1976) *Schooling in Capitalist America: Educational Reform and the Contradictions of Economic Life*, London, Routledge and Kegan Paul; Carnoy, M (1974) *Education as Cultural Imperialism*, New York, David McKay.
17. Husén, T (1979) op.cit., pp.28-29.
18. Illich, ID (1970) *Deschooling Society*, New York, Harper & Row; Reimer, E (1971) *School is Dead*, Harmonsworth, Penguin; Christie, N (1971) *Hvis Skolen ikke Fantes* (If the school did not exist), Oslo, Universitetsförlag.
19. Huss-Moback-Hallgren (1977). (in Swedish)
20. Husén, T et. al. (1973) op.cit. (in Swedish)
21. Husén, T (1979) op.cit., p.100.
22. Ibid., pp.110-111.
23. CERI (1971)
24. OECD (1979) op.cit.
25. *Lärartidningen Svensk Skoltidning* 27/1980 p.35.

APPENDIX 1

Sweden: Counties

COUNTY	POPULATION	DENSITY PER KM2
AB Stockholm	1,519,114	230
C Uppsala	239,090	33
D Södermanland	252,067	42
E Östergötland	392,057	37
F Jönköping	302,407	30
G Kronoberg	171,434	20
H Kalmar	241,340	22
I Gotland	54,935	17
K Blekinge	154,368	53
L Kristianstad	276,983	45
M Malmöhus	742,738	151
N Halland	227,175	40
O Gbg. & Bohus	713,469	140
P Älvsborg	422,828	37
R Skaraborg	267,342	33
S Värmland	284,892	16
T Örebro	274,268	32
U Västmanland	259,692	41
W Kopparberg	284,490	10
X Gävleborg	294,288	16
Y Västernorrland	268,110	12
Z Jämtland	134,420	3
AC Västerbotten	240,601	4
BD Norrbotten	266,329	4
TOTAL	8,284,437	20

APPENDIX II

Swedish Towns
Names in Text

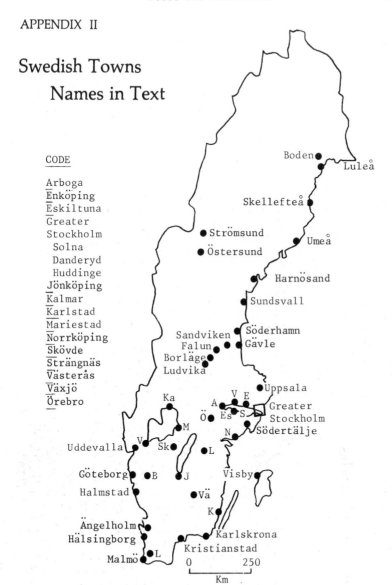

CODE

Arboga
Enköping
Eskiltuna
Greater
Stockholm
Solna
Danderyd
Huddinge
Jönköping
Kalmar
Karlstad
Mariestad
Norrköping
Skövde
Strängnäs
Västerås
Växjö
Örebro

Boden
Luleå

Skellefteå

Strömsund
Umeå
Östersund

Harnösand

Sundsvall

Söderhamn
Sandviken
Falun   Gävle
Borläge
Ludvika

Uppsala
Ka
V E
A
Ö Es S   Greater
M   Stockholm
N   Södertälje
Uddevalla V Sk   L
Göteborg B   J   Visby
Halmstad
Vä
K
Ängelholm
Hälsingborg   Karlskrona
Kristianstad
Malmö L   0   250
Km

APPENDIX III

The Structure of Swedish Schooling 1842-1971

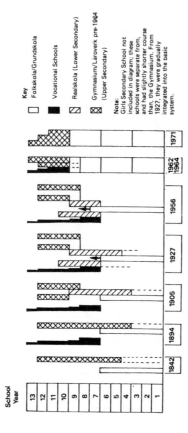

Key

☐ Folkskola/Grundskola

■ Vocational Schools

▨ Realskola (Lower Secondary)

⊠ Gymnasium/Laroverk pre-1964 (Upper Secondary)

Note:
Girls Secondary School not included in diagram; these schools were separate from, and had slightly shorter course than, the Gymnasium. From 1927, they were gradually integrated into the basic system.

1842 Separate and parallel systems; laroverk could be entered via private elementary school.

1894 Technical and Commercial Schools developing; Laroverk linked to the Folkskola, but private elementary school remained.

1905 Laroverk divided into 3- or 4-year Upper Gymnasium following 5- or 6-year Realskola; private elementary school remained.

1927 Technical and Commercial Schools now part of the 'system'; Realskola became either 4-year or 6-year, following 4-year or 6-year Folkskola; some 7-year and 8-year Folkskolor established.

1956 Minimum 7-year Folkskola as base for 3- or 4-year Realskola; Some 8-year and 9-year Folkskolor established; private elementary school largely vanished.

1962 9 year Grundskola established; 3 lines in final year, as base for *separate* vocational schools or gymnasium.

1964 Introduction of 2-year Continuation School as third alternative in post-Grundskola system.

1971 Integrated 2-year/3-year/4-year Gymnasieskolan established, following integrated 9-year Grundskola.

(Chart based on Marklund, S., Vär Nya Skola, p. 26)

From Boucher L, *in* Cook TG (Ed.) The History of Education in Europe, 1974, p. 69.

Proposals for Reorganisation of the Administration of the School System, 1981

On the basis of two committees of enquiry, *Skolan, Staten och kommunerna, SSK* (1978) and *Skoladministrativa Kommittén, SAK* (1980), proposals were laid before Parliament in Spring 1981 for reorganising the administration of the public school system. The main changes would be:

1. The responsibility of Parliament, *Riksdag,* and Government, *Kungl Maj:t* and *Utbildningsdepartment,* to direct the administration of schools. This is done through the school law, *skollag;* school decrees, *skolförordningar,* and qualification regulations, *behörighetsföreskrifter.*

2. The responsibility of the National Board of Education, *Skolöverstyrelsen,* for planning and evaluation of regional and local authority activities.

3. The responsibility of the County School Boards, *Länskolnämnderna,* for development of local authority activities.

4. The responsibility of the local authority boards, *skolstyrelserna,* for implementation and development at the local level.

Changes at NBE

a) Composition of the Board to be the General Director, Managing Director (*Överdirektör*), 5 representatives of the political parties, 1 representative of the local authorities, 1 representative of the county councils.

b) Two 'secretariats', one for finance, one for planning.

c) Four divisions, *avdelningar* - for the compulsory school, post compulsory school, adult education, administration (economic, legal and organisational aspects).

d)   Reduction of departments, *bryåer*, from 17 at present to a
       maximum of 8.

e)   Abolition of NBE *Gymnasieinspektörer* and *Skolkonsulent*
       posts, but provision for short-time (6 month) secondments
       for pedagogical work at NBE.

f)   Reduction of posts from 654 to 450.

Changes at County Board Level

a)   Retain the present lay board with the County School
       Inspector as Head of its office.

b)   Two School Inspectors, one for compulsory schooling, one
       for voluntary schooling.

c)   i   responsibility for the development, co-ordination and
            planning of schools (including the scale and disposi-
            tion of post-compulsory schooling within the framework
            decided by NBE)

       ii   stimulation, support and advice to the local author-
            ities

       iii evaluation of the schools' activities

       iv   promotion of developmental work

       v   responsibility for the achievement of the goals and
            guide lines of the schools.

d)   Abolition in-service *konsulent* posts, but short-time sec-
       ondment for pedagogical work at county level.

Changes at School Board Level

Responsibility for appointment of teachers and school management
staff (heads and directors of studies).

The justification for these changes is the desire to extend the
decentralising tendencies of the 1970's in *SIA*, the revised
grant system and Lgr 80. It is argued that the proposals
increase public influence over the schools, make it easier for
schools to adapt to local circumstances, and make it possible
to use resources more effectively. Strong central control,

however, would ensure the maintenance of national standards, partly at the level of Government and partly through the NBE which would now become essentially a lay body.

A parallel proposition by Government on school research and staff development purposes, from 1st July, 1982, provides for:

a) annual determination by NBE, following Government guidelines, of those in-service courses for which *B-avdrag* (minimum loss of pay) would be allowed.

b) local school boards, not county boards as now, to decide who should have leave of absence with *B-avdrag* (at present, some 3,300 per year have leave of absence for study, 2,500 with *B-avdrag*).

c) institutes of higher education to be the main providers of further education courses, *fortbildning*, with places guaranteed for those for whom *B-avdrag* has been granted.

d) NBE to allocate research funds, but will no longer conduct its own research.

The elimination on the National Board of Education of employer and employee representatives (*LO, TCO, SACQ/SR, SAF*), of higher education (*UHÄ*), and of the Labour Board (*AMS*) was fiercely criticised when *SAK* reported in 1980. The teacher associations, *LR, SL, SFL*, are also totally opposed to teacher appointments being a local authority responsibility, and to the proposed abolition of established, *ordinarie*, posts.

Study Loans and Grants in Sweden

The details below were correct as at April 1980. Swedish rates of pay for unskilled workers aged 16/18/21 were then approximately 20/25/30 kr. per hour (10 Sv.kr. = £1.00).

In 1979/80, 6% of debtors were defaulting on repayments, of whom 1% had left the country. (SCB, September 1980).

A. STUDY HELP (*STUDIEHJÄLP*)

Available for: 16-19 year olds in full-time study for at least 8 weeks, at upper secondary school, folk high school or state adult school.

Forms of help:-

Extended child allowance: 233 kr. per month for 9 months per year; no means test for self or parents (normal child allowance stops at age 16).

Grant: 233 kr. per month in lieu of child allowance: no means test.

Travel supplement: 140-354 kr. per month, depending on distance; minimum 6 kms.

Accommodation supplement: 315 kr. per month in lieu of travel for those whose homes are far away or are difficult to reach.

Travel allowance: free return home for those in lodgings: 4 times a month up to 250 kms., fortnightly over 250 kms.

Income based supplement: maximum 155 kr. per month; for over 17's only; available if income of self, parents or, if married, husband or wife, is below 40-48,000 kr., depending on number of dependants.

Supplementary allowance: maximum 215 kr. per month; income limit of self, parents or partner of maximum 48,000 kr. per year; available only if there is special need for further help.

Loans: a) for 16-17's: maximum 556 kr. per month: related
            to own and parental income, below 50-65,000 kr.
            depending on number of dependants; repayable.

        b) for 18-19's related to parental income: maximum
            1,111 kr. per month; income below 50-91,000 kr.
            depending on number of dependants; repayable.

        c) for 18-19's independent of parental income:
            maximum 1,708 kr. per month; own income below
            15,290-51,442 kr. per year depending on number of
            dependants; repayable.

Swedish parents overseas: 1-5,000 kr. per academic year for
pupil studying in Sweden.

B. STUDY AID (*STUDIEMEDEL*)

Available for: students in higher education and those aged over
20 taking school level courses. Applicants normally under age
45.

Grants: maximum 242 kr. per month for full-time study, 121 kr.
for part-time study: no means test.

Loans: maximum 2,076 kr. per month for full-time study,
1,038 kr. for part-time study: based on income (applicant
only); repayable.

Additional child allowance: repayable; maximum 414 kr. per
month.

Supplementary loan: applications for special cases (e.g. to
cover special study costs) may be granted; sums allowed are
repayable.

Income limits:

	Full-time study	Part-time Study	Reduction effect on loan
Own income	8,194 kr. p.a.	20,860 kr. p.a.	1/9th of excess per month
Own capital	89,400 kr.	89,400 kr.	2/45th's of excess per month

Conditions of loans:

a)   payment is made twice a term (4 times a year)

b)   study of minimum 15 days full-time, 30 days part-time

c)   scholastic aptitude test for those taking school level
     courses for the first time, other than in an upper
     secondary school

d)   continuation of grant/loan at higher education needs evi-
     dence of satisfactory completion of studies at a "normal"
     pace (student receives transcript from university/college)

e)   grant/loan can be reclaimed if the recipient breaks off
     studies or has increase of income/capital during the
     period of aid.

C.   STUDY PAYMENT (*STUDIEPENNING*)

Available for: adults in employment who lose income when taking study leave. The amount of aid available is limited and
awards are discretionary. Criteria for award of grant include
level of education and difficulty of taking part-time study.
Aid is for courses at school level in municipal (or if necessary at State) adult schools, and for vocational-technical
higher studies.

Applicants must have 4 year's work experience (can include care
of dependants at home), and take a scholastic aptitude test for
school level courses taken for the first time other than in an
upper secondary school. Continuation of grant requires evidence
of satisfactory completion of studies at a "normal" pace.

Special adult study support:

Grant: 2,360-2,932 kr. per month. Taxable.

Loan: within range of approximately 776-853 kr. per month;   not
taxable but repayable.

Aid available for at least 15 days of full-time study, 30 days
of part-time study, during one term.

Day release support: maximum 198 kr. per day, taxable, to
replace loss of income (available only to employees), for study
of up to 10 days in a year at Folk High School. Payment is made
for 2 extra days for those who have significant travel costs or
loss of income.

Accommodation grant: 165 kr. per day, not taxable, for those
taking part in study circle courses in Swedish, English,
Mathematics, Civics, trade union studies, mother tongue for
immigrants, special studies for handicapped persons; maximum
70 hours per year, plus a further 20 hours for those who have
significant travel costs or loss of income. (Similar support,
for a maximum 28 hours per week, 2,220 hours per year, is
available for adults taking basic literacy and numeracy courses:
taxable grants of 33 kr. per hour for loss of income, 13 kr.
per hour for those over 20 but not employed).

D. STUDY ABROAD (i.e. outside Nordic countries – Denmark,
          Norway, Finland and Iceland)

Available only to Swedish citizens:

a) Extended child allowance for those aged 16-19.

b) Help as for 16-19's for those residing abroad with their
    parents or if applicant is seeking vocational training not
    available in Sweden.

c) For applicants over 20, aid is for those in Sweden for
    courses not offered in Sweden and judged to be of value, or
    for study in certain shortage fields, e.g. medicine, chem-
    istry, physiotherapy, where places in Sweden are selective.

E. ASSISTANCE FOR NON-SWEDISH CITIZENS

Aid is available as for Swedish citizens if:

a) Applicant has been resident and employed at least half-time
    in Sweden for two consecutive years (limitation does not
    apply to applicants qualifying to teach two languages at
    higher education level).

b) Applicant is deemed to be a refugee.

c) Applicant is under 20 and whose parents satisfy condition a).

d)   Applicant is married or is living with and has a child with
     a Swedish citizen and has been resident in Sweden for a year.

Citizens of the Nordic countries do not require residence or
work permits in each other's countries, and can seek assistance
in their own country for study in one or other of the other
countries.

F.   REPAYMENT OF LOANS

1.   Repayment begins 2 calendar years after the completion of
     the initial period of loan: if studies are "completed"
     (i.e. not officially recognised as "interrupted") and a
     further loan is taken for "new" study, there is no further
     2-year period of grace before repayments fall due.

2.   The period of repayment depends on the age of the debtor
     when repayment begins:

     a)   under age 36, payment due by age 50
     b)   age 36-51, payment due within 15 years
     c)   over 51, payment due by age 65

3.   Size of debt is notified at the end of January each year;
     the annual amount to be repaid is based on a "regulating
     figure" related to the annual index of consumer prices. In
     April 1980 it was 1.032 - i.e. the debt is multiplied by 3.2%
     per year. (If the price index increases were less than 3.2%,
     the annual "interest" would be lower).

4.   Repayment is deferred if the debtor's annual income is less
     than 48,000 kr. p.a. (without dependants); and cannot
     exceed certain percentages of disposable income (percentages
     depend on levels of taxable income).

5.   The loan is cancelled at age 65, or in cases of handicap or
     illnesses preventing employment.

6.   Repayment at a rate in excess of that due earns a discount.

7.   The "interest" on the loan qualifies for tax relief.

The Official Curriculum for
Grundskolan, LGR 80

The official curriculum is in two parts. The first general
(*Allmän Del*) part, is prescriptive, and contains the goals and
guidelines (*mål och riktlinjer*), subject syllabuses (*kursplaner*)
and schedules allocating the time for each subject (*timplaner*).
This is "the controlling instrument for school and its personnel"
(Lgr 80, p.9). The second part, which appears periodically,
contains a commentary on the syllabus, and is not prescriptive.
Both parts are published by the National Board of Education, in
accordance with the decree SFS 1980: 64 of 14th February, 1980.
The goals, syllabuses, and schedules were published in November
1980 as Läroplan:1, 2, 3 respectively.

The Goals and Guidelines are the basis for planning in all local
school boards, school management areas (*rektors områderna*),
school units (*skolenheter*), working units within the school
(*arbetsenheter*) and class councils (*klassråd*).

The syllabuses for each subject area begin with a brief statement in two or three short sentences stating why the subject is
included in the basic curriculum. There are then a number of
sentences, of between 200–500 words, stating the goals (*mål*)
for the subject, followed by a list of the main items of content, divided between the three stages of *grundskolan*, for ages
7–10, 10–13 and 13–16. This content is no longer subdivided
into each year, and should be read in conjunction with the relevant parts of the Guidelines to indicate how the teaching and
learning should be carried out. Each subject is given some
five to ten sides.

The schedules give only the number of teaching periods for each
subject throughout each stage, not year by year: an allocation
of, for example, 13 periods (as for Mathematics in Years 1–3,
ages 7–10) could be divided 4-4-5, 5-4-4, 4-5-4 or any other
pattern decided by the school, as long as the total allocation
for that subject is correct and the total for all subjects in
a year is not exceeded (Year 1 –20; Year 2 - 24; Year 3 -
30; Years 4-6 - 35; Years 7-9 - 33-34).

The contents page of Lgr 80 is as follows:

Lgr 80: Läroplan för Grundskolan, Allman Del - Innehåll
(Lgr 80: Curriculum for the Basic School, General Part -
Contents), pp. 6-7.

Lines of Study, *Gymnasieskolan*, 1980

ARTS AND SOCIAL STUDIES SECTOR

2 Year Lines	Basic Course	Options	
Consumer	Term 1	Terms 2-4	Management
			Textiles
	Terms 1-4		Restaurant/Catering
Nursing	Term 1	Terms 2-4	Medical Services/
			Geriatrics
			Mental Nursing
			Mentally Retd. Adults
			Child-Youth Welfare/
			Nursing
Music	Terms 1-4	(General Course)	
Social	Terms 1-4	(General Course)	
3 Year Lines			
Arts	Terms 1-6	(General Course)	
	Terms 1-2	Terms 3-6	Semi classical
			Classical
			Aesthetic
			Social
Social	Terms 1-6	(General Course)	
Sciences	Terms 1-2	Terms 3-6	Aesthetic
			Social

Special Courses		
Play Leaders	Term 1	
Physiotherapy	Terms 1-4	
Occupational Therapy	Terms 1-6	

ECONOMICS SECTOR

2 Year Lines			
Distribution	Terms 1-2	Terms 3-4	Distribution
- Clerical			Accountancy
			Typing
Economics	Terms 1-6		
3 Year Lines			
Economics	Terms 1-4	Terms 5-6	Accountancy
			Distribution
			Administration
			Languages
	Terms 1-2	Terms 3-6	Aesthetic

Special Courses

Decorating	)	
Pharmacy Assistants	)	Courses of various lengths of
Receptionists	)	study
Plus courses for local need)		

TECHNICAL AND SCIENTIFIC SECTOR

2 Year Lines	Basic Course	Options	
Clothing Manufacture	Terms 1-2	Terms 3-4	Women Clothing Men's Clothing
Foodstuffs	Term 1	Terms 2-4	Services
	Terms 1-2	Terms 3-4	Catering Restaurants Baking/Pastry Cook Butchery
Workshop Techniques	Terms 1-2	Terms 3-4	Mechanics Metal/Welding Heavy Plate Steel Mills
Motor Engineering	Terms 1-2	Terms 3-4	Motor Mechanics Mechanical Engineers Spare Parts Aircraft Mechanics
Woodwork	Terms 1-2	Terms 3-4	Joiners Pattern Makers Boat Builders
Building Construction	Terms 1-2	Terms 3-4	Concrete Joiners Bricklayers Streets/Roads Mining/Metallurgy
	Terms 1-4		Heating & Sanitary Fitters Painters Platers Floor Layers
Operational Engineering	Terms 1-2	Terms 3-4	Energy Technology Marine Engineering Power Production
Electro Tele- Communications	Term 1	Terms 2-4	Electricians Tele-comm. repair Regulating devices Fitters Office Machinery
Process Engineering	Terms 1-2	Terms 3-4	Chemistry Food Processing

TECHNICAL AND SCIENTIFIC SECTOR, Continued

			Paper/Pulp
			Metallurgy
			Building Materials

| Forestry | Terms 1-6 | (General Course) | |
| Agriculture | Terms 1-6 | (General Course) | |

2 Year Lines	Basic Courses	Options	
Technical	Terms 1-6		Mech. Engineering
			Building
			Electro-technical:
			Power
			Telecommunication
			Chemical

| 3 Year Lines | | | |
| Science | Terms 1-9 | (General Course) | |

4 Year Lines			
Technology	Terms 1-4	Terms 5-8	Mech. Engineering
			Building Construc-tion
			Housing
			Electro-technical:
			Power
			Telecommunication
			Chemical

Special Lines

Cartography	Terms 1-2
Furriers	Terms 1-6
Hairdressing	Terms 1-6

(plus courses for local need, of various length)

APPENDIX VIII

Higher Education: NATIONAL COURSES OF STUDY: AUTUMN TERM 1980

Line	Points 1 Yr=40	S	U	Li	Lu	G	Um
Agronomy	220	x					
Architecture	160	x		x	x		x x
Mining	160	x					
Biology	120	x x x			x		x x
Building Tech.	60	x					x
Computing	160		x				
Management	40						
Electrotechnology	160	x x		x x			x x
Fishery	80				x		x
Aeronautics	160	x					
Vehicle Technology	60	x					
Physics	120	x x x		x x			x x
Geotechnology	160						x
Geology	120	x x		x			x x
Horticulture	220	x		x			
Environmental Health	120						x
Industrial Economics	160			x			
Forestry	160	x					x x
Chemistry	120	x x x		x x			x x

Technology Sector

Line	Points 1 Yr=40	S	U	Li	Lu	G	Um
Chemico Technology	160	x				x	x
Landscape Architecture	220		x		x		
Surveying	160	x					
Food Technology	40/60	x x		x	x	x	x
Machine Technology	160	x x		x x	x	x	x
Mathematics	120			x			
Paper & Pulp Tech.	40					x	
Environmental Construct.	160	x				x	x
Marine Engineering	80	x x		x x	x	x	x
Seamanship	80	x					
Factory Industry Tech.	60					x	
Forestry Commission	60	x		x	x	x	x
Steel Industry Tech.	60			x	x		
Forestry Technology	60	x x		x x	x	x	x
Timber Technology	60	x		x			
Physics Technology	160	x x			x		
Physics Electrotech.	160					x	
Garden Architecture	40	x			x		
Roads and Water	160	x x x		x x	x	x	x

*Regions: Stockholm   Lund
           Uppsala   Göteborg
           Linköping   Umeå

Administration, Accounting & Personnel Sector

Line	Points 1 Yr=40	S	U	Li	Lu	G	Um
Electronic Data Process	40/60	x	x	x	x	x	x
Behavioural Science	120	x	x	x	x	x	
Economics	120	x	x	x	x	x	
International Economics	140		x	x	x	x	
Consumer Economics	100				x	x	
Administration	140/150	x	x	x	x	x	
Public Administration	140	x	x	x	x	x	
Psychology	120	x	x				
Accountancy	80	x	x	x	x	x	
Social Planning	140	x		x		x	
Social Science	120		x		x	x	
Social Service	140/150	x		x	x	x	
Systems Analysis	120	x	x	x	x	x	
Transport Administration	80	x	x				x
Advanced Guidance Couns.	20	x			x		

Care Services Sector

Line	Points 1 Yr=40	S	U	Li	Lu	G	Um
Pharmacy	160		x				
Work Therapy	80/120		x			x	x
Hearing Aid Asst.	80	x		x		x	x
Lab. Tech. (5 lines)	100	x					
Speech Therapy	120	x		x			
Medicine	220	x	x	x		x	x
Medicine for nurses	180	x					
Radiotherapy	100	x				x	
Radiology	100	x		x	x	x	x
Opthalmic Assistant	80		x	x			
Operating Assistant	100		x		x	x	x
Receptionist	100		x				
Physiotherapy	100	x	x		x	x	x
Nursing	63/105	x	x	x	x	x	x
Social Work	60/100	x	x	x	x	x	x
Dental Hygienist	40	x	x	x	x	x	x
Dentistry	200	x	x		x	x	x
Veterinary Science	200	x					
Advanced Courses							
Blood Grouping	3 x 2	x		x		x	x
Clinical Cytology	24	x	x			x	x
Orthopaedics	40	x					
Psycho-Therapy	30/60	x					x
Advanced Nursing	10 - 15	x		x		x	x
Toxology	60	x					

*Regions: Stockholm
             Uppsala
             Linköping
             Lund
             Göteborg
             Umeå

Education Sector

Line	Points 1 Yr=40	S	U	Li	Lu	G	Um
Child Care	120	x				x	x
Folk High School	40			x			
Leisure Teacher	50-100	x	x	x	x	x	x
Pre-School Teacher	50-100	x	x	x	x	x	x
Gymnastics-1 subject	80	x	x				
-2/3 subjects	160				x	x	x
Commercial Studies	40	x			x	x	x
Home Econ.-1subject	120	x				x	x
-2/3 subjects	160						x
Industrial Crafts	40	x			x	x	x
7-10 Class Teacher	100	x		x	x	x	x
10-13 Class Teacher	120	x	x	x	x	x	x
Music-1 subject	160	x	x		x	x	x
-2 subjects	160-180			x	x		
Craft-1 subject	40			x	x		
-2 subjects	160			x	x		
Study & Voc. Guidance	60/120	x			x		x
Art	120	x					x
Textiles-1 subject	120		x			x	x
-2 subjects	160						x
Care Services	60	x		x	x	x	x
Subjects-Hist./Civics Gp.	160	x		x	x	x	x
-Maths/Nat.Sc.Gp.	160	x		x	x	x	x
-Languages Group	160	x		x	x	x	x
Advanced Courses							
Agric./Forestry/Gardening	20		x				
Ped/Meth for Pre/Leisure	20	x			x		
Special Educ. (3 lines)	20/100	x	x	x	x	x	x

Cultural and Information Sector

Line	Points 1 Yr=40	S	U	Li	Lu	G	Um
Media Studies	40	x					
Librarianship	80		x				
Dance	120	x				x	
Design	160					x	
Free Art	200	x				x	
Graphics	40/80	x				x	
Pottery/Prints Arts	80	x				x	
Journalism	80	x				x	x
Cultural Communication	160	x	x	x	x	x	x
Church Music	120	x			x		
Film/TV/Radio/Theatre	160	x				x	
Musical Drama	80	x			x	x	
Music	120	x			x		x
-2 subjects	80/160						
Advertising	60		x			x	
Religious Studies	140		x			x	
Drama	120	x				x	
Interpreter	120	x				x	x
Advanced Courses							
Architecture	40	x	x				
Practical Theology	20					x	

*Regions: Stockholm — S
Uppsala — U
Linköping — Li
Lund — Lu
Göteborg — G
Umeå — Um

LOCAL COURSES OF STUDY: AUTUMN TERM 1980

Technology Sector

Line	Points 1 Yr=40	S	U	Li	Lu	G	Um
Biology/Geology	120	x					
Computing	80						x
Energy Economics	120			x			
Chemical Economics	140			x			
Materials	80			x			
Environmental Ecology	100				x		
Natural Resources	60/80						x
Process Programming	80						x
Production Economics	80		x				
Safety Engineering	60/80			x			
Control Engineering	80		x				
Textile Engineering	80				x		
Timber Technology	80/100						x
Development Engineering	100			x			

Administrative Sector

Line	Points 1 Yr=40	S	U	Li	Lu	G	Um
Languages for Admin.	60	x					
Economics and Accounts	80						x
Company & Admin. Law	160						x
Health Administration	60		x				
International Soc. Serv.	120	x					
Marketing	80		x				
Maths-Economics	120				x		
Personnel Admin.	80		x				
Educational Admin.	80		x				
Auditing	60				x		
Small Industry Econ.	40/80			x			
Small Industry Tech.	80				x		
Social Leadership	120				x		
Transport & Traffic	120		x				
Tourism	80		x				
Tourism & Recreation	80					x	
Tourism	80						x

Cultural Sector

Line	Points 1 Yr=40	S	U	Li	Lu	G	Um
Ancient Buildings	120			x			
Information	60/100	x	x				
Cultural Work	40/120	x					
Language Consultant	80		x				
Values & Life Orientation	140			x			

*Regions: Stockholm
         Uppsala
         Linköping
         Lund
         Göteborg
         Umeå

APPENDIX IX

Categories of Teachers

Teachers in *Grundskolan*

1. Class Teacher, *Lågstadiet*
2. Class Teacher, *Mellanstadiet*
3. Special Education, Grades 1-6
4. Special Education, Grades 4-9
5. Gymnastics
6. Music
7. Drawing (*Bild*)
8. Wood and Metal Crafts
9. Textile Crafts
10. Home Economics
11. Child Care
12. Drawing with Wood and Metal Crafts
13. Drawing with Textile Crafts
14. Home Economics with Wood and Metal Crafts
15. Home Economics with Textile Crafts

16-18. Two or three of the following at *Hogstadiet*:- Swedish, Mathematics, English, French, RK, Civics, History, Geography, Biology, Chemistry, Physics (plus Finnish, but only as non-established)

19. At *Högstadiet* (Grades 7-9) Mathematics and Technology, with Physics or Chemistry

20. Typing – non-established post only

21. Two of Gymnastics, Music, Drawing, Wood and Metal Craft, Textile Craft, Home Economics and Child Care in combinations other than in cateogries 12-15 – non-established post only

Gymnasieskolan

101. Women's Clothing
102. Men's Clothing
103. Stone Technology
104. Cement Technology
105. Building panel beater
106. Building carpentry
107. Road construction
108. Flooring
109. Plasterer
110. Painter
111. Heating installation
112. Electrician

113. Office machinery
114. Control machinery
115. TV installation
116. TV repair
117. Car machanics
118. Aircraft technician
119. Machine Tools
120. Stores
121. Baking
122. Butchery
123. Restaurant
124. Waiters

125. Caterer
126. Building Technology
127. Chemical Technology
128. Food Technology
129. Metallurgy
130. Pulp Technology
131. Boat Building
132. Model maker
133. Factory carpenter
134. Iron trades
135. Welding
136. Workshop mechanic
137. One or more of: typing, office skills, secretarial work
138. At least one of distributive trades with consumer marketing
139. One or more of plant care and agricultural machinery
140. As 139 with Farm Economics
141. Ecology and Production
142. Textiles: Sewing
143. Textiles: Weaving
144. Textiles: Sewing and weaving
145. Care Services
146. At least one of child care and youth care
147-8. One or more of machinery, forestry, surveying, nature care
149. Gymnastics
150. Music
151. Drawing
152. For 3-4 Year lines, one, two or three of: Swedish, English, German, French, Linguistics, Latin, History, RK, Philosophy, Psychology, Civics, Social Welfare, Mathematics, Biology, Natural Science and,

where appropriate, Finnish, Spanish, Portuguese, Italian, Russian, Greek
153. As 152, for other lines
154. For 3-4 Year lines, one or two of Business Economics, distribution, accountancy, administration, law
155. As 154 for other lines
156-7. For 4 Year line, one or two of technology, energy, production, regulatory technology, electronics, building technology, construction, town planning, installation, etc.
158. At least one of 152 with at least one of 154
159. At least one of 153 with at least one of 155
160. At least one of 152 with at least one of 156
161. At least one of 153 with at least one of 157

Non-established posts are also available in:
162. Industry and handicrafts
163. Agriculture, forestry and horticulture
164. Care Services
165. Domestic Services
166. Office and Shop trades
167-9. Two or three of Swedish, English, German, French, History, RK, Civics, Mathematics, Chemistry, Biology
170. Two or more of Mathematics, Physics, Chemistry, Technology, Building Technology, with professional theory in subjects 101-136

171. Business Economics and Economics for 2 Year line
172. Professional theory in subjects 101-136
173. One or more of typing, office skills, practical secretarial skills
174. Subjects with Pharmaceutical studies
175. Subjects in 2 Year Consumers Line
176. Wood and Metal Craft
177. Two of Gymnastics, Music, Drawing, Wood and Metal Craft, Textile Craft, Home Economics, Child Care
178. Work Therapy
179. Leisure Organisers
180. Computing
181. Physiotherapy

APPENDIX X

Glossary of Swedish Terms

Notes:

a)   The vowels *å*, *ä*, and *ö* are placed, as in Swedish, in that order at the end of any alphabetical list.

b)   Swedish has two genders, common and neuter. The difference is clear when a noun is used with the indefinite article, which is a separate word placed before the noun - e.g. common: *en klass* (a class);   neuter: *ett hus* (a house).

c)   The definite article is a suffix to the noun - e.g. in singular common: *klassen* (the class);   neuter: *huset* (the house). Nouns ending in a vowel add *-n* or *-t* as appropriate.

d)   Nouns are classified into five declensions, differentiated largely by the ways in which the indefinite and definite plurals are formed. The rules are complex and there are several exceptions. The basic constructions are as follows:

Declension	e.g. (a ——)	(the ——)	(——s)	(the ——s)
		Singular	**Plural**	
1st	*en* ——	—— *n*	—— *or*	—— *orna*
2nd	*en* ——	—— *n*	—— *ar*	—— *arna*
		—— *en*		
3rd	*en* ——	—— *n*	—— *er*	—— *erna*
		—— *en*		
	ett ——	—— *et*		
4th	*ett* ——	—— *t*	—— *en*	—— *na*
5th	*en* ——	—— *n*	——	—— *na*
		—— *en*		—— *en*
	ett ——	—— *et*		

Unstressed or weakly stressed final vowels are dropped in forming plurals (*en fröken - två fröknar*).

Foreign words ending in -ium in the indefinite singular drop the 'um' in forming the definite singular and all plurals (*gymnasium - gymnasiet, gymnasier, gymnasierna*).

e)   Except for proper nouns, all nouns listed in the glossary below are given with their root spelling, followed in brackets by the appropriate endings for the definite singular and for both plural endings.

SCHOOLS AND COLLEGES

Brevskolan   the correspondence school run by the cooperative movement.

Enhetsskola (*-n, -or, -orna*) unity school. (The term used in the 1960's for the emerging common school for 7-16's).

Experiment Gymnasiet, EG the experimental upper secondary school in Göteborg 1969-73.

Fackskola (*-n, -or, -orna*) continuation school, set up in 1964 and incorporated in the integrated upper secondary school in 1971.

Flickskola (*-n, -or, -orna*) girls school, incorporated in the basic school in 1962.

Folkhögskola (*-n, -or, -orna*) folk high school, the adult education college originating in Denmark in 1844.

Folkskoleseminarium (-(~~ium~~)*et, -*(~~ium~~)*er, -*(~~ium~~)*erna*) elementary teachers training college (until 1967).

Förskola (*-n, -or, -orna*) pre-school, either nursery or kindergarten.

Grundskola (*-n, -or, -orna*) basic school, since 1962, for 7-16's; it is a generic term to describe the school-form covering the whole age-range.

Gymnasieskola (*-n, -or, -orna*) integrated upper secondary school, with courses of up to four years' duration following class 9 of the basic school.

Gymnasium (-(~~ium~~)*et, -*(~~ium~~)*er, -*(~~ium~~)*erna*) academic upper secondary school, until 1971.

Gymnastik-och Idrottshögskola, GIH the university college for the study of physical education; it has one centre in Stockholm and a newer one in Örebro.

Handelshögskola (*-n, -or, -orna*) university college for commercial and economic studies.

Hermods   the oldest correspondence college in Sweden, founded 1898.

Högskola (*-n, -or, -orna*) university college.

Högstadium (*-(um)et, -(um)er, -(um)erna*) 13-16 stage of the basic school.

Konstfack   the university college for art in Stockholm.

Lågstadium (*-(um)et, -(um)er, -(um)erna*) 7-10 stage of the basic school.

Läroverk (*-et, ——, -en*) academic secondary school until 1962.

Mellanstadium (*-(um)et, -(um)er, -(um)erna*) 10-13 stage of the basic school.

Realskola (*-n, -or, -orna*) academic lower secondary school until 1962.

Seminarium (*-(um)et, -(um)er, -(um)erna*) training college.

Skolenhet (*-en, -er, -erna*) school unit comprising one or more stages of the basic school or one or more sectors of the upper secondary school.

Småskola (*-n, -or, -orna*) 7-9 stage of the elementary school until 1962.

Trivialskola (*-n, -or, -orna*) pre-19th century lower academic school, teaching the medieval "trivium".

Vuxenskola (*-n, -or, -orna*) school for adults.

Yrkesskola (*-n, -or, -orna*) trade school, incorporated into the upper secondary school in 1971.

TITLES OF SCHOOL AND COLLEGE STAFF

Adjunkt (*-en, -er, -erna*) teacher of 2-3 academic subjects from age 13; traditionally with *fil.mag.* (MA) degree.

Extra   temporary full-time appointment.

Extra ordinarie permanent non-established appointment.

Folkskollärare (*-n, ——, -(ø)na*) elementary school teacher.

Fritidslärare (*-n, ——. -(ø)na*) teacher for leisure activities.

Förskollärare (*-n, ——, -(ø)na*) pre-school teacher.

Huvudlärare (*-n, ——, -(ø)na*) head of department.

Inspektör (*-en, -er, -erna*) inspector.

Konsulent (*-en, -er, -erna*) consultant, adviser.

Lektor (*-n, -er, -erna*) senior teacher of one academic subject in the upper secondary school, normally with a higher degree.

Lågstadielärare (*-n, ——, -(ø)na*) teacher of 7-10's in the basic school.

Ordinarie   permanent established appointment.

Prefekt   academic head of a unit in a university/college (e.g. a major department; analagous to dean of a faculty).

Rektor (*-n, -er, -erna*) head of a school unit (*enhet*) or head
         of a university/college.
Skoldirektör (*-en, -er, -erna*) Director of Education in a local
         authority (*kommun*).
Småskollärare (*-n, ——, -(ø)na*) teacher of 7-9's in the pre-
         1962 elementary school.
Studierektor (*-n, -er, -erna*) director of studies in a school or
         unit of higher education.
Syokonsulent (*-en, -er, -erna*) consultant for study and work
         guidance.
Tillsynslärare (*-n, ——. -(ø)na*) teacher responsible for equip-
         ment and maintenance.
Timlärare (*-n, ——, -(ø)na*) teacher appointed for part-time work
         by the hour.
Yrkeslärare (*-n, ——, -(ø)na*) teacher of trade subjects.
Ämneslärare (*-n, ——, -(ø)na*) teacher of academic subjects from
         age 13, requiring one year (40 points) of higher
         education in each subject.

TECHNICAL TERMS

Aktuellt   current news; the official circular notifying
                 new regulations.
Avdrag   deduction of salary (in 3 categories, known as A,
                 B and C depending on circumstances).
Behörig   qualified.
Bestämmelser (*-n, ——, -erna*) official instruction.
Betyg (*-et, ——, -en*) mark or grade.
Bidrag (*-et, ——, -en*) grant in aid.
Fortbildning   in-service training for continued education rather
                 than for furthering formal qualifications.
Förordning   official decree.
Kollegium (*-(um)et, -(um)er, -(um)erna*) staff meeting.
Kungl. brev   letter in the name of the Crown, i.e. H.M.
                 Government.
Lag   Law.
Läroplan (*-en, -er, -erna*) official curriculum (i.e. Lgr 62,
                 Lgr 69, Lgr 80).
Mål (*-et, ——, -en*) goal, aim.
Protokoll (*-et, ——, -en*) minutes, proceedings.
Råd (*-et, ——, -en*) advisory body.
Remiss   review, official response, to an official com-
                 mittee of enquiry.
Riktlinjer   guidelines.
Skrivning (*-en, -ar, -arna*) written test.
Stadga (*-n, -at, -arna*) regulations.

Sakkunniga   body of experts.
SOU   *Statens Offentliga Utredning*, a "Royal
                  Commission" report listed by year of publica-
                  tion and number (e.g. SOU 1944:20 - the report
                  of the 1940 school committee).
SFS   *Svensk Författingssamling*, the official
                  codification of laws and decrees, listed by year
                  and number (e.g. SFS 1962:319 - the 1962 School
                  Law).
Studiebidrag (*-et*, ——, *-en*) study grant.
Studielan (*-et*, ——, *-en*) study loan.
Tenta   formal test at university/college.
Tätort   built up area of 200 inhabitants.
UFB   *Utbildnings Författningsbok*, the annual hand-
                  book of educational laws, decrees, regulations
                  and instructions.
Utredning (*-en*, *-ar*, *-arna*) enquiry.
Vidareutbildning further education, leading to a formal
                  qualification.

PUBLIC OFFICES AND ORGANISATIONS

Arbetmarknadsstyrelsen, *AMS* The Labour Market Board.
Bibliotek   Library.
Bondeförbundet The Farmers' Party (until 1970's).
Centerpartiet The Center Party, successor to the Farmers' Party.
Folkbildningsförbundet   The Adult Education Association.
Ecklesiastikdepartmentet The Ministry of (Education and) Church
                  Affairs, until 1958.
Finansdepartmentet The Ministry of Finance.
Folkpartiet   The Liberal Party (literally "People's Party").
Högern   The Conservative Party until 1970's (literally
                  "Right Party").
Justiciedepartmentet The Ministry of Justice.
Kommun   Local Authority (literally "commune",
                  municipality).
Kungl. Maj:t   The Crown, i.e. H.M. Government.
Köping   Market town; now used as a suffix to the name
                  of some towns (e.g. Jönköping). There is a
                  town called Köping.
Landsorganisationen, *LO* The coordinating organisation for the
                  manual and skilled trades unions.
Landsting   County Council.
Län   County.
Länsskolnämnd   County School Board.

Lärarnas Riksförbund, LR Academic subject teachers association.
Medbestämmandelagen, MBL The law on joint participation in
    working life.
Moderaterna   The Conservative Party, successor to *Högern*;
    (literally "the Moderates").
Pastorsämbetet The Parish Office, used as the official Registry
    of births, marriages and deaths, and of the
    annual census.
Riksdag   Parliament.
Skolöverstyrelsen, SÖ The National Board of Education, NBE.
Statsråd   Minister of the Crown.
Sveriges Akademikers Centralorganisation, SACO The composite
    union of those whose employment requires a
    degree qualification (class teachers belong to
    TCO – see below).
Sveriges Elevers Centralorganisation, SECO The composite
    union for school pupils, founded 1952.
Sveriges Lärarförbund, SL Class teachers association.
Skolstyrelse School Board in a Local Authority.
Socialstyrelsen The National Board of Social Welfare.
Tjänstemännens Centralorganisation, TCO The composite union for
    salaried employees.
Universitets- och Högskoleämbetet, UHÄ The Office of Universi-
    ties and Colleges.
Utbildningsdepartmentet The Ministry of Education.
Utrikesdepartmentet The Ministry of Foreign Affairs.
Vänsterpartiet Kommunisterna, VPK The Communist Party (literally
    the "Communists of the party of the left; there
    are two other, progressively more left wing,
    communist parties).

Bibliography

The bibliography is arranged as follows:

A. Material in Swedish

    1. *Statens Offentliga Utredningar, SOU* (State Official Enquiries; all published by Government Printing House)

    2. *Lag och Forördningar: Statens Författningssamling, SFS* (Laws and Decrees, State Administrative Collection)

    3. *Riksdagen* (Parliamentary papers)

    4. *Utbildningsdepartmentet* (Ministry of Education)

    5. *Skolöverstyrelsen* (National Board of Education)

    6. *Universitetskansli ämbetet/Universitets- och Högskoleämbetet, UKÄ/UHÄ* (Office of University Chancery/ Office of Universities and Colleges)

    7. *Statistiska Centralbyrån, SCB* (Central Statistics Office)

    8. Journals and Newspapers

    9. Books and Articles

B. Material in English

    1. Books and large pamphlets

    2. Articles and small pamphlets

@@@@@@@@

A. MATERIAL IN SWEDISH

1. *STATENS OFFENTLIGA UTREDNINGAR, SOU*

SOU 1944:20   *Skolan i samhällets tjänst: frågeställningar och problemläge* (School in the service of society: questions and problems; 1940 School Committee)

247

SOU 1944:21   *Sambandet mellan folkskola och högre skola* (The
               connection between the elementary school and the
               higher school;   1940 School Committee)

SOU 1945:60   *Skolpliktstidens skolformer* (The length of com-
               pulsory schooling in different types of school;
               1940 School Committee)

SOU 1946:31   *Skolans inre arbete* (The inner workings of the
               school;   1940 School Committee)

SOU 1948:27   *Betänkande med förslag till riktlinjer för det
               Svenska skolväsendets utveckling* (Report with
               proposals for guidelines for the development of
               the Swedish school system;   1946 School
               Commission)

SOU 1952:33   *Den första lärarhögskolan* (The first teacher
               high school;   1946 School Commission)

SOU 1958:11   Härnqvist, K (1958) *Beräkning av reserver för
               högre utbildning* (Calculations of reserves for
               higher education)

SOU 1959:35   Orring, J (1959) *Flyttning, kvarsittning och
               utkuggning: högre skolor i relation till folk-
               skolans betygsättning* (Promotion, grade repeat-
               ing and drop-outs in higher schools in relation
               to school grades in the elementary school)

SOU 1960:13   Härnqvist, K (1960) *Individuella differenser och
               skoldifferentiering* (Individual differences and
               school differentiation)

SOU 1960:15   Dahllöf, U (1960) *Kursplansundersökningar i
               matematik och modersmålet* (Syllabus studies in
               Mathematics and Mother Tongue)

SOU 1960:42   Johannesson, I (1960) *Differentiering och social
               utveckling: social psykologiska aspekter på
               skolans differentieringsproblem* (Differentiation
               and social development: social psychological
               aspects of differentiation in school)

SOU 1961:30   *Grundskolan. Betänkande angivit av 1957 års
               skolberedning* (The Basic School. Report on the
               1957 School Preparatory Committee)

SOU 1963: 5   Härnqvist, K and Grahm, Å (1966) *Vägen genom
               gymnasiet: elevernas syn på valsituationer och
               skolformer* (Ways through the upper secondary
               school: pupils' views of choice possibilities
               and modes of study)

SOU 1963:22   Dahll f, U (1963) *Kraven på gymnasiet. Under-
               sökningar vid universitet och högskolor, för-
               valtning och näringsliv* (Demands on the upper
               secondary school. Enquiries at university,

college, administration and commerce.

SOU 1963:42   *Ett nytt gymnasium* (A new upper secondary school; 1960 Upper Secondary School Enquiry)

SOU 1963:50   *Fackskolan* (Continuation school)

SOU 1964:44   *Skolans försörjning med lärare* (The supply of teachers for schools)

SOU 1965:25   *Studieplaner för lärarutbildning* (Courses of study for teacher education)

SOU 1965:29   *Lärarutbildning: Huvudbetänkandet* (Teacher education: Main Report)

SOU 1965:30   *Lärarutbildning: tekniska beräkningar till huvudbebetänkandet* (Teacher education: technical calculations for the main report)

SOU 1965:31   *Specialundersökningar om lärarutbildning* (Special enquiries on teacher education)

SOU 1966: 3   *1963 års Yrkesutbildningsberedningen* (1963 Trade Training Enquiry)

SOU 1971:61   Bengtsson, J and Gesser, B (1971) *Val av utbildning och yrke* (Choice of education and work)

SOU 1972:26   *Förskolan* (Pre-school)

SOU 1973: 2   *Högskolan: betänkande av 1968 års utbildningsberedningen* (Higher Education: Report of the 1968 Educational Enquiry)

SOU 1973:42   *Utbildning av lärarutbildare* (Education of teacher educators)

SOU 1974:53   *Skolans inre arbete* (The inner workings of the school)

SOU 1975: 1   *Demokrati på arbetsplats* (Democracy at places of work)

SOU 1975:90   *Arbete åt alla* (Work for all; 1974 Employment Enquiry)

SOU 1976:16   *Folkhögskolan 1: Folkhögskoleutredningen* (Folk High School 1: the Folk High School Enquiry)

SOU 1977: 2   *Folkhögskolan 2* (Folk High School 2)

SOU 1977: 9   *Betygsutrednings betänkande: Betyg i Skolan* (Report of the School Marks Enquiry, BU73: Marks in school)

SOU 1977:38   *Folkbildningen i framtiden* (Adult education in the future)

SOU 1977:53   *Sektorsanknutenforskning och utveckling: Expertbilaga 1* (Research and development related to sectors: Expert appendix 1)

SOU 1977:54   *Information om pågående forskning: Expertbilaga 2* (Information on current research: Expert appendix 2)

SOU 1977:55   *Forskning i kontakt med samhället: Expertbilaga 3* (Research in contact with society. Expert appendix 3)

SOU 1978:44   *Arbete åt handikappade* (Work for the handicapped; 1974 Employment Enquiry)

SOU 1978:62   *Regional-politisk stödformer och styrmedel* (Regional-political forms of aid and control; 1974 Employment Enquiry)

SOU 1978:86   *Lärare för en skola i utveckling* (Teachers for a school in transition; 1974 Teacher Education Enquiry)

SOU 1979:24   *Sysselsättningspolitik för arbete åt alla* (The politics of employment for all; 1974 Employment Enquiry)

SOU 1979:85   *Folkbildning för 80-talet* (Adult education for the 1980's)

2. *LAG OCH FÖRORDNINGAR; STATENS FÖRFATTNINGSSAMLING, SFS*
    (The basic laws and decrees, with subsequent amendments)

Laws
SFS 1960:97   *Samhällets vård av barn och ungdom* (Law on society's care of children and youth)
SFS 1962:319   *Skollag* (School Law)
SFS 1973:1205   *Förskoleverksamhet* (Law on pre-school activity)
SFS 1976:580   *Medbestämmande i arbetslivet* (Law on joint participation in working life)
SFS 1976:600   *Offentlig anställning* (Law on official appointments)

Decrees
SFS 1949:381   *Föräldrarbalk* (Decree on parental duties)
SFS 1958:478   *Folkhögskoleförordning* (Decree on Folk High Schools)
SFS 1965:478   *Specialskolförordning* (Decree on special schools)
SFS 1967:216   *Nomadsskolförordning* (Decree on schooling for nomads)
SFS 1967:270   *Privatskolförordning* (Decree on private schooling)
SFS 1971:235   *Skolförordning* (Decree on schools)
SFS 1971:273   *Tryckfrihetsförordning* (Decree on freedom of publication)
SFS 1976:863   *Anställningsförordning* (Decree on appointments)

3. *RIKSDAGEN*

Propositions

Prop. 1950:70   *Riktlinjer för den svenska skolväsendets utveckling* (Guidelines for the development of the Swedish school system)

Prop. 1957:106   *Grundskolan* (The Basic School)

Prop. 1967:4   *Lärarutbildning* (Teacher education)

Prop. 1975/6:39   *Skolans inre arbete, SIA* (The inner workings of school, SIA)

Prop. 1975/6:105 *Arbetsrättsreform* (Reform of employment law)

Prop. 1976/7:59   *Utbildning och forskning inom högskolan m.m.* (Education and research in higher education etc.)

Prop. 1978/9:80   *Läroplan för grundskolan* (Syllabus for the basic school)

Committee Reports

SäU   1950:1   *Särskilt utskottets utlåtande* (Special committee's report; on Unity School Act, 1950)

SU   1956:102   *Särskilt utskott* (Special committee; on interpretation of the 1950 Unity School Act)

IU   1975/6:45   *Inrikesutskottets betänkande*; *arbetsreform* (Home Affairs Committee report: reform of employment law)

4. *UTBILDNINGSDEPARTMENTET*

Marklund, S (1961)   *Skolreformen och Lärarutbildningen* (School Reform and Teacher Education; 1957 School Preparatory Committee)

Dr U   (1977:20) *Medinflytande i skolan. Förslag med anledning av Riksdagens beslut om skolans inre arbete m.m.* (Joint participation in school. Proposals following the parliamentary decision on the inner workings of school, etc.)

Utbildningsdepartment (1979) *Skolan skall fostra: en debattskrift. Arbetsgrupp kring normbildning och normöverföring i skolan* (The school is to educate: a paper for discussion. Working Party on the formation and transmission of norms in school.)

Rådmark, J (1980)   *Hur ska vi har det? Ett arbetsmaterial för på högstadiet och i gymnasieskolan. Arbetsgrupp kring normbildning och normöverföring* i skolan (How do we want it to be? Working papers for pupils at the senior stage and the upper secondary school. Working Party on the formation and transmission of norms in school)

Utbildningsdepartmentet (1977) *Lärarutbildnings specialiserings-grad* (The degree of specialisation in teacher education; study made for LUT Teacher Education Enquiry)

5. *SKOLÖVERSTYRELSEN*

(1959)   *Försöksverksamhet med nioårig enhetsskolan. Sammanfattande redgörelse för läsåren 1949/50-1958/59.* (Experiments with the nine year unity school. Summary for the academic years 1949/50-1958/59)

(1962)   *Läroplan för Grundskolan, Lgr 62* (Syllabus for the Basic School, Lgr 62), Skriftserie 60.

(1965)   *Läroplan för Gymnasiet, Lgr 65* (Syllabus for the Academic Upper Secondary School, Lgr 65), Skriftserie 80

(1967)   *Läroplans översyn: Grundskolan* (Syllabus review: Basic School)

(1968a) *Klasslärarutbildning: studieplaner m.m.* (Class teacher training: courses of study etc.)

(1968b) *Ämneslärarutbildning: studieplaner m.m.* (Subject teacher training: courses of study etc.)

(1969)   *Läroplan för Grundskolan, Lgr 69: Allmän del* (Syllabus for the Basic School, Lgr 69: General Part)

(1970)   *Läroplan för Gymnasieskolan, Lgr 70* (Syllabus for the Upper Secondary School, Lgr 70)

(1971a) *Utbildningsplan för klasslärarlinjer vid lärar-högskolor* (Curriculum for class teacher lines of study at Teacher High Schools; revised 1974)

(1971b) *Utbildningsplan för ämneslärarlinjer vid lärar-högskolor* (Curriculum for subject teacher lines of study at Teacher High Schools; revised 1975)

(1975)   *PLUS:1; PLUS:11* (Plan for the training of school leaders)

(1976/7) *Vi och vår skola: översikt; skoldagen; skola-arbetsliv; elever och fritiden; arbetssätt och arbetsformer; friare resursanvändning* (We and our school; the school day; school and working life; pupils and leisure; ways of working; freer use

of resources)   six pamphlets on the SIA decision.
(1978a)   *Förslag till förändring av grundskolans läroplan*
(Proposals for the revision of the syllabus of
the basic school)

(1978b)   *Svensk Utbildningsforskning 1977/78* (Swedish
educational research 1977/78)

(1980a)   *Läroplan för Grundskolan, Lgr 80: Allmänn del*
(Syllabus for the Basic School, Lgr 80:   General
Part)

(1980b)   Börjesson, B (1980) *Gymnasieskolans dimensionering
1980-85:   central och regional planering* (The
scale of upper secondary school provision 1980-
85:   central and regional planning), Pl 80:5, Dnr
P80:945, 10th April.

(1980c)   *Högskoleprovet 1980:   orientering och exempel*
(Scholastic Aptitude Test for Higher Education:
orientation and example)

(Annual) *Petita* (annual estimates)

(Annual) *Att välja studieväg* (To select the course of
study: for entry to upper secondary school)

6. *UKÄ/UHÄ*

UKA   (1975:4)   *Utbildningsplanering för förnyelse.   Problem och
grundprinciper* (Educational planning for renewal.
Problems and basic principles)

UKA   (1975:20) *Utbildningsplanering för förnyelse.   Regional och
central nivå* (Educational planning for renewal.
Regional and central level).

UHA   (1975/6:2) *Direktiv till organisationskommittée m.m.   för
högskolereformen* (Directive to the organisation
committee for the reform of higher education)

UHA   (1977a)   *Reform information* (Information on reform)

UHA   (1977b)   *Ledamot av högskoleorgan* (Membership of boards
of Higher Education)

UHA   (1977c)   *Högskolans organisation* (The organisation of
higher education)

UHA   (1979a)   *Siffror från CA HT 1979* (Numbers from the Central
Admissions Office, Autumn Term, 1979), *Byrå för
Centralantagning*

UHA   (1979b)   Kim, L (1979) *Två års erfarenheter av de nya
tillträdesreglarna till högskoleutbildning* (Two
year's experience of the new entry rules to
higher education)

UHA   (Annual) *Högskolan* (Higher Education)

UHA   (Termly)   *Anvisningar för anmälan till högskolan,*
                höstterminen/vårterminen (Instructions for
                applications to higher education, autumn term/
                spring term)

UHA   (Annual)   *Att studera i Sverige - högskoleutbildning för
                invandrare och politiska flyktningar* (To study
                in Sweden - higher education for immigrants and
                political refugees)

UHA   (Annual)   *Utbildning för tekniska yrken: översikt -
                allmänna utbildningslinje - arbetsmarknad* (Educa-
                tion for technical work - summary - general lines
                of study - the labour market)

UHA   (Annual)   *Utbildning för administrativa, ekonomiska och
                sociala yrken:* ... (Education for administrative,
                economic and social work:...)

UHA   (Annual)   *Utbildning för vårdyrken:*... (Education for work
                in the Care Services:...)

UHA   (Annual)   *Utbildning för undervisningsyrken:*... (Education
                for teaching:...)

UHA   (Annual)   *Utbildning för kultur och informations yrken:*...
                (Education for cultural and information service
                work:...)

7. *STATISTISKA CENTRALBYRÅN, SCB*

SCB   (1960)   *Historisk Statistik för Sverige* (Historical
               Statistics for Sweden)

SCB   (1974)   *Obligatoriska Skolor 1847-1962* (Compulsory
               Schools 1847-1962), Promemoria Nr 1974:5

SCB   (1976)   *Högskolestatistik 11: Social bakgrund för
               studerande vid universitet och högskolor 1962/3 -
               1972/3* (Higher Education Statistics 11: Social
               background of students at universities and
               colleges 1962/3 - 1972/3), Promemoria 1976:5

SCB   (Annual)   *Meddelanden - klasser och elever* (Communications -
               classes and pupils)

SCB   (Annual)   *Meddelanden - lärare* (Communications - teachers)
SCB   (Annual)   *Statistisk Årsbok för Sverige* (Statistical Year-
               book for Sweden)

8. JOURNALS AND NEWSPAPERS

Lärarnas Riksförbund   *Skolvärlden* (The World of the School:
                                circa 45 issues per year)
                                Årsbok (Annual)

Sveriges Lärarförbund	*Lärartidningen Svensk Skoltidning* (Teachers Journal Swedish School Journal: circa 45 issues per year) *Årsbok* (Annual)
Sveriges Facklärarförbund	*Årsbok* (Annual)
Göteborgs Posten	(Daily; liberal; Göteborg)
Dagans Nyheter	(Daily; liberal; Stockholm)
Stockholms Tidningen	(Daily; conservative; Stockholm)
Svenska Dagbladet	(Daily; conservative; Stockholm - with issue from Malmö, *Sydsvenska Dagbladet*)

9. BOOKS AND ARTICLES

Bengtsson, J and Lundgren, UP (1969) *Utbildningsplanering och jämförelser av skolsystem* (Educational Planning and Comparison of School Systems) Lund, Studentlitteratur.

Berg, F (1883) *Folkskolan som Bottenskola: ett inlägg i en viktig samhällsfråga* (The Elementary School as a Basic School: a contribution to an important social question), Stockholm, Allmänna Folkskollärar Förening.

Bergstrand, N-OG (1972) *Analys av Läroverkens Målsättning 1898–1927* (Analysis of the Goals of Grammar Schools 1898-1927) fil. lic. avhandling, University of Lund.

Boalt, G and Husén, T (1964) *Skolans Sociologi* (The Sociology of the School), Stockholm, Almqvist & Wiksell.

Bolander, H (n.d.) *Ur Brevskolans Historia* (From the History of Brevskolan), Stockholm, mimeo (published in 1960's)

Bromsjö, B (1961) *Kursplansundersökningar i samhällskunskap* (Curriculum Study in Civics) 1957 års skolbereding, stencil

Carlberg, T (1978) *En studie av Fortbildning i Lag* (a study of in-service training in teams) Department of Educational Research, University of Linköping

DAG (1979) *Undersök Själva* (Know Yourself), Stockholm, Rabén & Sjögren

Dahllöf, U (1971) *Svensk Utbildningsplanering under 25 år* (Swedish Educational Planning for 25 years), Lund, Student-litteratur

Danielsson, A (1891) *Främlingen: ett besök i det nya samhället* (The Stranger: a visit to the new society), Stockholm

Egidius, H (1969) *Den Svenska Skolreformen: betänkande och propositioner i urval* (The Swedish School Reform: selected recommendations and propositions) Pedagogiska Orientering och Debatt 26, Lund, Uniskol.

Egidius, H (1978a) *Pedagogiska Utvecklingslinjer* (Developmental Trends in Education), Pedagogiska Orientering och Debatt 8, Lund, Scandinavian University Books, 5th Edit.

Egidius, H (1978b) *Riktlinjer i Modern Pedagogik* (Guidelines in Modern Pedagogy), Stockholm Natur och Kultur.

Ekholm, Mats (1977) *Social Utveckling i Skolan:* studier och diskussion (Social Development in School: studies and discussion) Stockholm, AWE/Gebers.

Emmanuelsson, Ingemar (1977) *Utbildning för Anpassade:* skolan i långtidsperspektiv: analys och debatt (Education for the Adjusted: the school in long term perspective: analysis and debate) Stockholm, Rabén & Sjögren

Erasmie, Thord (1977) *Pedagogik för Besuttna* (Pedagogy for the Privileged), Stockholm, Rabén & Sjögren.

Erlander, T (1973) *Memoarer 1940-1949* (Memoirs 1940-49), Stockholm, Tiden.

Grundin, HU (1975) *Läs och Skrivförmågans Utveckling genom Skolaren* (The Development of Reading and Writing Skills throughout the years of schooling), Utbildningsforskning rapport 20, Stockholm, Liber.

Hedin, A (1883) *Om Latin-herraväldet:* (On the Dominance of Latin), Stockholm.

Husén, T (1977) *Jämlighet genom Utbildning?* Perspektiv på utbildningsreformerna (Education for Equality? Perspectives on the educational reforms), Stockholm, Natur & Kultur.

Husén, T et. al. (1973) *Svensk Skola i Internationell Belysning 1: Naturorienterande ämnen* (The Swedish School in International perspective 1: Natural Science subjects), Stockholm, Almqvist & Wiksell.

Husén, T and Carlson I (Eds.) (1964) *Det Nya Gymnasiet* (The New Upper Secondary Grammar School), Stockholm, Almqvist & Wiksell.

Huss-Moback-Hallgren (1977) *Fran Skolupprop till Skolupprör: Experimentgymnasiet i Göteborg 1969-75* (From Calling up the School to School Revolt: the experimental school in Göteborg 1969-75), Stockholm, Rabén & Sjögren.

Isling, Å (1973) *Samhällsutveckling och Bildningsideal* (The Development of Society and Educational Ideals), Pedagogiska Skrifter 252, Stockholm, Sveriges Lärarförbund.

Israel, J and Lindskog, B (1967) *Elevstyre på eldprov* (Pupil Government Tested in the Fire), Stockholm, Bonniers.

Johansson, E (1961) *Kursplansundersökning i fysik och kemi* (Curriculum Studies in Physics and Chemistry)

Jägerskiold, S (1959) *Från Prästskolan till Enhetsskolan* (From Church School to Unity School), Stockholm, Almqvist & Wiksell.

Lander, R (1978) *Profeter i Egen Skola* (Prophets in your own schol) Report No.168, Institute of Education, University of Göteborg.

Landqvist, J (1946) *Pedagogikens Historia* (The History of Education), Lund, Gleerups.
Lund, A (1975) *Utvärdering av syo-funktion:* (Evaluation of the study and work guidance function), Umeå, Informations Psykologi AB.
Marklund, S (1961) see *Utbildningdepartment* list.
Marklund, S (1968) *Lärarlämplighet* (Teacher suitability), Stockholm, Liber.
Marklund, S (1970) *Vår Nya Skola* (Our New School), Stockholm, Bonniers.
Marklund, S and Paulston, R G (197), *Grundskolans Förhistoria* (The pre-history of the Basic School), Historielärarnasförenings Årskrift 1969/70.
Moberg, V (1949) *Utvandrarna* (The Emigrants), Stockholm.
Moberg, V (1952) *Invandrarna* (The Immigrants), Stockholm.
Moberg, V (1956) *Nybyggarna* (The Settlers), Stockholm.
Moberg, V (1959) *Sista Brev till Sverige* (The Last Letter to Sweden), Stockholm.
Richardson, G (1978) *Svensk Skolpolitik 1940-45* (Swedish School Politics 1940-45), Stockholm, Liber.
Reuterberg, S E (1968) *Val av Teoretisk Utbildning i Relation till Sociala och Regionala Bakgrundsfaktorer* (Choice of theoretical education in relation to social and regional background factors), Institute of Education, University of Göteborg, mimeo.
Sjöberg, Chris (1977) *Klassens Liv* (The life of the Class), Stockholm, Raben & Sjögren.
Skaraborgs *Länskolnämnd* (1978) *Information om reformarbeter inom skolan samt om fortbildnings verksamheten under läsaret 1978-79* (Information on school reform work and in-service activities, academic year 1978-79).
Stenholm, B (1968) *Skolans Ledning* (The Management of Schools), Stockholm, Liber.
Stockholm Universitet (twice monthly) *Meddelanden* (News).
Stockholm Universitet (termly) *Katalog* (Catalogue of courses).
Svensson, Allan (1977) *Jämlighet och högskoleutbildning. En studie av olika bakgrundsfaktorers betydelse för den post-gymnasiala utbildningen* (Equality and Higher Education. A study of the importance of different background factors in post upper secondary school education), Institute of Education, University of Göteborg.
Sveriges Lärarförbund (1971) *Insyn i Skolan* (Insight into the School), Stockholm, SLF.
Wennäs, O (1966) *Striden om Latin-herraväldet:* ideer och intressen: Svensk Skolpolitik under 1800-talet (The Fight over the Dominance of Latin: ideas and interests: Swedish educational politics in the 19th Century), Uppsala, AWE.

Åberg, Gertrud (1978) *Sveriges Småskollärare och deras Förbund 1918-1966* (Sweden's Infant Teachers and their Association 1918-1966), Pedagogiska Skrifter Nr 259, Stockholm, Sveriges Lärarförbund.

Åsemar, C (1977) *Studie- och Yrkesorienteringens Framväxt i Grundskolan och Gymnasieskolan:* en beskrivning av mål, organisation och metoder (The Growth of Study and Work Guidance in the Basic and Upper Secondary Schools: a description of goals, organisation and Methods), Pedagogiska monograf Nr 19, University of Umeå.

Åsemar, C (1978) *Kunskaper och Attityder till Dagens Syomål:* Rapport från Syo-Projektet (Knowledge and Attitudes to the Goals of Study and Work Guidance Today: report from the study and work guidance project), Pedagogiska Institutet, University of Umeå.

B.   MATERIAL IN ENGLISH

2.   BOOKS AND LARGE PAMPHLETS

Arvidson, Stellan (1955) *Education in Sweden,* Stockholm, Swedish Institute.

Bereday GXF and Lauwerys JA (Eds.) (1962), *The Yearbook of Education: The Gifted Child,* London, Evans.

Bereday GXF and Lauwerys JA (Eds.) (1963), *The Yearbook of Education:* The Education and Training of Teachers, London, Evans.

Bergendal, Gunnar (1977) *Higher Education and Manpower Planning in Sweden,* Stockholm, UH .

Bjerstedt, Å (1968) *Twelve Years of Educational and Psychological Research in Sweden,* Lund, CWK Gleerups.

CERI (1971) *Equal Educational Opportunity:* a statement of the problem with special reference to recurrent education, Paris, OECD.

Cook, TG (1974) *The History of Education in Europe,* London, Methuen, for History of Education Society.

Dahllöf, U (1971a) *Ability Grouping, Content Validity and Curriculum Process Analysis,* New York, Teachers College Press.

Dahllöf, U (1977) *Reforming Higher Education and External Studies in Sweden and Australia,* Uppsala, Acta Universitatis Uppsaliensis.

Dahlöff, U and Lundgren, UP (1970) *Macro and Micro Approaches Combined for Curriculum Process Analysis,* Project Compass 23, 10, Pedagogical Institute, University of Göteborg.

Dahlöff, U et.al. (1966) *Secondary Education in Sweden: A survey of Reforms,* Stockholm, SO-förlaget.

Dixon, W (1965) *Society, Schools and Progress in Scandinavia,*
Oxford, Pergamon.
Ekholm, Mats (1976) *Social Development in School:* Summary and
Excerpts, Report Nr 48:17, Institute of Education, University
of Göteborg.
Elmgren, J (1952) *School and Psychology:* a Report of the
Research Work of the 1946 School Commission, Stockholm,
Ecklesiastikdepartmentet.
Glatter, R (Ed.) (1977) *Control of the Curriculum:* issues and
trends in Britain and Europe, Proceedings of the 5th Annual
Conference of the British Educational Administration Society,
London, NFER for Institute of Education, University of London.
Hermods (n.d.) *Hermods of Sweden,* Malmö, Hermods. (published
in 1960's).
Husén, T (1962) *Problems of Differentiation in Swedish Com-*
pulsory Schools, Stockholm, Svenska Bokförlaget.
Husén, T (1967) *International Study of Achievement in Mathem-*
atics: a comparison in twelve countries, Vols. 1-11, Stockholm,
Almqvist & Wiksell.
Husén, T (1974) *The Learning Society,* London, Methuen.
Husén, T (1979) *The School in Question:* a comparative study of
the school and its future in Western Society, Oxford, University
Press.
Husén, T and Boalt, G (1968) *Educational Research and Educational*
Change: The Case of Sweden, New York, John Wiley (translation
of Boalt and Husén (1964), *Skolans Sociologi*).
Hoyle, E and Megrarry, J (Eds.) (1980) *The World Yearbook of*
Education: Professional Development of Teachers, London,
Kogan Page.
King, EJ, Moor, CH and Mundy, JA (1974) *Post-Compulsory*
Education I: A New Analysis in Western Europe, London, Sage.
King, EJ, Moor, CH and Mundy, JA (1975) *Post-Compulsory*
Education II: The Way Ahead, London, Sage.
Maclure, S (1971) *Innovation in Education: Sweden,* Paris,
OECD.
Marklund, S (1979) *Educational Administration and Educational*
Development, Institute of International Education, University
of Stockholm.
Marklund, S and Bergendal, G (1979) *Trends in Swedish Educa-*
tional Policy, Stockholm, Swedish Institute.
Marklund, S and Söderberg, P (1967) *The Swedish Comprehensive*
School, London, Longmans (translated from the Swedish edition,
1964).
Ministry of Education and Cultural Affairs (*Utbildnings-*
departmentet) (1973) *U68: Higher Education:* Proposals by the
Swedish 1968 Educational Commission, Stockholm, Allmänna
Förlaget (translation of the Swedish Summary of the U68 Report,

SOU 1973:2).

National Board of Education (*Skolöverstyrelsen*) (1979) *Teachers for a School in Transition:* a summary of viewpoints and proposals presented by the 1974 Swedish Commission on Teacher Education, Stockholm, National Board of Education, mimeo.

National Library for Psychology and Education (1978) *Swedish Behavioural Science Research Reports 1977/78,* Statens Psikologiska-Pedagogiska Bibliotek.

OECD (1967) *Educational Policy and Planning in Sweden,* Paris, OECD.

OECD (1968) *Study on Teachers: Sweden, Austria, Greece,* Paris, OECD.

OECD (1969) *Reviews of National Policy for Education: Sweden,* Paris, OECD.

OECD (1971) *Innovation in Education: Sweden,* Paris, OECD (see Maclure S).

OECD (1974) *Reports on Policies for Higher Education,* Paris, OECD.

OECD (1979) *Goals for Educational Policy in Sweden:* a status report on the compulsory school and higher education, Stockholm, mimeo.

Orring, J (1971) *School in Sweden,* Stockholm, SÖ-förlaget.

Paulston, Rolland G (1968) *Educational Change in Sweden,* New York Teachers College Press.

Scase, R (Ed.) (1976) *Readings in the Swedish Class Structure,* Oxford, Pergamon.

Spolton, L (1967) *The Upper Secondary School: a comparative survey,* Oxford, Pergamon Press.

Stenholm, B (1970) *Education in Sweden,* Stockholm, Swedish Institute.

Stukat, K-G (1976) *Current Trends in European Pre-School Research,* London, NFER.

Svensson N-E (1962) *Ability Grouping and Scholastic Attainment:* a report of a five-year follow-up study in Stockholm, Acta Universitatis Stockholmiensis, Studies in Educational Psychology 5, Stockholm, Almqvist & Wiksell.

Woodhead, M (1976) *Pre-School Education in Western Europe;* Issues, Policies and Trends, London, NFER.

Östergren, B (1979) *The Management of Change in Swedish Higher Education,* Paris, Unesco.

2. ARTICLES AND SMALL PAMPHLETS

Alkin, MC (1973) Analysis of national curriculum and instructional reform: application to Sweden, *International Review of Education,* 19, 1, 208-217.

Anderson, CA (1974) Sweden re-examines higher education: a
critique of the U68 report, *Comparative Education*, 10,3, 167-
180.

Anderson, CA (1975) Expanding Educational opportunity: con-
ceptualisation and measurement, *Higher Education*, 4,4 393-408.

Arvidson, Stellan (1951) Education for democracy, in Lauwerys
JA (Ed.), *Scandinavian Democracy*, Copenhagen, The Danish
Institute.

Axelsson, Rune (1979) Evaluation of vocational education in the
Swedish upper secondary school, *Scandinavian Journal of
Educational Research*, 23,4, 169-184.

Belding, RE (1975) Pryo - Sweden's unique careers education for
all secondary school students, *Western European Education*, 7,3,
37-45.

Bergsten, Urban (1980) Interest in education among adults with
short previous formal schooling, *Adult Education*, 30,3, 131-151.

Bjerstedt, Å (Ed.) (twice a year) *Didakometry and Sociometry*,
Research Reports, Department of Educational and Psychological
Research, School of Education, Malmö.

Björklund, E and Svensson, N-E (1967) Educational Research in
Sweden, *International Review of Education*, 13,2, 184-197.

Boucher, L (1968) Curriculum reform in Sweden, *CESE (British
Section) Conference Report*, The Changing School Curriculum,
68-96.

Boucher, L (1972) Assessment of scholastic achievement in
Swedish schools, *Compare*, 3,1, 20-23.

Boucher, L (1973) School marks in Sweden: the continued debate,
Compare, 3,2, 25-26.

Boucher, L (1974) Tradition and change in Swedish education, in
Cook TG (ed.), op.cit., 67-84.

Boucher, L (1975) Some aspects of teacher education and teacher
supply in contemporary Sweden, *British Journal of Teacher
Education*, 1,3, 377-382.

Boucher, L (1974) A case study of higher education reform in
Sweden, *Compare*, 5,1, 35-39.

Callewaert, S and Kallos, D (1976) The rose coloured wave in
Swedish pedagogy, *Educational Studies*, 2,3, 178-184.

Carlsson, G and Gesser, B (1965) Universities as selective and
socialising agents: some recent Swedish data, *Acta Sociologica*,
9, 25.37.

Current Sweden (periodically), Swedish Institute.

Dahllöf, U et al. (1971b) Reform implementation studies as a
basis for curriculum theory: three Swedish approaches,
Curriculum Theory Network, 7, 99-117.

Dahllöf, U (1973) The curriculum development system in Sweden,
International Review of Education, 19, 1, 218-231.

Erholm, Mats (198) The impact of research on an educational programme for school leaders in Sweden, in Hoyle, E and Megarry, J,
op. cit., 193-203.

Erikson, H (1966) Adult education and Swedish political leadership, *International Review of Education*, 12, 2, 129-143.

Fraser, SE and Fraser, BJ (1973) Scandinavian education: a
bibliography of English language materials: Sweden, *Western
European Education*, 5, 2-3, 163-271.

Gellerstam, Göand Köllerström, B (1979) Towards closer contact
between universities and work, *European Journal of Education*,
14, 4, 323-328.

Heidenheimer, A (1974) The politics of educational reform:
explaining different outcomes of school comprehensivation
attempts in Sweden and West Germany, *Comparative Education
Review*, 18, 3, 388-410.

Holmberg, B (1967) Correspondence instruction and the use of
self instructional media in schools, *Comparative Education*,
3, 3, 225-230.

Hultman, Glen (1980) The school from the viewpoint of organisational theory and its prerequisities for change: notes on the
evaluation of planned change in Swedish schools, *Educational
Studies*, 2, 127-140.

Husen, T (1962) Detection of ability and selection for educational purposes in Sweden, in Bereday GZF and Lauwreys JA
(Eds.). op. cit., 295-314.

Husén, T (1963) Social determinants of the comprehensive
school, *International Review of Education*, 9, 2, 158-174.

Husén, T (1964) Current trends in the Swedish teacher training,
International Review of Education, 10, 2, 206-211.

Husén, T (1965a) Educational change in Sweden, *Comparative
Education*, 1, 3, 181-191.

Husén, T (1965b) Curriculum research in Sweden, *International
Review of Education*, 11, 2, 189-208.

Husén, T (1969) Responsibilities and resistance in the education
system to the changing needs of society: some Swedish experiences, *International Review of Education*, 15, 4, 476-487.

Husén, T (1971) The comprehensive versus selective school
issue: introductory remarks, International Review of Education,
17, 1, 3-10.

Husén, T, Dahllöf, U and Bromsjö, B (1965) Curriculum research
in Sweden, *Educational Research*, 7, 3, 165-185.

Härnkvist, K (1961) Recent educational research in connection
with the Swedish school reform, *International Review of Education*, 7, 1, 85-90.

Härnkvist, K and Bengtsson, J (1976) Educational reform and
educational equality, in Scase, R (d.), op. cit., 305-232.

Johannesson, I (1975) Bilingual-bicultural education of immigrant children in Sweden, International Review of Education, 21, 3, 347-355.

Jones, W (1976) Swedish adult education observed, *Adult Education*, 49, 1, 24-31.

Kim, L (1979) Widened admission to higher education in Sweden, *European Journal of Education*, 14, 2, 181-192.

Lane, J-E (1979) Power in the university, *European Journal of Education*, 14, 4, 389-402.

Lauglo, Jon (1977) Educational change and aspects of bureaucratic organisation in the Scandinavian school reforms, in Glatter, R (Ed.), op. cit., 76-95.

Mallea, JR (1970) The implementation of Swedish educational policy and planning, *Comparative Education*, 6,2, 99-114.

Marklund, S (1963) The attitudes of intending teachers to school reform in Sweden, in Bereday, GZF and Lauwerys, JA, op. cit., 432-442.

Marklund, S (1966) Educational reform and research in Sweden, *Educational Research*, 9, 3, 16-21.

Marklund, S (1971) Comparative school research and the Swedish school of reform, *International Review of Education*, 17, 1, 39-49.

Marklund, S (1978) Differentiation and integration in the Swedish upper secondary school, *International Review of Education*, 24, 2, 197-206.

Marklund, S (1980) The role of central government in educational development in Sweden, in Hoyle, E and Megarry, J op. cit., 115-130.

Marklund, S and Boucher, L (1980) The curriculum for 13-16's in Sweden: a review of changes 1950-1980, *Compare*, 10, 2, 161-177.

Ministry of Education, Utbildningdepartmentet (1980a) Making schools safe for everyone, *Committee against violence in the School*.

Ministry of Education (1980b) A summary of the goals and guidelines in Lgr 80, the new Primary school curriculum.

National Board of Education (1970) Physical Education in Sweden, Stockholm, Liber.

National Board of Education (1975) The autonomous work of pupils, 17th November.

National Board of Education (periodically) Information sheets (on current aspects of schooling).

Paulston, RG (1976) Ethnic revival and educational conflict in Swedish Lappland, *Comparative Education Review*, 20,2, 179-192.

Polidaro, JR (1977) Professional preparation of PE teachers in Norway, Sweden and Denmark, *Research Quarterly*, 48, 3, 640-646.

Premfors, RIT (1979) The politics of higher education in Sweden: recent developments 1976-78, *European Journal of Education*, 14, 1, 81-106.
Premfors, RIT (1980) How much higher education is enough? A comparison of policy in France, Sweden and the UK, *Comparative Education Review*, 24,3, 302-322.
Rosengren, B (1974) Better environment for children, *Current Sweden*, Swedish Institute.
Rosengren, B (1976) More time for the children, *Current Sweden*, Swedish Institute.
Sundén, CG (1973) The experimental upper secondary school 1969-73, *Göteborgs School Administration*.
Svensson, Allan (1980) On equality and university education in Sweden, *Scandinavian Journal of Education*, 24, 2, 79-92.
Swedish Institute (various dates) *Fact Sheets on Sweden*.
Swedish Institute (various dates) *Current Sweden*.
Thorsell, Gunnar (1977) Response (to Lauglo) in Glatter R (30), op. cit., 96-100.
Times Education Supplement (weekly).
Trow, M (1972) The expansion and transformation of higher education, *International Review of Education*, 18, 1, 61-84.
Trow, M (1974) Problems in the transition from elite to mass higher education, in OECD, op. cit.
Wilke, I (1975) Schooling of immigrant children in Germany, Sweden, England, *International Review of Education*, 21, 358-382.
Willman, B (1977) Educational reform and the world of work: economic change, educational needs and secondary school reform, *Western European Education*, 9,2, 3-112.
Willman, B (1978) Cooperation and individualisation as principles of instruction in the Swedish school, *Western European Education*, 10, 2, 90-118.
UHÄ (1973) Internationalising the universities: a Swedish approach. Summary of a preliminary report from the *Internationalisation Committee*, Stockholm, Liber.